STORE WARS

STORE WARS

THE WORLDWIDE BATTLE FOR MINDSPACE

AND SHELFSPACE, ONLINE AND IN-STORE

SECOND EDITION

GREG THAIN AND
JOHN BRADLEY

A John Wiley & Sons, Ltd., Publication

This edition first published 2012
© 2012 John Wiley & Sons

Registered office
John Wiley & Sons Ltd, The Atrium, Southern Gate, Chichester, West Sussex, PO19 8SQ, United Kingdom

For details of our global editorial offices, for customer services and for information about how to apply for permission to reuse the copyright material in this book please see our website at www.wiley.com.

Wiley publishes in a variety of print and electronic formats and by print-on-demand. Some material included with standard print versions of this book may not be included in e-books or in print-on-demand. If this book refers to media such as a CD or DVD that is not included in the version you purchased, you may download this material at http://booksupport.wiley.com. For more information about Wiley products, visit www.wiley.com.

Library of Congress Cataloging-in-Publication Data

Thain, Greg, 1954–
  Store wars : the Worldwide Battle for Mindspace and Shelfspace, Online and In-store / Greg Thain and John Bradley.
        p. cm.
  Includes index.
  ISBN 978-1-118-37406-1 (cloth)
  1. Retail trade.   2. Marketing.   3. Consumer goods.   I. Bradley, John, 1957–
II. Title.
  HF5429.T37 2012
  381.'1–dc23
                             2012018039

A catalogue record for this book is available from the British Library.

ISBN 978-1-118-37406-1 (hbk) ISBN 978-1-118-37424-5 (ebk)
ISBN 978-1-118-37480-1 (ebk) ISBN 978-1-118-37481-8 (ebk)

Set in 11/15.5 pt FF Scala by Toppan Best-set Premedia Limited
Printed in Great Britain by TJ International Ltd, Padstow, Cornwall, UK

TABLE OF CONTENTS

ACKNOWLEDGEMENTS

We would like to thank all the team that have assisted us over the last three years in the creation of this book.

Especial thanks go to Alexandra Skey, our researcher, who diligently uncovered much new information; Alex Utochkin, who made our initial charts; Ludmila Belokonova, the manager of the StoreWars Business Simulation; and the other members of our team, Ekaterina Voitenkova, Lavrenyuk Anastasia and Dariusz Kepczynski.

On the expert and academic side, we would like to thank Professor Niraj Dawar of the Richard Ivey School of Business for his valuable input and suggestions; Chen Junsong, professor of marketing CEIBS, China, who gave us extremely valuable help on the China and Asian markets; Nuno Bouça, our partner at Excel Formação in Brazil, who helped us with information from South America; Tim Munnion, our partner in Portugal; Stephen Kreeger, Managing Director of Metro, Almaty, Kazakhstan, who gave invaluable insights into Russia and CIS; and Fernando Zerboni, PhD and Dirección Comercial at IAE Business School, Universidad Austral; Mikołaj Budzyński, our partner at Inspiraction, Poland; Marika Taishoff, PhD and Director of the Monaco MBA at IUM, and Ben Aris in Moscow.

Thanks also to Planet Retail and AC Nielsen for their assistance with charts and data, and our editor Tim Bettsworth.

John would like to thank his wife Audrey and daughter Georgina for their unstinting support in all his endeavours. I would like to thank my wife Katya and children, Sarah, Nick, Poppy, James and Magnolia for their understanding.

Greg Thain
April 2012

INTRODUCTION

SINCE THE ORIGINAL edition of *Store Wars* was published in 1995, much has changed in the fast-moving consumer goods (FMCG) industry, both for manufacturers and retailers.

Many iconic brand companies, such as Gillette and Cadbury, have lost their independence, swallowed up by bigger players, who see size as crucial in dealing with another of the major changes: gigantic retailers. Wal-Mart's 1995 sales of $93 billion more than quadrupled to a staggering $405 billion in 2010, with $100 billion coming from outside the United States. This leads to another massive change in the FMCG industry: the rise of emerging markets such as Russia, China, India and Brazil, which have been, and still are, a modern-day Klondike gold-rush for FMCG players, where fortunes can be made and lost. The rapid development of such markets is the prime reason behind global retail sales space more than trebling from 40 million m² in 2001 to 130 million in 2011.[1]

Many of the tools used by both manufacturers and retailers in 1995 now have dramatically different levels of potency. Television advertising, the mainstay of the branded manufacturer, can now no longer be relied upon to drive retail listings; instead, marketing budgets have been moving to the Internet and social media. *Private label*, an almost insignificant factor in 1995, has ascended to undreamt-of heights and is the cornerstone of virtually every major retailer's strategy, in some cases over 50% of their sales. Behind the tools, the information war has swung decisively in favour of the retailer as the combination of product scanning with loyalty cards has given the retailer almost perfect buying information at the level of individual shoppers.

The purpose of this second edition is to come to the aid of FMCG professionals, both manufacturers and retailers, to put into context and perspective the key events and changes which have taken place within their industry since the mid-1990s. This book will also be invaluable to academics and students who wish to better understand the shifting dynamics within the FMCG, retail and consumer-facing industries.

We shall see that much has changed at the operational level, and we will dig deeper to uncover and highlight the underlying strategic factors of these changes, while demonstrating how they should now be applied in the new reality of the twenty-first century. With over 100 examples and case studies from dozens of markets, we present the most comprehensive insight into the modern-day FMCG industry.

In Chapter 1, we take a strategic overview of the evolution of the FMCG industry and see how power has shifted not just in one direction from manufacturer to retailer but also in both ways at various times, driven by technological innovation, social change and, most crucially, innovation within the industry itself as each party seeks to increase its share of transaction profits. A crucial constant in the battle between manufacturers and retailers for a share of profits is the battle to win and hold consumer trust in an era when brand loyalties are more fragile than ever before.

In Chapter 2, we take a close look at the differences between manufacturers and retailers, and we learn how the friction characterising most of their dealings is not a result of similar organisations pursuing different, conflicting goals but of very different organisations pursuing the same goals by very different means. In particular, a lack of understanding of their contrasting financial structures is often the reason why they can respond acrimoniously to the same set of circumstances.

We focus on the manufacturing side and examine how and why manufacturers adopt the types of strategies they do, in Chapter 3. We look at the crucial role of *segmentation*, when properly applied, in moving companies from the deadly battlefield of price competition to the sunny uplands of profitable growth. However, such markets are very dynamic and we see how companies can easily be tempted by the siren-song of price competition to address failing top and bottom lines. But we also see how price competition can be a profitable and attractive strategy in the fast-moving *emerging markets*.

We then switch to look at retailer strategic positionings, in Chapter 4, to see that they are much more limited than manufacturers are. Retail chains need to occupy very broad swathes of the market, so tend to be much more closely grouped than manufacturer brands, which can profitably occupy many small differentiated niches. We then examine the emergence of the retailers' ability to segment their store types by shopping need, meaning that one retail banner can cover anything from a 100 ft² convenience outlet to a 100 000 SKU hypermarket, and see how this *multi-format strategy* is affecting the retailer–manufacturer interface.

In Chapter 5, we examine in detail the two retailer–manufacturer battlegrounds of *shelfspace* and *mindspace*. Previously, these two commodities were fought over between manufacturers, but now the battle rages between retailers and manufacturers. We see how the combination of retailer size, brand-building and robust private label strategies has tilted the playing field heavily in favour of the retailer. Manufacturers now have to be savvier in their approach to winning mindspace, including the retailers' brands within their competitive sets.

In Chapter 6, we go on to dig deeper into the battle for mindspace and the relative advantages held by manufacturers and retailers. We explore different strategies in building mindspace and look at categories where one or the other player has a built-in head-start. We also highlight the increasing skills overlap between manufacturers and retailers, a consequence of brand-building becoming a core strategy for retailers in recent years.

We deep-dive into the fight for shelfspace in Chapter 7, where we expose the overused delisting threat as being largely hollow. We encourage a systematic approach based on the relative concepts of the cost of switching brands versus the cost of switching stores so that both parties better understand where they have leverage and where they don't. We show how manufacturers must seek to increase the consumers' cost of switching brands through their brand-building activities and reduce their cost of switching stores through their distribution strategies. Similarly, retailers must strive to achieve the opposite.

In Chapter 8, we dissect the various means by which retailers can build a sustainable advantage in a category where dominance has been fleeting. The world's two largest retailers were both founded in the 1960s, a situation unthinkable on the manufacturer side; they tend to be much older and more enduring. We explore the possibilities of fresh produce, multi-segmentation, loyalty cards and price as defendable strategies, we also show how each market has three price positionings, one of which every retailer must choose.

Chapter 9 concentrates on providing an in-depth understanding of the retailer's single most important competitive weapon: private label. We explain the roles of the five different types of private label offering and how each has a specific role to play in positioning the retailer against its competitors and against manufacturer brands. We also explore the impact on manufacturers of the resurgence of private label as a retail strategy and their need to have a clear strategy on the matter and how its impact can be mitigated.

We then look, in Chapter 10, at the thorny issue of *trade marketing* for manufacturers, which for some has become their second-largest expenditure, as an interface between their business and the retailers. We explore how trade marketing and brand marketing inherently conflict as they serve different groups – consumers and retailers – who have different interests. Strategies for controlling the spiralling costs of trade marketing are explored, tied into the organisational challenges of accommodating it within a brand-focused organisation.

In Chapter 11, we step back to look at the internationalisation of the FMCG industry, especially with regard to emerging markets, with examples and illustrations from China, Russia, Brazil, India and further afield. We contrast the different rates of internationalisation of manufacturers and retailers, showing how this creates opportunities for the manufacturer. We show how internationalisation for the retailer can be a huge challenge, demanding a new set of skills and attitudes. As we focus on the emerging markets, we show how those markets are evolving at a much faster pace and along differing paths compared to the history of developed markets. We also note the emergence of strong manufacturers and retailers from those markets and the threat they pose to the established global players.

We switch, in Chapter 12, to the virtual marketplace of the Internet and examine the rapid rise of *e-retailing* and the emergence of *e-grocery*. We explore the reasons behind the phenomenal growth of *e-commerce* and look in detail at lessons from successful and unsuccessful e-retailing and e-grocery ventures to better understand the impact this channel will have on the FMCG category. We see how having the right business model is critical for retailers and how mobile presents enormous opportunities for retailers.

Finally, in Chapter 13, we pull together all the insights and predict what the future will be like for manufacturers, retailers and e-retailers. We see how consumers will be much more brand-neutral, in that they will be happy with the right branding from any party. This will force manufacturers to make much harder choices about their brand portfolios and force them to adopt genuine premium, value or industrial strategies, and we explore the organisational implications of each. Similarly, retailers will have to embrace e-retailing and fight off the challenge of the vertically integrated specialist, category-killer retailer, or suffer the consequences. Finally, we make a series of predictions of how we see the FMCG category evolving in the next 5 to 10 years.

The insights and lessons from this *Store Wars* book can be explored in a highly realistic setting in the StoreWars Business Simulation, which, since the mid-1990s, has been recognised as one of the world's leading business simulations for executives, senior managers and directors of consumer-facing businesses. The simulation has been run in 43 countries in excess of 700 times and has been used by 60% of the world's leading FMCG and retail businesses. Academically, the StoreWars simulation has been used by universities across five continents. Full details can be found at the website (www.STOREWARS. net). In addition, this website contains all the charts and tables in this book in full colour, and these will be updated annually to keep you abreast of the inevitable changes in the FMCG world.

Greg Thain
John Bradley

Note

1. http://www.atkearney.com/index.php/Publications/retail-global-expansion-a-portfolio-of-opportunities2011-global-retail-development-index.html. Accessed 12 December 2011.

Chapter 1

D URING THE LATTER half of the twentieth century, manufacturers had control of virtually all the marketing variables – such as price, promotions and presence on shelf – that resided within the retail environment. Brand-positioning strategies always included the consumer price point for the brand, which could then be counted on to appear in-store. A shortfall in distribution was seen as a tactical failure of the manufacturer's sales department to negotiate properly with their customers, a failure that could be easily rectified. Manufacturers cared little in whose shops their brands were bought as distribution was near universal. However, shifts in the balance of power between manufacturers and retailers have made this era obsolete. In June 2009, Progressive Grocer reported:

> Five years ago, manufacturers and retailers say they held equal
> shares of power in their partnerships, but today, manufacturers
> believe that retailers control almost two-thirds of the overall
> power and will extend their control to 71 percent five years from
> now, while retailers believe they currently control 60 percent of
> the overall power, and expect to control nearly two-thirds in five
> years' time.[1]

Manufacturers' sources of power from the past no longer work today. They used to be the sole provider of consumer knowledge, but they have been overtaken by retailers' own information, analysed by experts. For example, 28.5 million shoppers use Tesco's loyalty pro-grammes.[2] In 1994 Tesco's hired dunnhumby to help them analyse their database, and within three months then Tesco Chairman Lord MacLaurin was moved to say, 'What scares me about this is that you know more about my customers after three months than I know after 30 years.'[3]

The conversation between retailers and manufacturers used to be dominated by the manufacturers' latest brand initiatives, but it is now dominated by retailers' latest supply chain initiatives. Retailers used to welcome brand innovation for the store traffic it would drive, now they often lead the way innovating under their store brands. Whereas the marketing budget used to be dominated by television advertising, now manufacturers pay more for retailer-related costs than consumer-related costs, spending anywhere between 10 and 25% of their annual revenues on trade deals, the second-biggest cost after manufacturing. Savings from reducing overheads and improving productivity have been generated to help offset the increase in trade spending, but many manufacturers are forced to spend less on consumer marketing to balance the books and remain profitable.

The outcome of these shifts is that manufacturers now have to consider retailers as a separate and dominant force in the market rather than compliant minions who could be relied upon to do their bidding. Thanks to the success of private label strategies (see Chapter 9), five of the top eight FMCG manufacturers in the world are actually retailers; giants such as Unilever and Coca-Cola are no longer even in the top ten, their global sales dwarfed by products under the names of Wal-Mart (now the world's largest FMCG manufacturer), Carrefour, Tesco, Aldi and Lidl. The branded manufacturers who have been tempted to produce private label are in no doubt where the power now lies. Indeed, it is rare for a branded company to even admit to being involved in private label; Weetabix are an example of one being open about their involvement.[4] Unilever, PepsiCo, Nestlé, Heinz, Playtex, Ralston Purina, Hershey, RJR Nabisco and McCain are less public about their move to the dark side.

But such shifts are neither a recent phenomenon nor an irreversible tide of history. To better understand how and why they have occurred we need to analyse the basis of retail power and examine how and why the balance of power in the value chain has shifted over time between manufacturers, distributors and retailers.

The emergence of branding as a value chain weapon

The history of trade is dominated by a struggle for the control of profits between producers, distributors and retailers. In the early days of the consumer economy, 'Mom and Pop' retailers were serviced by a complex network of middlemen who supplied mostly generic products sourced from a multitude of small-scale manufacturers. The anonymity of the products meant that manufacturer accountability for product quality was non-existent; shoppers neither knew nor really cared who made them. Retailers were the key players. Since they were the last stop in the supply chain, they were the only party the shopper could hold accountable as guarantor of the quality of goods purchased. As a counterbalance to retailers' necks being on the line with regards to quality, they had the ability to set prices, most often individually by shopper, which gave them a large degree of control on the transaction profits.

The more enlightened retailers realised they could increase turnover and hence profits by becoming an attractive destination. One way of achieving this was by gathering themselves under one roof, where their combined pulling power benefited all with the extra shoppers who thronged in their thousands. While the first recognisably modern shopping mall was the Southdale Shopping Centre, opened in Minneapolis in 1956, London's Royal Exchange, opened in 1568, fulfilled a very similar purpose. The invention of plate glass revolutionised retailing and was used to impressive effect in Paris' Palais Royal in the late eighteenth century, which spawned the nineteenth-century retail cathedrals that were to be found in London, Paris, Vienna and most large cities, attracting shoppers from far and wide.

The only way for distributors and manufacturers to end this relative dictatorship of the retailers on the size of the cake and their taking the biggest slice, was to take away their status as the 'agents of trust'. If a member of the supply chain was willing to take responsibility for product quality and to stake their reputation on it, they could then inform the consumer of the product's quality by placing some kind of mark on the product and (it was hoped) thus create a demand for their products as opposed to anyone else's – and the notion of brands evolved.

The first brand used on packaged goods was created almost 2000 years ago in Pompeii. The product, Vesuvinum, which combined Mt Vesuvius with the Latin word for wine, *vinum*, was a type of red wine – a category highly vulnerable to middlemen adulterating the quality with cheaper wine, water or worse. Rome's brick-makers also employed branding devices imprinted onto the bricks such that buyers in the city's brick market could recognise those bricks built to last. The United Kingdom's first brand trademark was registered in the late eighteenth century: the red triangle on bottles of Bass Pale Ale Beer, sold around the world.

It was essential that the branded manufacturer be able to package their product securely if their guarantee of quality was to be worth anything. Many packaging breakthroughs came about as a result of the demands of warfare. Foods became practical for mass manufacturing and branding with the invention of airtight food preservation in bottles by Nicholas Appert, in response to a prize offered by France's Napoleonic government as a means of feeding the Emperor's armies. The process for canning food was patented in 1810 but was slow to catch on, not least because the can opener was not invented for another 45 years. Similarly, the American Civil War gave a huge boost to embryonic food producers as the massive military orders forced them to scale up and reap huge economies of scale; prices consequently plummeted, making their products much more affordable when peace returned.

Many of the famous early consumer brands, such as Procter & Gamble's Ivory Soap in the United States, and Pear's Soap in Britain, came from the first manufacturers in the value chain to stake ownership of product quality. Their competition was not other brands – theirs was the first – it was the unbranded and largely untrustworthy generics.

Towards the end of the nineteenth century, after industry manufacturers grasped both the advantages of economics and technology to make branding synonymous with manufacturing, they were able to take the initiative ahead of distributors and retailers because of the scale economies of mass manufacturing combined with developments in packaging and transportation technologies. Together, these enabled the efficient production, transportation and retailing of individually sealed, branded packages, giving the manufacturer a route with which to build and own the relationship of trust with the consumer, and thus leverage with which to squeeze the distributor and have some influence over the shopkeeper.

The demise of the middleman

The middleman had had a good life in the nineteenth century. His monopoly on distribution, particularly in America, gave him substantial leverage over the manufacturer, who was a distant third in the battle for power. But, as middleman, he was vulnerable as he had no direct contact with the consumer and did not have the means to establish branding on the thousands of product lines in which he dealt.

When Procter & Gamble (P&G) were building their new soap brand, Ivory, their route to market was through the middleman. The early advertising was not just singing the praises of Ivory, but directing the shopper to make sure it was Ivory they were buying, thus hoping to generate a pressure on the retailer to ask for it specifically from the distributor.

EXAMINE BEFORE YOU BUY.

Figure 1.1 'Examine Before You Buy'. *Century Magazine*, printed in 1886. *Source*: The National Museum.

This advertisement (Figure 1.1),[5] 'Examine Before You Buy', ran in the *Century Magazine* in 1886 – it indirectly encouraged grocers to stock Ivory Soap so that their customers would not be fooled into buying soap of a lesser quality.

The brand sold well with this approach, but P&G were still the poor relation in the value chain and had not been able to shake the grip of the retailer and the middleman on the profits. Despite increasing the investment in consumer advertising – up to $146 000 in 1886, Harley Procter reported that 'soap is in excellent demand but prices are low and profits small.'[6]

P&G began to experiment in 1913 with cutting out the middleman by selling and delivering to retailers direct, and by 1921 they adopted the approach nationwide. This was a big bet by P&G.

Overnight, the sales force had to be expanded from 150 to 600, 125 more warehouses had to be acquired, 2000 contracts had to be written for deliveries by trucks and the accounting department had to be reorganised to handle 450 000 accounts.[7]

A boycott of P&G products by enraged distributors meant that the initiative was on a knife-edge for a while, but ultimately the gamble proved a success. Many other major goods manufacturers were able to follow P&G's lead to reap the benefits of greater profits of doing distribution for themselves, as well as the incremental benefits of having their own salespeople and merchandisers regularly visiting shops and building relationships with the shop owners. The original reason for P&G considering the initiative – greater predictability in orders and shipments – paled into insignificance with the benefits that influence over the point of sale were to bring.

A battle that had always been biased in favour of retailers because of their ability to influence the consumer and the middlemen for control of the route to market now began to swing inexorably in favour of the producer. This switch prompted innovation within the retail sector to fight back against the increasing power of the manufacturers.

An early appearance by private label

The Atlantic and Pacific Tea Company (A&P) opened their first store in 1859, founded on the principle of importing tea direct from China and Japan, thus cutting out the middleman and passing on the extra profits in the form of lower prices. This was an early example of the retailer realising that, having the key position of being in direct contact with the shopper, they had the potential to cut out one or even both of the other players in the value chain.

Within six years, they had expanded to 25 stores and decided that the same principle could be extended to other grocery items, which, for the most part, they executed by selling under a private label strategy. By 1930, A&P had become the largest retailer in the world, selling over a billion dollars' worth of goods a year through their 15700 stores.[8] While they did sell the most popular brands from manufacturers, slightly over half of the 300 products they sold were under the A&P private label – a ratio that a modern retailer would see today as a reasonable target to aim for. As part of their strategy, A&P had vertically integrated back into producing their private label products, thus also cutting out the manufacturer from the equation. They owned and operated coffee roasting plants, bakeries, food factories, cheese warehouses and salmon canneries, making them, at their peak, one of the world's largest FMCG manufacturers.

However, within the strength and success of the A&P retail model was the Trojan horse that would lead to it being eclipsed: manufacturer brands.

The rise of the brand retailer

The Piggly Wiggly chain pioneered the supermarket concept in terms of layout and self-service in the 1920s. But it wasn't until 1930, when Michael J. Cullen, an imaginative retailer then working for Kroger, came up with the idea to have a supermarket stocked with nothing but well-known manufacturers' brands sold at wafer-thin margins, an idea he enthusiastically proposed to Kroger's senior management:

> Can you imagine how the public would respond to a store of this kind? To think of it – a man selling 300 (branded) items at cost and another 200 at 5% above cost – nobody in the world ever did this before . . . People would break down the doors to get in, it would be a riot. I would have to call out the police and let the public in so many at a time.[9]

Kroger, who had a large private label business themselves, failed to see the potential of Cullen's idea of only stocking 1000 branded items and selling half of them at cost or marginally above: they thought him a lunatic. But Cullen realised that, as manufacturer brands were by then being advertised nationally via the powerful medium of radio, they would do all of the selling for him. So he left to develop the idea in his new grocery chain, the King Kullen Grocery Company. His prices on the most popular 500 lines substantially undercut other retailers, leaving A&P and Kroger, with all of their vast upstream costs associated with the private label, high and dry. The core of Cullen's idea has endured to this day: most major retailers today will have 400–500 lines they sell at or below cost.

Cullen was doubly fortunate in the timing of his idea: not only was radio advertising, the most powerful medium the world had yet seen, selling his stock for him, courtesy of the manufacturers' marketing budgets but rapidly increasing car penetration meant shoppers would gladly drive past their local A&P to reach his store and buy their favourite brands for less. He thus was able to overcome the two biggest challenges to succeeding in retail: attracting shoppers and the limitations of location. His formula was widely copied immediately. Independent store owners who could not hope to match the new grocery chains' prices and private label specialists who were not selling the advertised brands people wanted to buy both stood no chance and began a long, inexorable decline.

The triumph of branded manufacturers

Cullen had created a concept that was successful in horizontal competition with other retailers, but he had sown the seeds of retailers losing the vertical battle for profits to the manufacturer. He had unwittingly created the situation where power, consumer influence and consequently the bulk of the profits increasingly rested with the branded manufacturers. As manufacturers and retailers got accustomed to retailers earning uniformly thin margins, pricing control also fell into the hands of the brand owners via their list pricing, which translated into a very predictable on-shelf price.

Broadcast media for advertisers provided a perfect marriage of the economies associated with scale of production and communication – for the first time advertisers could talk to millions of customers at once, and fill the retailers' shelves with thousands of products to satisfy their needs. The brand message delivered repeatedly had a mesmerising effect on consumers, and on corporate bottom lines. By 1965, Coca-Cola were selling an annual average of 260 drinks per person in America, Camel dominated with 33% market share and Pampers were raking in $14.4 million. The manufacturers seemed unstoppable.

The dazzling power of mass media and the allure of branded products in self-service stores meant that there was no real need for someone in the value chain to engage the consumer and listen to their individual needs: everyone wanted to buy the big brands. This love affair with brands negated the one real source of advantage previously held by retailers: direct contact with their shoppers.

Retailers battle for the scraps

By the 1960s, retailers found themselves hopelessly outgunned by the branded manufacturers, who dictated the terms on what they should stock, how and where it should be displayed, at what price, how much they would be allowed to order and how much of the selling price they could keep as profit. As the branded manufacturers became financial goliaths with easy access to capital, retailers, especially in Europe, remained predominantly family businesses reluctant or unable to borrow substantial funds to fuel growth, thus widening further the scale mismatch between manufacturers and retailers. Rendered almost powerless, retailers disengaged from the vertical value chain battle for transaction profits and focused almost entirely on the horizontal battle with other retailers for market share, primarily in a race to be seen as the cheapest place to buy well-known brands.

Retailers thus embarked on a discounter strategy by developing large sites and maximising efficiency, building high volume with low prices and then negotiating appropriate discounts from manufacturers, investing in technology and reducing logistics costs. This strategy has worked across the globe, from Coles in Australia to Carrefour in Brazil and Loblaws in Canada, and across the sectors (e.g. food, electrical appliances, toys, pet care), but left most of the power and profits with the brand manufacturers.

The retailers' discounter strategy is most successful and appropriate when there is share to be taken from smaller, less efficient competitors. Sam Walton's US Wal-Mart chain grew dramatically through the 1970s and 1980s by being the epitome of this model. He placed many of his new stores in small towns where they could all but close down an entire Main Street of specialist shops.

This development of large, efficient retailers was not initially a threat to manufacturers. In fact, the efficient stores were better customers, shifting greater volumes per location and often increasing overall consumption. The better deals given by the manufacturers were justified by their savings servicing the high-volume discounter, compared to the costs of servicing a multitude of smaller, less tightly managed stores.

Discounters' profits came and still come from buying competitively while handling financial operations, logistics and property business more astutely than other retailers can. The high-volume, low-operating-cost model allowed them to offer lower prices and more choice, while maintaining acceptable service levels; their goal was to move a lot of product and make small percentage profits on high volumes, which improves efficiency and gives them the power to negotiate with manufacturers.

Manufacturers encouraged and favoured these 'model traders' with discounts, advantageous delivery arrangements and information technology link-ups. Most large manufacturers introduced systems where their computers were linked directly with the stock controlling computers in their clients' stores. Stock sold was reordered automatically as the goods moved out of the shop. Inventories could be minimised and administration reduced. The independents stood no chance. By the end of the 1950s, grocery chain stores had accounted for 50% of US food sales, which then rose steadily to 80% by the early 1990s; today, US grocery chain stores account for 89.6% of all food sales.[10] Elsewhere, Russia went from a situation in 1990 of virtually all trade being through small, grossly inefficient shops to 30% being through modern chain supermarkets within the space of 20 years.

The discounter strategy was unstoppable when there exist weaker competitors to crush, and the better discounters did very well because their sales were always increasing. Consumer demand for discount retailers was greater than supply, with towns begging retailers to open big-box stores in their vicinity. The competition between the discounters centred on being the first to develop new sites servicing these consumers who were waiting to benefit from the retail revolution.

The same situation exists today in the rapidly expanding emerging markets. The Russian retail food market, worth $239 billion in 2011, is growing at 13% a year, and yet the leading 10 retailers are growing at between 30 and 40% as they build upon their current modest 11% share. In India, organised chain retailers account for only 7% of the $435 billion market, a share forecast to rise to 20% by 2020.[11] The discounter model is unstoppable in fragmented, unorganised markets.

The end of the golden age for discounters

But all good things must come to an end. Once there is supermarket or hypermarket saturation, profitable growth via the discounter strategy becomes almost impossible. New sites have to be placed not in virgin discounter territory but in areas already served by other discounters. In saturated markets, such as Germany, this led to the emergence of the hard discounter as being a new way to compete.

Discounters have powerful differential advantages compared to traditional small stores, but as protection from each other all they have is location. As long as they stay apart, and the consumer isn't too mobile, they are differentiated by the cost involved in travelling to competitive stores. As the accessibility of transport increases, the advantage of location decreases. Even in countries like Australia, where a relatively small population is distributed across a continent, location is no longer a meaningful advantage. Coles and Woolworths compete toe to toe for the vast majority of grocery dollars spent in every major town and city. Retail competitors face each other with similar offerings of similar stores selling similar products at similar prices. Since there are no new supermarket shoppers, growth implies taking share away from competitive stores. The golden age of discount retailing, where developing a store in a well-chosen location was a formula for printing money, has come to an end.

The shift to selling orientation

The fastest route to maintain sales volume in such a competitive retail environment is a transition to selling, or 'hustle', strategies. *Hustling* means holding the basic product offering (store, range, service) constant while increasing the selling pressure. This involves price cutting, promotions, special 'discount' days, dump bins, checkout displays, piles of stock on the main floor with special offer etc., etc.

These techniques do not create greater value, except in impulse-buy categories such as soft drinks and confectionery, because most of them are easy to copy. The simplest way to increase sales volume is by dropping your prices, and the easiest way for competitors to recover their lost sales volume is by copying your strategy and dropping their prices even lower. Hence the price wars of the 1980s, which reduced retailers' margins to the bone. Hustle techniques almost always escalate beyond their break-even point: the value of the total market does not increase enough, if at all, to repay the combined investments of the participants.

Competing retailers thus hope to outdo each other in this situation by becoming more sophisticated. By analysing their promotions better than the competition does, they believe they can adjust their offers more efficiently to create greater profits. This is true for some competitors at some points, but it can't sustain the FMCG retail industry over time. As the techniques for analysing the effects and costs diffuse to the slower retailers, the outcome is similar layouts and promotions across the board.

At first glance the consumer would seem to benefit from such a competitive climate. However, the resulting oversupply of retail outlets is inefficient: supermarkets working at below-optimal capacity have higher fixed costs. They also have less money to invest in efficient technology. Selling strategies also tend to breed other, more complicated, inefficiencies.

Inefficiencies of the selling orientation

Selling strategies have detrimental effects on logistics. For example, they encourage forward buying. This practice is a result of regular and significant promotions, which are supposedly forced on manufacturers by the price-obsessed retailers. Once an expectation of promotions is established, retailers are motivated to buy as much of their turnover as possible during promotions, often to be resold later at regular prices, this being known as the *bull-whip effect*.

In simple terms, the trade start buying the product on discount to hold in stock for future sale at a higher margin rather than sell immediately. They make money by taking advantage of contradicting discounts and promotional schedules and then selling the product for a higher price at a later date. This is not uncommon. If a manufacturer offers promotional prices every other month, a retailer will forward buy five weeks' supply at the end of each promotional month. It is not unknown for a retailer to buy a year's supply ahead of a major price rise. At the extreme, forward buying necessitates special warehousing capacity, and the stop–go purchasing creates inventory inefficiencies both for the manufacturer and for the retailer: the average FMCG product spends more than 100 days in inventory supply. Freelance warehousing companies can generate a separate, parasitic business. These 'brokers' buy in bulk during promotions and sell to retailers out of promotion time.

Although forward buying is still a problem today, the opportunity to make money from it isn't as viable as it once was, because manufacturers have realised the costs to their business of such inefficiencies. In October 2011, John DeJesus, president of Foodmaster, explained that this is due to recent changes in the relationship between retailers and manufacturers:[12]

> We used to be able to take a [forward buying] position but manufacturers are getting smart now and saying no . . . If you sell everything on sale, no one will make any money, and if the manufacturer sells everything on deal, he won't make any money.

Retailers in a selling war sometimes ask manufacturers to create artificial differences in a product sold through competing chains (e.g. different-size packs) so that direct price comparison becomes more difficult. In the 1980s, Woolworths in the United Kingdom had major cost and thus selling price disadvantages compared to the 'selling' retailers who were pushing the same products at lower prices. They responded by demanding exclusive presentations of products from the main manufacturers. The strategy worked for a while as Woolworths had the size to order economically efficient quantities of such 'exclusives' in specific product categories where Woolworths were strong, while their competitors did not. But this approach added extra costs to the manufacturers, who soon began to regret agreeing to the idea. It also only masked Woolworths' cost inefficiencies rather than addressed them and no retailer can carry major cost inefficiencies forever, as

Woolworths demonstrated by finally closing the doors on its 800+ UK stores in January 2009.

Manufacturers and selling strategies

Selling strategies by retailers are not all bad news for manufacturers. Discounting big brands makes them exceptionally good value and, when advertised in flyers by retailers, reinforces the brand's advertising presence, and thus share of mind (mindspace) together with the retailer usually devoting more space to the promoted lines, increasing their shelfspace. Meanwhile, since these popular brands are so essential to selling-oriented retailers, the manufacturers can hold out for high margins in their negotiations.

In the long term it is a disadvantage to the manufacturer for big brands to be sold at a loss, because the retailer loses the incentive to merchandise the brands in favourable, high-traffic locations. The retailer features them in advertising to generate store traffic, but once the shopper is in the store the retailer has every incentive via prominent merchandising to sell that person a competitive brand, one on which they will make a profit. Manufacturers who cultivate high added-value, brand-building strategies are undermined when the retail trade promotes their brands with aggressive price promotion. This is because the exaggerated importance attached to price overwhelms the other attributes, encouraging brand switching and substitutability.

The gradual commoditisation of brands has been the outcome, a fact epitomised by specialist retailers such as Costco and Sam's Club, who might only stock one brand per category and are more than happy to switch that brand by the month if the right selling price/margin is on offer. Their customers do not mind which brand is stocked as the scale of the price discount trumps any brand preference.

Selling-oriented retailers can be tough to deal with because they are determined to secure better terms than their quasi-identical competitors. Their biggest fear during negotiations is that they did not squeeze manufacturers hard enough and left some margin on the table that may be given up to a more determined competitor, who will use it to undercut them on price.

However, during negotiations, retailers can sometimes focus on their competition so much that they are often less astute when buying (i.e. their competitive effort is directed horizontally rather than vertically). In these circumstances it is not unusual for a manufacturer to find that it is possible to raise the list price offered to all retailers without being criticised. The retailers are focusing on the discount from the given list price, as the list price is known to be common to all retailers. Thus, the objective for retailers in the negotiations is to win greater discounts, bonuses, promotions support, delays of payment and so on than other retailers, but not primarily to compete for profit with the manufacturer.

The winners of the selling phase and the quest for market orientation

Retailer selling strategies can dominate for a long time, but not indefinitely. Eventually, all the weaker competitors get squeezed out or bought up. In the late 1990s, the pace of consolidation accelerated in America when Kroger acquired Fred Meyer, the sixth-largest retailer, and Albertsons, the fourth-largest; they gained 4700 stores and became the country's second-biggest grocery retailer.[13] Consolidation was also happening in all other mature markets, especially in Europe, as Wal-Mart, Carrefour and Ahold were pushing out smaller chains, and Australia, which became dominated by two retailers, Coles and Woolworths.

The United States, while being by far the largest national grocery market, is still a series of regional markets, which accounts for the relatively low percentage of sales held by the top four grocery chains (Figure 1.2).

In the smaller European markets a greater degree of retail concentration has occurred.

Divestitures and internal growth contributed to rising shares in recent years

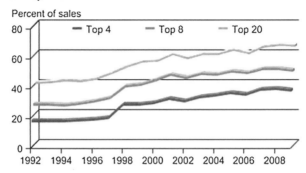

Figure 1.2 Top 4, 8 and 20 firms' share of US grocery store sales, 1992–2009.[14]
Note: Sales based on North American Industry Classification System (NAICS).
Source: USDA, ERS calculations using data from US Census Bureau, Monthly Retail Trade Survey, 1992–2009 and company annual reports.

While Sweden has the highest level of concentration among the top five grocery retailers, it is interesting to note that the concentration among those five is intense. The top three retailers, ICA, KF Group and D-Group, have 70% of the market share (35%, 20% and 15% respectively), leaving the fourth- and fifth-largest retailers, Hemkop and Bereghals, with the remaining 18%.

Once sufficient concentration and merging have taken place, the winners hope to be free to establish a more orderly form of competition between themselves, one where they create differential advantages for their stores, so that 'their shoppers' no longer see one store as substitutable for any other.

The information revolution

The biggest change that enabled the transfer of power from manufacturers to retailers was the introduction of UPC scanning and its universal adoption across FMCG. Described as the industry's Manhattan

Project,[15] UPCs and the supporting technologies took 20 years to develop before a pack of Wrigley's gum became the first product ever scanned in a grocery store on 26 June 1974.

Originally developed as a cost-saving efficiency tool, once all product categories adopted UPCs and computing became powerful and cheap enough to handle the unimaginable quantity of data, the benefits of retail information dwarfed the anticipated cost benefits from efficiencies. Real-time knowledge of sales at the item level dramatically illustrated the truism of knowledge equating to power, especially when the data could be measured at the individual shopper level through loyalty cards.

Perhaps the next information revolution in FMCG will be QR codes, short for 'quick response'. Whereas the utility of UPC codes is confined to retailers and manufacturers, QR codes can be used by end consumers, who scan them with their smart phones and can be directed to anything: a website, a promotional video, even an in-store coupon. This opens up a direct channel of communication with the consumer that can be used by both manufacturer and retailer.

The concept is in its infancy, but will undoubtedly have a huge effect on the retail market. For example, in 2011, AaramShop, an Indian online retail platform for small independent stores, added another dimension to what can be done with a QR code. Consumers can now scan the code on the product when they are running low, and it will be ordered and delivered within hours to their home, completely side-lining all the tools and techniques of competing manufacturers who would wish to get the consumer to brand switch. Tesco's Homeplus in South Korea also launched a campaign that engages shoppers to buy products using QR codes. Homeplus created virtual billboards of their store aisles in subway stations, allowing passengers to shop while they waited by scanning the products' QR codes – the groceries being delivered when they arrived home. The goal of the campaign was to help Homeplus compete with the number-one retailer, E-MART, without increasing their store numbers. Since the launch, their online sales have increased 130%, making them the top online retailer in

South Korea, and a close second offline.[16] For the 2011 Christmas season, J. C. Penney gave each shopper a 'Santa Tag' with every gift purchase containing an individualised QR code. The shopper could use the QR code to record a personalised gift message that could be heard by the recipient when they scanned the code after receiving it with the gift. The commercial uses of QR technology continue to evolve, illustrating that the battle between retailers and manufacturers is never static.

Key learnings

- The fact that **retailers are expanding their influence** and control over the value chain is not a new phenomenon; it is the **latest episode in a struggle for power and profits** that began over 200 years ago.
- The **shift of power to retailers is not an inevitable phenomenon**: technological changes and associated innovative ideas have been instrumental in moving power and profits in both directions around the value chain at different times.
- It is crucial to earn the consumer's trust ahead of horizontal competitors and ahead of other players in the value chain. It is not enough to be trustworthy, or even more trusted than one's direct competitors; **one must be the *most trustworthy* player in the value chain**. For example, Wal-Mart's strategy is that their commitment to EDLP (Every Day Low Prices) will make them the most trustworthy player because it confirms their honesty; in 2011, when a magnitude 9.0 earthquake devastated large areas of Japan, prices for items like bottled water stayed the same after Wal-Mart Seiyu outlets in the hit region reopened, while rival shops raised their rates.

- The days when manufacturers had a de facto advantage in winning consumer trust are over. All other things being equal, **the retailer will have an advantage** because of their direct contact with the shopper.
- The manufacturers' **old branding tools are now insufficient** to win the battle of the value chain. In order to develop new, more effective approaches, a much deeper understanding of the modern retailer is needed than has hitherto been the case.
- Brand **loyalty is not an absolute**; it can be bought for a price, a feature display or an optimal shelf location.

While much has changed over time in the relationship between retailers and manufacturers, one thing that has not changed is that they are very different kinds of businesses. They are structured differently, operate differently and are financed differently, all of which are at the root of much of the tension that exists between the two. In the next chapter, we will explore these differences and how a better understanding of them can lead to more productive retailer–manufacturer interactions and relationships.

Notes

1. Progressive Grocer (USA), 10 June 2009 (2009 Category Management Study).
2. www.marketingmagazine.co.uk/news/943397/Tesco-Clubcard-signs-one-million-customers-relaunch/. Accessed 27 July 2006.
3. Mesure, S (2003) 'Loyalty card costs Tesco £1bn of profits – but is worth every penny', *The Independent*, 10 October 2003.
4. http://www.weetabixusa.com/index2.html. Accessed 29 July 2006.
5. http://www.americanhistory.si.edu/archives/Ivory/index.asp. Accessed 30 March 2006.

6. Dyer D, Dalzell F, Olegario R (2004) *Rising Tide: Lessons from 165 years of brand building at Procter and Gamble*. Harvard Business School Press, Boston, p. 35.

7. Chandler AD (2004) *Scale and Scope: The dynamics of industrial capitalism*. Harvard University Press, Boston, p. 156.

8. Tedlow RS (1990) *New and Improved: The story of mass marketing in America*. Basic Books Inc., New York, p. 194.

9. Tedlow RS (1990) *New and Improved: The story of mass marketing in America*. Basic Books Inc., New York, p. 383.

10. http://www.ers.usda.gov/publications/aer811/aer811e.pdf. Accessed 30 March 2006.

11. http://www.atkearney.com/index.php/News-media/buying-less-frozen-food.html. Accessed 30 March 2006.

12. http://supermarketnews.com/retail_financial/retailers_fewer_opportunities_1010/index1.html. Accessed 30 October 2011.

13. http://www.ers.usda.gov/briefing/FoodMarketStructures/foodretailing.htm. Accessed 30 March 2006.

14. http://farmfutures.com/blogs.aspx/food-retailers-continue-rapid-consolidation-2446. Accessed 30 October 2011.

15. Tony Seideman; *Barcodes Sweep the World*, www.barcoding.com/Information/barcode_history.shtml. Accessed 31 March 2006.

16. http://design-milk.com/the-future-of-grocery-shopping. Accessed 3 August 2011.

Chapter 2

RETAILERS AND MANUFACTURERS are very different kinds of businesses. They view and act upon the same situations differently, many times at odds with each other. This creates friction in their relationships. If advantage is to be gained by one party or the other, it is crucial to understand the other's business model and their key drivers.

Historically, manufacturers and retailers have known little about each other. For most of the twentieth century, what little knowledge there was about how the other operated was confined to specialists who interacted with each other: sales operatives and buyers. But today, such is the sophistication of both parties, it is essential that everyone has a thorough understanding of the other's business model.

The differing realities of retailing and manufacturing are driven by four fundamental factors: financial structure, cost structure, physical network and the role of price.

Financial structure differences

The biggest difference between manufacturers and retailers is how they generate their profits. If we consider the equation:

Return on equity (ROE) = Net profit margin × Asset turnover × Leverage

Table 2.1 Comparison of return on equity between a typical retailer and manufacturer

	Net profit	Asset turnover	Leverage	ROE
Retailer	3%	1.9	3.2	18%
Manufacturer	13%	0.9	2.7	31%

Source: Average figures over 2008–2009 based on public data from companies' annual reports and financial results presentations.

Table 2.2 Property and other tangible assets of major retailers, 2011 or latest

Retailer	US$ billion	Percentage of sales
Tesco	42	43
J Sainsbury	14	41
Wal-Mart	109	26
Metro Group	16	19
Carrefour	20	17

Source: Average figures based on public data from companies' annual reports.

and look at a representative sample of the top retailers and manufacturers, we will notice some significant differences (Table 2.1).

Manufacturers, in general, have a higher ROE than retailers do, which retailers partially compensate for in the eyes of investors by having higher growth rates. But the more relevant fact is that ROE is derived quite differently across the two groups. Despite the complaints from manufacturers about the rising power of the retailers, manufacturers still have a large share of the value-chain profits, as demonstrated by the huge difference in net profit margins. Retailers rely on a higher asset turn and leverage to compensate for their much smaller profit margins. Retailers also have large property portfolios, which add immense value to their businesses, as shown in Table 2.2.

As can be seen by comparing Tables 2.3 and 2.4, some retailers, such as Ahold and Marks & Spencer, have achieved profit margins

Table 2.3 Return on equity for manufacturers

	Net profit margin	Asset turnover	Leverage	Return on equity
Procter & Gamble	14%	0.6	2.1	16%
Unilever	12%	1.1	3.2	41%
Coca-Cola	19%	0.7	2.0	28%
Kraft Foods	7%	0.6	2.7	11%
Philip Morris	11%	1.7	2.0	39%
Kellogg's	9%	1.0	4.5	44%

Source: Average figures over 2008–2009 based on public data from companies' annual reports and financial results presentations.

Table 2.4 Return on equity for retailers

	Net profit margin	Asset turnover	Leverage	Return on equity
Wal-Mart	3%	2.3	2.5	19%
Tesco	4%	1.6	2.4	18%
Carrefour	2%	1.6	4.6	18%
Auchan	2%	1.5	3.7	12%
Ahold	8%	1.8	3.2	48%
Marks & Spencer	8%	1.4	3.5	41%

Source: Average figures over 2008–2009 based on public data from companies' annual reports and financial results presentations.

similar to giants from the golden age of manufacturer brands, such as Kellogg's and Kraft, but it is not yet common.

However, this could very well change as retailers are developing their own brand equities via impressive private label strategies (see Chapter 9) and will begin seeing brand premiums being factored into their profit margins.

These fundamental differences in financial structure affect the way retailers think and operate, which is a source of friction between them and manufacturers. The most important consequences are that retailer profits are much more sensitive to volume, pricing decisions and finely controlling costs than is the case for manufacturers.

Volume Sensitivity

Retailers are more vulnerable than manufacturers to small changes in volume because it adversely affects their asset turnover, which is a much bigger driver of their profits. When a manufacturer has supply issues and leaves a retailer out of stock, the impact on the retailer is greater than it is on the manufacturer because of the difference in the importance of asset turnover combined with their lower overall profitability. Consequently, it is not unusual for retailers to get more upset than the manufacturer anticipated. According to the Grocery Manufacturers Association of America, US grocers lose almost $20 billion a year due to out-of-stocks, a loss that hurts their bottom lines much more than it does those of the manufacturers. This sensitivity to volume also translates into retailers' vulnerability towards price battles instigated by the manufacturer or between themselves.

The vulnerability of a retailer's profits to relatively small downturns in sales was vividly demonstrated by Tesco at the end of 2011 when they reported a fall in underlying UK sales of 2.3% for the crucial last six weeks of the year, partly caused by their 'Big Price Drop' promotion failing to pull in more shoppers.[1] While such a decline would not be welcome in a manufacturing company, in a retailer it is seen as catastrophic. The news sent Tesco's share price plummeting 16%, wiping £5 billion off their value as a projected 10% increase in their profits in 2012 was hastily revised to zero.

Price Support

A reduction of the net profit margin by one percentage point from 3% to 2% will reduce the retailer's ROE by one-third, from 18% to 12%, using the numbers in Table 2.1 as an example, which explains why lowering prices to face hard discounters can be a disaster. A similar reduction of one percentage point in the net profit margin of the manufacturer will only reduce its ROE from 31% to 29%, which is a problem, but is a much more manageable drop for the manufacturer than the retailer. While a manufacturer may be tempted to fund price reductions demanded by a hard discounter as the increased volume would cover their reduced margins, retailers who felt compelled to match the lower price would be outraged because of the cataclysmic impact on their profit margin. In many mature markets it is common for retailers to assume that the manufacturer funded a lower price in a competing retailer, and instead of taking the loss with lower profit margins they will deduct the cost of reducing their prices from the manufacturer's outstanding invoices.

Operating Costs

With such thin margins, profits turn to losses if the retailer loses control of costs by even one or two percentage points. Thus, any activity by the manufacturer, even a change in packaging, will come under intense scrutiny for its impact on a retailer's in-store merchandising or supply-chain handling costs. There is little chance the product will be listed if it is more costly for the retailer to handle. Equally, any manufacturer who does not immediately jump through hoops to instigate packaging or handling changes required by a retailer for efficiency reasons will find the temperature in negotiations rapidly dropping.

Cost-structure differences

Modern retailing is no different from most other industries in terms of the benefits of size, which provides economies of scale and competitive strength. The difference for retailers compared to manufacturers is the level at which scale advantages accrue: at the company, chain or store level. The main points of difference driven by the different cost structures are size and breadth of product range and lack of flexibility in fixed costs.

Range and Assortment

The size and breadth of product range affects profit margins differently for retailers than for manufacturers. In FMCG manufacturers, large product ranges are frequently seen as a cost burden and often come under cost-reduction pressures owing to perceived but hard-to-quantify 'costs of complexity'. In retailing, more is (mostly) seen as better. Competition is fiercest on the most basic grocery items: some 400 lines, which in many cases are still sold at Michael Cullen-type margins. If a store stocks only 1000 lines, only a maximum of 600 can be sold at a higher margin. A store with several thousand lines has more scope for making good margins for the vast majority of its lines (in particular fresh foods and non-food). Thus, a larger retail unit, all other things being equal, will make better margins than a smaller one. A typical European hypermarket will carry 40000 SKUs; the largest Wal-Marts in the United States can carry over 100000 SKUs. In contrast, a manufacturer will usually make better margins on its biggest products and be constantly looking to rationalise its tail of lower-volume lines. This difference can cause much conflict when a manufacturer wants to discontinue a low-volume product because of poor profitability, whereas those retailers who sell it see no reason why it should go as it will be one of their higher-margin lines.

Fixed-Costs Inflexibility

As retailing becomes more sophisticated, the fixed costs in property and technology at each location increase. For the large retailers, the value tied up in their stores is enormous (Table 2.5).

The lower the ratio of sales to fixed tangible assets, the more the retailer is exposed to these capital assets and needs to find ways to make them work harder. An in-store butcher or bakery cannot be

Table 2.5 Property/plant/equipment on the balance sheets of top retailers

Retailer	Property/plant/equipment, book value (depreciated) (US$ billion)	Sales (US$ billion)	Sales/Fixed tangible assets (US$ billion)
Wal-Mart	108	419	3.9
Tesco	42	98	2.4
Carrefour	20	112	5.7
Metro Group	16	86	5.3
Kroger	14	90	6.2
J Sainsbury	14	34	2.4
X5 Retail Group	4	11	2.8

Source: Corporate websites of retailers in 2011.

scaled down indefinitely, made more efficient by operating across several stores or outsourced to India. Retailers have to generate increased sales in each location to justify the investment, and every manufacturer has to demonstrate how their brands help to achieve this versus competitive brands, either through increasing store traffic or increasing basket size, or both.

Pricing and price perception differences

Price plays a larger role in the positioning of stores than it does in the positioning of brands. Price rarely provides a differential advantage for product brands: indeed, the more expensive brands are often category leaders, like Tropicana in chilled fruit juice, Pampers in disposable nappies (diapers) and Danone in Greek yogurt. In contrast, the price perception of a large retailing chain is a cornerstone of its image. This is the case not just for hard discounters with an unambiguous price positioning but also for those who aim at a mainstream compromise between price, quality and assortment.

Even chains committed to a high-quality image, like Russia's Green Perekrestok, continually have to remind shoppers of their commitment to price. Green Perekrestok offer a wide assortment of high-quality foods and services, including consultations for gourmet cheeses, meats and liquor. Their messaging is focused on providing service at the best prices, and they have regular deals on their website to help maintain a price-conscious image.

The world's largest member-based supermarket network, IGA, launched a premium private label range in Australia, promising 'Quality and Value'. Their new product line is built to confirm their dedication to quality as well as price, as they guarantee that 'all IGA Signature products are carefully selected and evaluated for best quality and value'. More generally, 90% of all retail advertising in Europe is price related and 70% is exclusively based on price.

There are four clear differentiating factors between the pricing of a product and the pricing policy of a store, and these are described below.

Split Baskets

Many shoppers regularly visit two or more stores and they 'split their baskets', or cherry pick promotions. Suppose a supermarket decides to invest in giving wide choice, and reflects the costs incurred via generally higher prices. Nearby, a competitor develops a low-choice, low-cost strategy. The more expensive store finds shoppers develop the habit of visiting the cheaper store to stock up on basics (e.g. milk, eggs, soft drinks) while continuing to buy more exotic and quality-sensitive items from them. The supermarket cannot destock basic products, for fear of alienating its remaining one-stop shopping segment, but it has profitability problems, as the basics account for 40% of its operating costs, but does not have the sales to match. When retailers stock directly comparable national brands, it is easy for shoppers to cherry pick, buying from the retailers that have the lowest price that week.

Manufacturers are relatively immune from this phenomenon because brand buyers find it harder to split their brand purchases based on marginal price differences: they either buy the brand or they don't.

Breaking the Price–Quality Relationship

In product marketing the price of a brand usually has an influence on its perceived quality. When stores that have different price positionings sell the same brands, this price–quality relationship can be broken. A store can position itself credibly as selling good-quality products and, through its own efficiency and good faith, delivering those products or brands at lower prices. In the words of Albert Gubay, the UK Kwik Save's founder, 'Our objective is not to sell cheap groceries, but to sell groceries cheaply.' Price as a guarantee of quality is a tactic that is now much harder for manufacturers to implement, as pricing is very much in the control of the retailer, who will decide it based on their own price perception objectives, not those of the brands. Retailers are not inclined to follow the manufacturer's price recommendations; hence, manufacturers can no longer rely on price to send signals on quality.

Managing Price Perceptions

Retail price perception is much more open to influence through advertising than it is from shoppers comparing actual prices between chains. Even a research company trying to make an objective comparison between pricing in two chains has to pick an arbitrary basket of goods and a particular date, and then as soon as it is published the retailers who compare unfavourably point out that it is out of date or unrepresentative.

Thus, the consumer is more inclined to rely on impressions gained from advertising, the store's promotional activity, the presentation of the store or comments in the media, as well as an idiosyncratic selection of actual price comparisons. This is why discount retailers, like Food Basics in Canada, Lidl in Europe and Vishal Megamart in India, have poor lighting, cheap signage and less modern displays: they send a message that they don't spend money on store appearance, so that shoppers believe they get the best prices. Retailers will focus their advertised price activity on the brands that help get their pricing message across, whether the manufacturer likes being discounted or not.

The Value of the Shopping Experience versus the Brand Experience

In a six-month period, 90% of German households visit an Aldi store. Thus Aldi, the retail brand with the cheapest positioning, has an almost universal penetration among the richest population in Europe who are unwavering in their support of premium brands such as Mercedes, BMW and Audi.

There are very few upscale grocery chains. Marks & Spencer in the United Kingdom, Russia's Azbuka Vkusa and Whole Foods Market in North America are exceptions, and each originally built their store traffic on niche positionings: Marks & Spencer via clothes and Whole Foods via organic foodstuffs. When you look at major supermarket chains, there are no 'Lexus' chains; there are not even 'Mercedes' chains. While it is possible for a grocery company to operate different chains that have different actual and perceived prices, for example the Loblaws Group in Canada own Fortinos at the higher end, Loblaws in the middle and No Frills at the cheaper end, the price differentials between them are small compared to the price differentials between product brands.

FMCG retailing is generally a low-added-value activity. Shoppers seek neither prestige nor pleasure from the experience. Shopping is a rational decision where price (or rather the shopper's perception of price) is destined to play a major role, much greater than between brands. Manufacturers need to be extremely sensitive to this.

Physical differences

Location is of the highest importance to retailers. No market analysis of a retailer is complete without a map showing the locations of their stores and those of their competitors. In studies on shop choice,

Table 2.6 Reasons for choosing a main supermarket among regular shoppers

Reason	2008	2009	2010
Price	58	62	72
Convenience	49	43	49
Parking	17	18	22
Late-night hours	8	9	9
Quality of product	11	10	12
Loyalty programmes	8	10	10
Support local shops	6	6	8

Source: National Consumer Agency, Grocery Shopping Market Research Findings in the United States, March 2011. Report by Amarach Research.

location is almost always one of the top two reasons behind price (Table 2.6).

The store's total potential target market – the group of consumers who could use one of the stores on a regular basis – is defined as their coverage. It depends on the number of stores, the population density, traffic flows and transport infrastructure. It is also affected by people's measures of convenience and willingness to travel. A retailer's competitive situation can change dramatically if its average relative location changes, for example when a strong major player buys a weak smaller player and rebrands all the stores it gains.

In the United Kingdom during the 1980s, the biggest chains, Sainsbury's and Tesco, were located within the nearest five supermarkets to more than half of UK households. This was a notable achievement, but still meant that each of these chains was only a serious competitor for 50% of UK grocery purchases. The difficulty and expense in gaining a lead in supermarket coverage led Tesco to enter a new channel by purchasing a chain of convenience stores, T&S Stores, in 2002. More than 500 were changed into Tesco Express, a format with a typical size of $2000\,\text{ft}^2$ that focuses on everyday essentials plus higher-margin convenience items, such as pre-prepared meals. This move, since extended and copied by Sainsbury's, also changed the dynamics for manufacturers who had been charging T&S Stores higher net prices than they had Tesco and so lost a more profitable customer. These smaller sites usually charge a 10–15% price premium over their out-of-town counterparts, partly owing to more complex supply chains that require more frequent store deliveries and partly because they are able to do so anyway.

A retailer's coverage consists of a set of geographical patches around its stores. This causes three problems for the retailer in targeting shoppers:

- **The patches do not always resemble each other.** For example, one store may be in an affluent area and another in a poor area. Some will be in urban areas; others, in rural areas.
- **Geographical segmentation** does not generally say a lot about people's preferences: no manufacturer segments its market on local geography.
- **Peripheral shoppers:** The key target market for any one store is not the people nearest to the store, who can mostly be counted on to come anyway, but the marginal shoppers located some distance away, who could just as easily visit another store.

Thus, a chain of stores is forced to service a widely heterogeneous target: the people for whom the set of stores is convenient. Manufacturers create perceptual maps of brands that suggest how their brand should be positioned to gain users, whereas stores are positioned on a real map. Whatever shopper segments a chain would *like* to choose, it *has* to serve the shoppers who live or work nearby. Hence, any one chain is unlikely to find a homogeneous socio-economic or lifestyle sub-group across all its stores. Since a retail chain is the sum of its individual stores, every retailer serves, to varying degrees, all groups:

- those customers who find it convenient, i.e. those living nearby or for whom the store is on a route
- customers who are attracted by the price policy, be it *every day low price* (EDLP), *high-low* or *premium*

- customers driven by special offers/promotions
- customers attracted by a specific, SKU, service or facility, e.g. fresh bread, meat, fish.

Retailers do not sit side by side on a shelf. They do not have an entire population from which to target their users; for their part, shoppers do not select stores from the complete range of retail chains on offer in the country.

Key learnings

- Retailers and manufacturers have **very different financial business models**. These differences drive many of the contrasting perceptions and behaviours of the two parties and are at the root of much of the friction: they see and respond to the same events in very different ways.
- Relative to manufacturers, retailers have huge fixed costs and miniscule margins: this makes their profits **more susceptible to small changes in volume and pricing**, both favourably and unfavourably, than is the case with manufacturers.
- The **price perception of a retail chain** is a critical success factor, and one that they cannot be seen to get wrong. Manufacturers who offer better deals to some retailers and not others take a huge risk.
- Retailers **control the pricing of brands** and will use price on leading brands to achieve their own objectives.
- Retailers **have much broader target markets** than do brands, and need to appeal to all target groups to achieve volume.

Note

1. http://www.guardian.co.uk/business/2012/jan/12/tesco-stores-shakeup-christmas-performance/print. Accessed 16 January 2012.

Chapter 3

I N A MATURE industry, manufacturers have to fight each other, and increasingly their retail customers, ever more aggressively to win sales. Slow or no market growth means sales have to be won directly from competitors, which is not easy because mature markets are dominated by two phenomena:

- **Product parity:** When technological development plateaus, advantages created by technology disappear and competitors produce goods of almost identical quality, from washing-up liquid to computers to lipstick. New entrants, both manufacturers and private label, are able to jump quality learning curves by using outsourced manufacturing, which just further increases the pressure on the market leaders. As far as shoppers can judge, brands become mostly indistinguishable. This leads to substitutability, a death sentence for profits in any industry. There is no longer blind loyalty to brands in more than a small minority of consumers. But there is preference, and preference will ordinarily weaken over time owing to innovation from competitors, the increase in availability/quality of private label options and brand fatigue, which all make it easier for the shopper to switch.

- **Overcapacity:** During periods of growth, companies focus on expanding capacity ahead of their competition to win. When demand plateaus, this expansion cannot be halted in time to avoid excess capacity. This overcapacity eventually destroys profits as manufacturers are more likely to make marginal cost-based decisions to regain volume.

Retailers play a role in both these phenomena. They are no longer interested in listing every brand, so every time they choose to delist one manufacturer's product in favour of another, new capacity is created and old capacity is left empty. In addition, to facilitate the ease with which retailers can switch listings, they are committed to the commoditisation of brands. Retailers want brands to be interchangeable and thus substitutable; otherwise, they are weakened in negotiations if the brand is so unique and popular it must be listed at all costs.

In mature markets, where overcapacity and brand substitutability have become prevalent, selling strategies seem much more attractive than stagnation, but selling-oriented manufacturers can all but destroy each other.

Selling orientation and hustle strategies

When overcapacity occurs in industries with high fixed costs, price cutting by one or two competitors often leads to a price war. Price wars are bloodiest in markets where volume is key to competitiveness and high fixed costs are involved (e.g. the auto industry, televisions, airlines, personal computers) or where barriers to exit (e.g. redundancy payments, write-offs) are high.

Hustle actions increase consumers' willingness to buy without adding value to the product; they tempt the buyer using price cuts, incentives and aggressive sales forces. Selling-oriented strategies work for the first competitors to use them, but they elicit a mirror response from the competition and often spiral out of control. As each offer escalates and destroys profitability, the benefits of any sales increase are more than lost as sales return to normal but at much lower margins. Each participant is motivated by the dream that losses will force some competitors into submission and the victors will inherit a profitable market.

The 2008 bailouts of GM and Chrysler in North America were in part precipitated by the price war initiated in 2005 by GM, and rapidly copied by Ford and Chrysler, to extend their employee pricing to all buyers. Although the initial sales response was excellent, with all three companies registering their highest month's sales for years, it became a trap from which no one dared to be the first to escape. The offer was repeated in subsequent years despite falling sales volumes, which dragged down prices and profits for all. More recently, owing to the economic downturn in 2008, many airlines had seen business travel drop 30% in three months, leaving spare capacity in a high fixed-cost industry. The airlines felt their only resort was to make massive price cuts to retain volume. British Airways cut fares by 25%, and others were panicked into offering prices that hadn't been seen since the 1980s.[1]

The conditions that drive such actions also often apply to retailing these days, as the fixed investment has risen to a point where a superstore costs as much as a factory. High fixed costs mean that high volumes are an ever-essential objective. One of the big strategic advantages of manufacturers outsourcing production is that they are not as vulnerable to fixed-cost pressures to fill the factories at any cost.

Market orientation

The key to profitability for manufacturers is to make their brands non-substitutable in the eyes of consumers, and the best way of achieving that is through segmentation. While the potential of segmentation to grow volume and profit is widely understood, it comes as a surprise to many to learn that segmentation was originally developed to negate price wars, a lesson that seems to have become neglected, so it is worth revisiting the origins of segmentation to remind ourselves of its original purpose, which is of critical importance today.

In 1890, there were 578 American soap manufacturers, one of which, P&G, had over 30 different kinds of soap on the market. New brands had been launched by all to fill capacity, not unmet consumer needs. After a post-World War I acquisition spree that consolidated the market, leaving Lever Bros., Palmolive and P&G as the dominant players, P&G ended up with a bloated portfolio of 140 soap brands, all of which purported to do the same thing: clean everything from lace tablecloths to the family dog.

With so many brands available, each claiming to address the whole range of washing needs, prices were falling as shoppers were choosing on the basis of price alone – the brands were completely substitutable.

To escape this death spiral, P&G decided to slash their brand portfolio and target each of the remaining brands at specific washing needs. Thus initially evolved separate brands for the washing of clothes, skin and hair, which further evolved over time into separate brands for work-clothes, delicates, colours, whites, oily skin, dry skin, sensitive skin, dry hair, oily hair, dandruff-laden hair, blonde hair, coloured hair *ad infinitum*.

This segmentation not only addressed the downward pressure on prices but also became a major engine for volume growth. Segmentation encouraged the consumer to buy not just one large slab of generic soap at a rock-bottom price but also a whole range of higher-priced offerings that performed different tasks or were targeted at different water conditions, usages or users. And once all that soap was in the house, washing frequency increased. Now differentiated, the brands could coexist on the shelf without being seen as substitutes for each other, each being able to maintain its appropriate price point.

Segmentation of usage occasion can be used within the same brand via differentiated packaging formats. Coca-Cola introduced the first six-pack carrier in 1923 to create a new place to enjoy their product – the home – and consumption rapidly increased. By the 1950s, additional sizes were available: families could buy the 755 mL bottle for home and the 195 mL bottles for picnics, and the products could coexist happily on the shelf with very different prices per litre. Their innovation in packaging continues to create new segments, for example creating the 100 mL can for people who feel too guilty to purchase a full size Coca-Cola. Not that Coca-Cola ignored the possibilities of segmenting by product variant. In 1982, they introduced Diet Coke to target the health-conscious population, and there are now over 23 flavours of Coke (including Coca-Cola, Diet Coke, Caffeine-Free Coca-Cola, Caffeine-Free Diet Coke, Coca-Cola Black Cherry Vanilla, Diet Coke Black Cherry Vanilla, Coca-Cola with Lime, Diet Coke with Lime, Coca-Cola with Lemon, Diet Coke with Lemon and Coca-Cola C2).[2]

P&G and Coca-Cola leveraged a profound consumer insight: shoppers don't buy products, they buy benefits. To get the most benefit from a segmentation strategy, marketers must focus on *why* consumers buy, not *what* they buy or *who* they are. Once you know what consumer preferences depend on, you can adapt your offering to those conditions.

A key element of a segmentation strategy is that a market-oriented producer is not jealous of the segments satisfied better by its competitors. The producer is pleased to have competitors who follow market-oriented strategies similar to its own, while despising competitors who want to copy its products and then compete on price.

The key to a competitive edge in a market-oriented industry is to understand consumers' buying decisions better than the competition, and to strive continually to increase that knowledge to combat the retailers' desire to commoditise. Apple are a terrific example. Instead of following the trend to push products when they opened their retail outlets in 2001, their goal was to create a place for people to gather and celebrate. They provided a great experience by being a hub of information instead of focusing on sales, and in 2006 they even replaced their check-out counters with handheld POS systems (now iPods) to minimise the sales push feel. Their stores generated 170 million visits in 2009 and created more revenue ($6.6 billion) than their total global sales when they first opened in 2001 ($5.4 billion).[3]

An industry's position on the selling–market orientation spectrum

Whether by latching onto emerging consumer trends and magnifying their impact or in training shoppers how to shop, the behaviour of an industry influences its consumers.

For example, many household cleaning brands have shifted their offering to respond to the environmental movement. Aldi Australia linked with Aussies Living Simply, a community focused on sustainability, permaculture and organic gardening. South Africa's Pick 'n Pay launched a line of eco-friendly cleaning products, and P&G launched Tide Free. New companies have also emerged, including Tri-nature lifestyle products in Australia and Method, a high-end range of naturally derived, biodegradable household cleaning products. Green cleaning products are currently projected to take 30% of the market in 2013.[4]

In other instances, long-term complementary strategies adopted by dominant industry players can create a new set of buying rules to their mutual advantage. In the US cola market, Coca-Cola and Pepsi have long waged a permanent advertising and public relations war. This has encouraged consumers to develop emotional loyalty for either supplier. Meanwhile, regular price promotions, often alternating between the two of them, tend to reduce the scope for smaller brands and private label trying to attract buyers willing to switch on the basis of low price. Coca-Cola and Pepsi were not competing on price with each other, but using price to minimise further competition. This kind of arrangement can still be profitable if the big brands have a group of loyal buyers who still buy at the normal price outside promotions. In fact, alternating price promotions between major competitors can defend their joint market share against smaller brands (or a retailer's own brand) who have fewer loyal purchasers. Dr Pepper, which looks exactly like a cola even if it has a somewhat unique flavour, has long struggled to breach this industry defence outside of its homeland of Texas.

But when matters are less orderly and the heat is on, the need for speed of response often dictates the types of action in a market. For example, if management is under pressure to deliver profits in the short term, quick-response promotions are a more attractive investment than design improvements. Short-term actions are also favoured in industries sensitive to changes in volume sales, like retailers. Shoppers tend to react more quickly to price promotions than to store layout changes.

The financial resources of competitors also dictate the choice of weapon. Retailers, even small ones, can initiate a disruptive price war to which all others must respond, whereas with manufacturers a sales force war, for example, can only be initiated by rich competitors. The prescription drug industry sends armies of competing salespeople into doctors' offices to push similar drugs. Only where profitability is high, like pharmaceuticals, can companies afford expensive tools such as large, well-trained sales forces. Out-of-patent drugs, such as Bayer's Aspirin, do not have the benefit of a huge sales force battering their way into doctors' offices to sing its praises and so have to battle it out on the shelves with generics and private label.

The more competitors focus on different reasons for purchase, and on segmenting their offerings, the more orderly the market becomes, and the more the opportunities for individual competitors to be profitable abound. However, it is hard for a single competitor to move away from a selling mode in isolation. In many cases it has to get to the point where competitors collectively become so tired of ongoing selling wars that they find ways of moving as an industry.

There are three ways for an industry to escape from the selling war: collusion, concentration and signalling.

- **Collusion:** Cartels such as OPEC (Organization of Petroleum Exporting Countries) are often formed in an attempt to end price wars. When OPEC discovered collusion in 1973, it more than quadrupled the price of a barrel of oil together with its members' incomes. Protectionism to reduce the competition from abroad is similarly attractive. Producers have long been convinced of the benefits of these methods; however, governments generally disapprove.

Beyond possible legal problems, there is the risk of falling back into selling strategies if the cartel crumbles. In a cartel, there is a permanent temptation for each member to break ranks and sell more or cheaper than agreed with the other members. The more producers involved, the more realistic it is that someone will crack, and thus the greater the temptation to be that one. De Beers operated a selling cartel for diamonds by using their control of the central selling organisations to manage prices by manipulating supply and demand. In the past, when a single country, such as Zaire, tried to break away and sell their diamonds independently, De Beers would flood the market with similar diamonds to drive down prices for Zaire, forcing them to return to the cartel. But the cartel crumbled in the 1990s, driven by the fragmentation of the Soviet Union, the discovery of diamonds in new countries such as Canada and the defection of Australia's huge Argyle mine. The cartel could cope with occasional defectors but not such a large number. With their market share reducing from 85% to 65%, De Beer's recognised that they could no longer manage the cartel and turned to brand building as an alternative.

- **Consolidation:** In a situation where intense, selling-focused competition is reducing profits, one solution is to buy up competitors until there are few left and each can see hope in cooperating with the others. This can, like cartels, be against the consumers' interests and most governments have some monopoly and mergers legislation. However, consolidation, coupled with a desire among the survivors to restore normal profit levels, helps to usher in an era of orderly competition based on serving the variety of wants.

In 1975, Carrefour became the first foreign retailer in Brazil. Through a period of aggressive mergers and acquisitions, they increased their market share and forced smaller competitors to leave or consolidate. In 1999, the largest national retailer, Companhia Brasileira de Distribuicao, merged with Casino Guichard Perrachon & Cie, to compete against the growing foreign chains, which now hold 40% of the market. The outcome has been a more orderly market where each is large and successful enough not to have to resort to permanent cut-throat price competition.

- **Signalling and 'Rules':** Firms can signal to one another their willingness, or unwillingness, to abide by certain rules. By making the right signals, they can sometimes collectively withdraw from unwinnable battlegrounds and create a competitive, but orderly, market. Implicit rules (if made explicit) would include:
  - avoiding hustle strategies or operating at a loss (predatory pricing)
  - not copying the products of competitors (me-tooing)
  - searching for and investing in non-price differences to promote products: invest in adding value (e.g. advertising) rather than selling pressure (e.g. promotions).

Announcements promising the most competitive prices are an invitation to the industry to start a price war. Asda's promise to be 15% cheaper than Tesco on a range of products forced Tesco to launch their 'Big Price Drop' series of price cuts in the latter part of 2011. On the other hand, a retailer announcing that it will match a competitor's low prices can be a signal to stop fighting on price. In an experiment in the United States, Big Star Supermarket promised to match Food Lion Supermarkets' prices on 100 specified product lines.[5] After two years, the prices for the matched products had risen significantly in both stores, compared to the prices on the unmatched lines. The trick that protects profitability is the promise to match, not to beat.

Swinging back to hustle strategies

A successful shift towards market orientation does not eliminate the risk of a swing back to hustling. This is not surprising when one considers the following situations, each capable of producing a price war:

- **A price war can re-occur because competitors become too good to each other.** If profitability makes the market unusually attractive, new competitors are bound to enter. Usually, they enter at the bottom of the market, serving price-sensitive segments. In retailing this process has been observed so frequently that it has been named the 'wheel of retailing'. But, as most large retailers move towards operating across a range of formats where price expectations of the shopper are different, this cycle is coming to an end as the large players are leaving fewer price gaps.
- **If competitors are determined to grow in a static market, they may start to break the orderly market rules.** Producing copies of rivals' products is tempting because in the short term it 'steals' share and makes money. Although competitors with strong technological and marketing skills are unlikely to launch exact copies of rival brands, it is estimated that 97% of new products are not genuine innovations.[6] The failure rate of new products is extremely high, around 90% two years after launch, so even though differentiated brands on the whole perform better than me-toos, me-toos are common in markets where innovation is slowing down. Once they get a hold in an industry, there is an inevitable downward pressure on prices.

The first E-reader was developed in the 1970s, although they weren't popular until the mid-2000s, when Amazon launched the Kindle, and then Barnes & Noble followed with the Nook, Sony with the Sony Reader Touch, Kobo with the eReader and Bookeen with Cybook Opus. Now there are so many E-readers offering similar functionality and benefits that the industry has moved to compete on price. In 2009, Amazon reduced their price of the Kindle from $359 to $259 with subsequent further reductions reaching $79 by January 2012 in response to Booken's progressive price reduction of their Cybook Opus from $349 in 2009 to $189 in 2011, and Kobo launched their eReader at $149 to steal market share.

Me-too strategies are very popular in fast-growing markets because they avoid one of the main barriers to successful innovation: consumer acceptance of the idea. Within FMCG categories, break-through performance from new products has always been difficult to achieve and seems to be getting harder. In the United States, on average, nearly 80% of new product introductions fail to generate more than $7.5 million in first-year sales, with less than 3% of products achieving 'mega hit' status of over $50 million in first-year sales.[7] Against that background, gate-crashing someone else's party can sound quite attractive.

- **If the consumers' desires or willingness to pay changes, marketers may find price competition unavoidable.** On Friday, 2 April 1993, Philip Morris, the maker of premium-priced Marlboro cigarettes, announced a 20% price reduction to restore a competitive position against private label and cheap brands that sold for up to a 40% discount and had been consistently eating into Marlboro's share. The company's stock price immediately fell by 26% as the move was widely hailed as a disaster for premium brands. But it was not; it was just the end of a premium brand being overpriced; the problem was that Marlboro had opened up too big of a price premium, opening the door for all kinds of competitors. The event precipitated the end of cigarette price wars because many competitors were unable to compete with a more affordable Marlboro. Within two years, Philip Morris's stock had fully recovered. The Canadian cola market has demonstrated time and again the consumer's willing-ness to switch from Coca-Cola or Pepsi to private label colas if the price differential were greater than $1 for a box of 12 cans. Opening too big a price differential begins a price war by increasing the volume that moves around the market because of price.
- **Price wars may be engaged intentionally by an aggressive competitor out to steal share.** This strategy is tempting to a competitor who has a more efficient cost structure. By fighting a war on price, a com-petitor may be able to drive other competitors to the wall, and the survivors can hope for profitable years to come. Philip Morris's price

cuts also could be seen as an aggressive action focused on driving RJR Nabisco from the cigarette market. RJR's domestic tobacco sales, and that division's operating profit, were dramatically affected, down 72% by the end of the year. In the retail sector, using a higher level of efficiency to fund lower prices had long been Wal-Mart's strategy. Costco and Sam's Club use a variant of this, where members' fees basically equate to the annual profit of the company with sales through the stores earning effectively zero margin. It is easy, however, to miscalculate the staying power of one's adversaries. Price wars drag on long and painfully, especially when the players have backers with deep pockets, for example PepsiCo's Frito-Lay versus Anheuser-Busch's Eagle Snacks in the US snacks market, a war that waged for over a decade with no one emerging as the winner.

- **A weak competitor may resort to dropping prices because it is the only available action for increasing its volume in the short term to stave off disaster.** By the late 1970s, Tesco had been suffering because of their legacy of small, town-centre sites but succeeded in taking the industry by storm with their 'check-out' campaign. The whole UK retail market became price-driven for several years, before it swung once again towards a market orientation with the battle being fought on location, format and service.

The damage done over time by a price war is twofold: everybody loses money unless there is dramatic growth in the overall market, and it can destroy the brand equities built during orderly competition. Communications focused on slashed prices push aside the messages focused on quality and function. Quality has to be trimmed to ensure price competitiveness: advertising, R & D and other brand differentiating investments are reduced in the drive to cut costs. This encourages the buyer to believe that all products are similar and increases the salience of price. Consumers are made more price-sensitive, destroying the added value of the whole market.

But this is the impact of price wars in slow-growing, highly developed Western markets, where the industry players are large and sophisticated and see price wars as a failure of management to come up with anything better. In fast-growing, emerging markets, such as China, price wars are more prevalent and are viewed as legitimate and effective business tools in certain circumstances.

The difference comes from the different market conditions. In a market such as China, it is not unusual for a category to have many small, inefficient manufacturers who operate as quasi-local monopolies under the protection of the local government. A price war in these circumstances, when initiated by the strongest player, can force many out of business and create opportunities for the survivors. When a category has not yet been significantly penetrated by Western, Korean or Japanese firms, the opportunity for a price war is even greater as these firms then hesitate to enter a market where price wars are common, especially considering Chinese consumers are, in general, more price-sensitive than Western consumers.

In the mid-1990s, this set of circumstances was faced by the colour TV manufacturer Changhong, the largest and most profitable of 130 local manufacturers. They believed they were the main target of the non-Chinese global firms, all of which were seeking routes into the market. As a consequence, on 16 March 1996, they announced a double-digit price cut on all 17–29 in. colour TVs. The outcome was a three-fold success for Changhong: their market share doubled to over 30%, one-third of their local competitors who operated on lower profit margins went out of business and foreign manufacturers, nervous of the now shrunken profit margins in the market, took a step back, allowing Changhong time and space to cement their position in the minds of Chinese consumers.[8]

Galanz, a Chinese manufacturer of microwave ovens, also initiated a series of substantial price cuts in the mid- to late 1990s. The move not only gave them a dominant share of the Chinese market but also resulted in their becoming the largest manufacturer in the world because they were able to use their increase in economies of scale to keep funding lower prices, a tactic Henry Ford would have been very familiar with.

Key learnings

- An **orderly retail market is very fragile** rather than one of long-term stability. Even during phases of marketing orientation, **markets are dynamic.**
- A **marketing orientation is a permanent struggle** because competitive initiatives are continually eroding competitive advantages and brand preferences.
- When companies feel themselves losing their position, they all too **easily panic and turn to selling strategies.**
- **Segmentation is the most effective route** out of a selling/hustle orientation to a marketing orientation
- Don't start a price war unless you have a substantial, long-term cost advantage, or you are in a rapidly growing market in need of consolidation.

Manufacturers have had a 50-year start on developing marketing-led strategies compared to retailers. However, retailers are catching up fast and in some cases overtaking their suppliers in their sophistication. Manufacturers need to understand the pace and nature of changes being adopted into retail strategies.

Notes

1. http://www.telegraph.co.uk/travel/travelnews/3918657/Airlines-launch-price-war-cutting-fares-by-up-to-25-per-cent.html. Accessed 27 July 2011.
2. http://www.thecoca-colacompany.com, http://www.thecoca-colacompany.com/investors/annual_review_2010.html. Accessed 27 July 2011.
3. http://www.business-strategy-innovation.com/2009/05/inside-look-at-apple-store.html. Accessed 30 June 2011.

4. http://www.xpedx.com/pdf/Ashkin%20White%20Paper.pdf, http://aussieslivingsimply.com.au/forum/natural-cleaners-and-products-for-the-home/200513-new-green-cleaning-line-at-aldi, http://www.methodhome.com/methodology/our-story. Accessed 29 July 2011.

5. http://test.cba.uh.edu/jhess/documents/10.pdf. Accessed 15 September 2011.

6. http://konzept-nalyse.de/download/CY775b842cX11f60988f3eXY20c4/Brand_positioning_in_established_markets.pdf. Accessed 11 August 2011.

7. IRI, 'Innovation Highlights From 15 Years of New Product Pacesetters'

8. http://executiveeducation.wharton.upenn.edu/resources/upload/marketing-determining-measuring-strategy.pdf. Accessed 29 July 2011.

Chapter 4

RETAILERS AND MANUFACTURERS not only differ in financing, and structure; they also follow very different consumer strategies. This is because their structural differences profoundly affect the power and relative importance of key elements of the marketing mix. In particular:

- **Segmentation:** Retailers cannot segment consumers to the degree that manufacturers do and, as a consequence, must favour broader rather than pointed positionings. However, to achieve a workable level of segmentation, retailers are increasingly moving towards multiple store formats across multiple channels, including online, that appeal to different shopping needs.
- **Brand proliferation** is very limited when applied to retail chains, where the predominant retail strategy is for one overarching retail brand with perhaps a handful of private label sub-brands. This is in complete contrast to the manufacturing world, where companies handle vast portfolios of distinct brands. Retailers, in general, welcome brand proliferation from manufacturers but are increasingly wary of SKU proliferation within brands. While the number of brands offered has been shown to exert a positive correlation on store choice, the number of SKUs per brand and the number of sizes per brand actually have a slightly inverse effect.[1] Based on our research, anything less than 1000 SKUs or more

than 40 000 in a store can present more negatives than positives for a retailer.

- **Role of quality:** The quality of the shopping experience provides weaker differential advantages than quality can bring to product brands, but it can still have an impact. As retailers add new services, such as banking, insurance etc., they can strengthen the quality of the shopping experience and enter new markets. Brands, on the other hand, have long covered virtually all viable quality positionings.

- **Importance of price:** Price is imperative for FMCG retailers, much more so than for manufacturers. Retailers must constantly keep their real prices competitive and put great effort into managing their price perceptions in the minds of their shoppers.

Retailers and segmentation

The common approach for manufacturers to the art of segmentation is to slice and dice a large target market into subgroups of homogeneous consumer needs in order to better serve with tightly targeted offerings. Manufacturers have the ability to target a small subgroup of consumers with a product brand and still generate viable sales. For example, the Head & Shoulders shampoo brand is targeted at consumers with dandruff, approximately 20% of the population. Within that 20%, further profitable segmentation is still possible. Thus, Head & Shoulders can successfully target people with dandruff and either sensitive, itchy or oily scalps, and then coloured, permed or natural hair etc., resulting in 12 versions of their shampoo.

But a retailer cannot slice and dice its customers *at the brand level* (i.e. chain) to the same degree. A retailer who seeks to target only 20% of the potential market is already on thin ice. Retail coverage (i.e. the physical footprint of a store's catchment area) dictates the target audience for each store, which means that the audience is relatively heterogeneous: everyone who lives within the store catchment area. A large mainstream store has to generate volume at each unit level as most of the costs, such as building, staff and stock, are local; therefore, because of retailers' sensitivity to small volume changes that we saw in Chapter 2, the more shoppers the better. Thus, a store cannot afford to alienate any substantial segment of shoppers in its 'covered area', and must aim to take a maximum proportion of the sales from all shoppers within easy reach of its stores. The fixed costs of a store targeting 100% of shoppers in its footprint are no different from one that targets only 20%. In contrast to manufacturers who continue to sub-segment, the profit pressure and high fixed costs of retailers prevent such micro-segmentation.

Another key difference which leads to hyper-segmentation on the product side, but not the retail side, is that a market-leading product brand is always vulnerable to more targeted, niche brands that nibble away at their target audience. Thus Head & Shoulders, despite decades of investing in owning the dandruff shampoo mindspace, now has to worry about ever more niche brands arising, such as Bumble and Bumble's line of dandruff shampoos that focus on scalp rebalancing therapy, which will no doubt result in a thirteenth Head & Shoulders variant. And so it continues.

However, it is not possible to attack, for example, Brazil's leading retailer Grupo Pão de Açúcar by launching a niche supermarket that 20% of their shoppers prefer, because it is physically impossible to offer this competitor to all Grupo Pão de Açúcar's shoppers: economics would not support matching their store numbers. Equally, while L'Oréal can target Mixa bébé shampoo at mums with children under five, no grocery retailer can open a chain, equipped with crèche and changing room, targeted only at shoppers with young children. Retailers do no sit side by side on the shelf as products do. Opportunities for a retailer to segment at the chain level exist, but their toolkit is limited.

A barrier to a retailer segmenting its offer at the local level is the issue of store consistency. A retailer does not want to position separate stores of a chain too differently from each other for fear of losing a coherent image and thus negating the power of its vast advertising budgets. If the retailer chooses to develop a more pointed positioning for each store to suit its local competition, it would not benefit from economies of scale in marketing. If it wants to maximise its profits by using a consistent pricing policy, national advertising and centrally run strategic thinking, it must compromise the ideal position for each store, which then results in a set of homogeneous stores. These aggregated 'ideal positions' for the main chains are likely to converge because they are targeting the same shoppers.

Retailers (with the exception of hard discounters) feel obliged to compete on all major dimensions: always trying to offer low prices, while striving to improve service, the quality/value of products and the convenience of the stores. They are driven towards a bland image partly because their positioning must attract all significant groups in their 'coverage' and partly because the same brand has to appeal across a range of different competitive situations. For example, one of the fastest-growing supermarkets in India, More., promotes a national message of 'more. quality, more. variety, more. convenience and more. value.' And who could object to that? While manufacturers can develop more pointed positionings ('rifle brands'), retailers must create a positioning on price or cultivate bland, umbrella positionings.

Manufacturers try to position their brands in a contrasting way to other brands in the minds of their consumers. Their aim is to differentiate their brands. A retailer's competitive position, by contrast, has been defined by location.

Suppose a hypermarket opens outside a town and is successful, and a competitor decides to open a hypermarket serving a similar town, 100 miles away. Assuming that the first retailer got its product offering and consumer positioning right, the second retailer's optimal offering will be the same as the first retailer's (i.e. to be a perfect me-too). At 100 miles apart there will be minimal direct competition, and if the towns' populations are similar, the optimal offering for one town will also be optimal for the other.

On a perceptual map, these chain brands look like me-toos who compete directly with each other. In contrast to manufacturer brands, where identical products fight for each other's sales, retail chains identical in format, quality and other offerings do not directly compete if they are geographically separated. This is how, in large countries such the United States, a retailer such as the HEB Grocery Company can thrive in its Texas and northern Mexican heartland without being too different from Wegmans on the eastern seaboard and most of the 100+ other regional grocery chains in America.

Hard discount chains Aldi and Lidl, which are very similar to each other, operate in the same countries without directly competing with each other; they compete for locations rather than for shoppers within the same location. Hard discounters, who compete solely on price, do not want to get into price wars with each other. Aldi follow that thinking within their structure. Originally founded in 1946 by two brothers, the company split into two separate companies, Aldi Nord and Aldi Süd, each run by a brother, after an irreconcilable dispute over whether to sell cigarettes at the checkout. They operate in separate countries apart from their 'home' country of Germany, where, perhaps not surprisingly, Aldi Nord operates in the north of the country and Aldi Süd in the south. While each brother may wish to triumph over the other, they both realise that competing head on will destroy both their companies.

The most successful way retailers have found to escape generic blandness through segmentation has been to develop several different store formats based on the needs of the shopping occasion (top-up versus main shop versus monthly shop etc.) and, less successfully, on discount versus mainstream quality and choice. The following is a summary of the main formats:

- **Hard Discounters:** Have a spartan atmosphere, the promise of rock-bottom prices and offer 700–1200 SKUs. Lidl were one of the first hard discounters in Europe in the 1970s, and are still one of the most popular. This format is sometimes inaccurately branded as offering low-quality products, whereas it actually offers good-quality products – sometimes the best – but with low levels of service and choice.

- **Convenience Stores (aka Superettes or Mini-Marts):** Offer a limited range of products, mostly food, with a focus on pre-prepared meals. Prices are higher but compensated for by convenience via proximity and extended hours. They offer 3000–4000 SKUs and generate approximately $1 million in annual sales. The most successful convenience chain in the world is 7–11.
- **Supermarkets (aka Grocery Stores):** Concentrate on food and provide more balance between prepared food and produce, offering quality at good price. They may also have a deli, a bakery and a pharmacy. They offer 15 000–30 000 SKUs and generate at least $2 million in annual sales. Foodworld are the largest supermarket chain in India and Kroger are the largest in North America.
- **Superstores:** A supermarket offering an expanded selection of non-food items, speciality departments and extensive services, like dry cleaning. They offer approximately 40 000–60 000 SKUs and generate around $12 million in annual sales from a selling space usually 2500 m^2 and higher. ParknShop in Hong Kong are a classic example.
- **Mass Merchandisers:** Primarily sell hardware, clothing, small furnishings, electronics and sporting goods, but they can also carry dry grocery items. This channel includes chains such as Wal-Mart and Target, which carry 60 000–100 000 SKUs.
- **Hypermarkets (aka Supercentres):** A hybrid of a Supermarket and a Mass Merchandiser. They offer a wide variety of food and non-food merchandise on an average of 170 000 ft^2. They offer 50 000–150 000 SKUs. Wal-Mart Supercentres are among the largest in the world. Their biggest store in the United States is more than 260 000 ft^2, the size of five football fields! The biggest hypermarket in Europe is a Tesco in the Irish town of Naas, which is 199 000 ft^2 and opened in November 2010. The biggest hypermarket in Asia,

and the world, is a Giant Tiger in Shah Alam, Malaysia, which spans 350 000 ft^2.

- **Warehouse Store:** A concept developed by Price Club in the United States, where members pay to shop for around 4000 items sold marginally above cost in a 9000–12 000 m^2 'bare bones' environment. Stock turnover is way above industry standards with very little listing of alternative brands. Costco and Sam's Club dominate the category, Costco becoming one of the world's top 10 retailers despite having been founded in only 1983.

- Many retail chains now cover several of these formats to maximise their coverage of different shopping occasions within the same towns and cities. In Belgium, GB have GB Maxi, GB Super, GB Partners, GB Express and GB Home Delivery; in India, RPG group have Spencer's Hyper, Spencer's Super, Spencer's Daily and Spencer's Express; and in China, the largest nationwide retailer have Lianhua Supermarket, Lianhua Quik and Century Mart.

Some retailers have also launched discount chains as a defensive measure against the hard discounters. Carrefour were the first with ED (Europa Discount) in 1978, and now have 6200 discount stores around the globe. In Russia, the X5 Retail Group launched a soft discounter in 2008 and then converted their Pyaterochka chains to hard discounters in 2009; in Australia, Coles launched BI-LO, and in Canada the Hudson's Bay Company acquired Fields.

However, *chain* proliferation for retailers, where they have completely distinctive retail brands, is now becoming an outdated approach as it has several inefficiencies, such as marketing/advertising, compared to a single chain that covers different store formats. First-mover advantage is very beneficial in launching more formats as there is a limit on the number of available, viable sites for each format in an area. Even if sites were available, the number of competitive stores in one area would be limited by the need to generate sufficient volume of sales at each unit. Store costs are high and retailers have to respect the density of stores that an area can justify: they cannot proliferate stores if the projected sales are too small.

Retail brand takeovers

The difference in the potential for retailers to brand proliferate is seen most acutely when one store chain takes over another. When a manufacturer takes over another manufacturer, it often buys it for its brands, and through these brands it gains valuable mindspace for which it will pay a large price premium over the value of the tangible assets of the acquired business. Many of the famous brands owned by Unilever and Nestlé were bought and developed in this way. They may change the house name, for example Nestlé replaced Rowntree as the maker of Kit Kat, but they would never dream of eradicating the Kit Kat name.

But when a retailer buys a competitor, it has to choose between keeping the goodwill that may exist for the bought brand and the chance to extend the coverage of its main chain. Generally, it is no contest. Tesco had no presence in Ireland prior to 1997; the market was dominated by a handful of local chains, primarily Quinnsworth and Dunnes. In 1997, Tesco purchased Quinnsworth and Crazy Prices (Quinnsworth's larger discount outlets) from Associated British Foods and immediately set about their Tesco-isation.

The first step was to remove Quinnsworth's private label brands and replace them with Tesco's, under the campaign 'Tesco at Quinnsworth'. Simultaneously, Tesco opened just one new Tesco store to gauge how much of the Tesco UK format would work in Ireland. Tesco quickly learnt that they could not replace Irish best-selling brands with the best-sellers from their UK stores: Lyons not Tetley was the best-selling tea; Batchelors Baked Beans trumped Heinz and 7UP was preferred to Sprite. Thus, Quinnsworth stores were progressively rebranded to 'Tesco Ireland' as stores were upgraded to Tesco standards, but with the best-selling Irish brands maintaining their dominance. More recently, the name has been changed to Tesco to complete the transition. Twenty-five years of the Quinnsworth's brand equity was worth nothing to Tesco. They paid for the real estate, the prime locations and the shoppers, not the brand.

The mechanism is different from manufacturer product brands because the physical market is different. Two brands of toothpaste can sell alongside each other on a shelf, and consolidating them into one brand would make few savings and no sense. Whereas a store buying another store has an incentive to consolidate to create one chain with improved coverage because a retail chain benefits substantially from increasing its critical mass.

The inability of chains to provide highly differentiated positionings does not imply uniformity in shoppers' preferences. Some shoppers will demand a wide choice of brands, some prefer convenience, some will be primarily price sensitive and some most influenced by the quality of fresh food. It just means that retailers cannot profitably serve these segments by developing separate, segmented chains of supermarkets specialising in each, but that they have to find the best balance in meeting them all within the same store.

Quality as a differential advantage

Retailers, driven by their need to attract as many shoppers as possible into each store, recognise the problems in creating a differential advantage based on store values. Store features cannot be limited to the shopper segment attracted by them: a retailer cannot provide carpets for one shopper and tiles for the next. Nor can it increase the staff available to shoppers selecting high-margin brands while teaching them to ignore shoppers looking for discounts. Some services, for example trained staff who advise customers, suffer from the problem of being separable from purchase. If customers are advised and allowed to browse without buying, nothing stops them from comparing prices in a number of stores and waiting for the cheapest offer. Some services are not separable from purchase, including late opening hours, after-sales service and guarantees. A store that offers its purchasers a 'no questions asked' money-back policy is building a stronger bond with its purchasers than a store that offers friendly advice to all-comers, most of whom just want to get in and out as fast as possible.

Unlike a brand, a supermarket cannot target too tightly. For example, life stage will indicate certain preferences:

- Families with children: supermarkets with play areas.
- Senior citizens: small packages, large print, shelf positions that do not involve reaching or bending and home deliveries.
- Lifestyle: trendy versus conservative, healthy versus convenience.

But while these are used successfully to target product brands, they are all too limiting to work in a retail context. A supermarket cannot afford to become too specific in terms of style. Segmentation is really about meeting some needs very strongly, even at the expense of others, which a retailer cannot afford to do. For example, playing loud rock music, dressing the checkout operators in funky outfits and tiling the floors black and pink will alienate certain important segments, even if it is strongly appealing to others. The store values have to appeal to the whole heterogeneous target.

Since retailers can't create tailored values, what else can they do to create a better shopping experience? Who wouldn't want an improvement in the attitude and availability of store personnel, more open checkouts, a wider range of products stocked and better parking? The problem, however, is that successful modifications could be copied by any competitor who had lost volume to the improved store. Since the improvements are broad in appeal, the improvements the competition makes are likely to keep the stores similar. Competitors are forced to match, reusable bag for reusable bag. The net effect of improving the shopping experience was seen historically by retailers as going 'back to square one' at a higher cost level than before.

However, this view has been challenged by the runaway success of Tesco in the United Kingdom over the last 20 years, especially since the introduction of their 'Every little helps' campaign in 1992. For most of the 1980s, Tesco was number two to Sainsbury's in the UK grocery market. With a major focus on improving their poor-quality image and simultaneously reducing prices, Tesco got back into the game and eventually caught up to Sainsbury's in market share. But a key part of their subsequent success was rooted in the insight that *continuous improvement to the shopping experience rather than any one particular improvement* had the potential to be a major competitive edge. Tesco's improvements included their 'One in front' commitment to effectively abolish checkout line-ups, baby-changing and bottle-warming facilities, ATMs, escorted searches for product requests and priority parking for pregnant mums. It was not that one improvement was more successful than another; it was the relentless implementation of a never-ending stream of small improvements that steadily improved Tesco's image relative to their competitors, who were left seemingly forever floundering in their wake. The scheme also got Tesco's staff more engaged in service delivery and coming up with ideas for further improvements. 'Every little helps' helped Tesco attract over a million new shoppers in the period from 1990–1995.

The retailers' price imperative

Even if a retailer does as much as it can to improve the shopping experience, there is always a significant segment of price-sensitive shoppers who will change stores to get a better deal. This segment gets larger as the perceived price difference between retailers increases. It can also grow larger during recessions, or owing to marketing efforts that draw attention to prices.

A supermarket cannot allow its price perception to rise too far from the bottom of the market or it will lose a significant segment of business (or run the risk of new competitors being enticed by attractive margins). This explains why it is easy for retailers to slip into price wars.

A classic example of the retailers' price problem occurred in September 2011 within the UK grocery market. Tesco, who as we just saw had rocketed from being a poor number two to being by far the United Kingdom's leading grocery chain with a 30% market share, had begun to lose share to Asda through Asda's pricing policy of being 15% cheaper on a range of basic grocery items. Tesco, whose success had been driven by elements other than price, such as Every Little Helps and their Clubcard, were becoming seen as being more expensive than Asda, which forced them into announcing their largest series of price reductions for 25 years. Prices on 1000 product lines in Tesco's private label range were cut by between 15 and 20% as a direct response to their loss of price perception versus Asda. Rival chains were quick to point out that these cuts were being funded by changes elsewhere to Tesco's overall offer, primarily from a halving of points awarded to Clubcard members, together with a drastic cutting back on buy-one-get-one-free offers (BOGOFs).[2] Such is the power of price in retail that a dominant player like Tesco has to respond to a competitor half its size. Even worse, the initiative didn't work as the damage to Tesco's price perception had already been done. This shows that price is imperative for all FMCG retailers. They must always do two things well:

- **Be genuinely price competitive** on the top 100 best-selling products where the shopper is most likely to make direct comparisons.
- **Perpetually make efforts to manage their price image** and must consider the impact of all marketing actions on that image. Wal-Mart still advertise their price Rollbacks even though everyone has known for decades they are good value.

It is extremely difficult for a non-hard discounter retailer to make permanently lower prices provide a long-term, sustainable differential advantage. This is surprising, but occurs because low prices are an imperative for everyone. Any competitor who tries to make a differential advantage of prices forces their competitors to match because no one can afford to be beaten on price.

However, there are now opportunities for retailers to use price as a stealth weapon. Information technology has provided the means for the first time for 100 years since set prices became the norm that price and price perception can be managed on a one-to-one basis with each customer. The price that each shopper pays no longer need be one arbitrary average but can reflect the value the store represents to the shopper, and vice versa, the shopper's real price sensitivity, and be related to extra services the store provides.

Tesco's Clubcard, which we shall discuss in more detail later, enabled Tesco to identify over 5000 customer needs segments with each receiving individually tailored price coupons via email. We should not be surprised by this. It has long been established by brands such as Coca-Cola that very different prices/relative value can be charged even within the same store for a 24-can value pack in the beverages aisle compared to a cold bottle from a checkout-located cooler, so it seems logical that different shoppers will pay significantly different prices for the same item.

Pushing the pricing opportunity further, while it may be controversial to charge different prices for the same products during different day-parts, it makes sense as grocery chains could, for example, maximise their profits by raising prices on certain lines after 6 p.m. when richer clientele may dominate. Although no one in the grocery market is using dynamic pricing, it is common in other industries, including transportation, electronics and even fashion. India's leading fashion and lifestyle retailers, Ebony Retail Holdings Ltd., have started incorporating dynamic pricing into their seasonal pricing mix. As nearly 25% of grocery inventory is perishable, shoppers are already used to the fact that retailers charge less on items that are about to expire.

Key learnings

- With the exception of hard discounters, retailers have to **cultivate a mainstream brand proposition** for their chains; they have to be attractive to all the main segments in terms of quality, convenience, value for money and price perception.
- Retailers cannot follow the key marketing ploy of manufacturers: segmentation via brand proliferation. Their advantage is **their ability to segment by shopping needs**, provided they have the data on their customer's shopping behaviour. This reconnection of the store with knowledge of its customers is at the root of manufacturers' loss of power.
- The emergence of **new retail formats** such as Hard Discount, Warehouse Clubs and the re-energising of the High Street convenience offer by the major grocery chains has provided scope for the large retailers to segment by shopping occasion/need.
- Because retail brands are barely differentiated, they are relatively fragile when compared to the largest manufacturer brands, despite having, in general, much higher awareness levels. Thus, there is much **more fluidity in retail branding**, with old names being quick to disappear once a better/stronger player muscles in. Retailers hope that, as they develop multi-format strategies and are now the largest advertising spenders, their brands will develop a greater permanence.
- Store values/ambiance per se cannot provide a sustainable advantage, as **copying is relatively easy**. But if a player commits to stay ahead of the pack through constant improvement, then significant advantage can accrue.

While retailers and manufacturers have very different business models and strategies, their battleground is situated in the twin currencies of the FMCG world: the mindspace owned by brands and the shelfspace owned by retailers. And it is to these we turn next.

Notes

1. Briesch RA, Chintagunta PK, Fox EL (2009) How does assortment affect grocery store choice? *Journal of Marketing Research* 46(2): 176–89.
2. http://www.Telegraph.co.uk/finance/newsbysector/retailandconsumer/8782931/Tesco-to-cut-prices-by-500m-claims-UK-head-Richard-Brasher.html. Accessed 12 December 2011.

Chapter 5

THE LONGEVITY OF product brands, even those having no apparent technological advantage, is a striking characteristic of FMCG markets, as can be shown by the launch dates of 25 of the top global brands, starting with Schweppes in 1783 (Table 5.1).

Brands such as these are aided by the knowledge and experience accumulated within the company, and the knowledge and experience built among the company's customers (consumers and distributors). In FMCG companies, competitors find it harder to replicate the latter, even when cost and technological parity or superiority has been achieved. For a consumer brand to succeed, it doesn't just need technical excellence and value; it needs a prolonged superiority in mindspace and shelfspace.

Mindspace and shelfspace

Over time, a successful consumer brand will build up a web of experiences, associations and buying habits among consumers, distributors and retailers. Big brands are omnipresent over a long period in the lives of consumers. They see the advertisements for the product; see, or even take part in, the promotions; pass the product on the shelves when they are shopping. This is mindspace. Shelfspace is simpler to grasp: the sum of the linear inches of retailers' shelving a company's

Table 5.1 Top 25 global brands by their year of launch

Brand	Category	Year of launch
Schweppes	Soft drinks	1783
Cadbury	Chocolate	1831
Budweiser	Beer	1876
Coca-Cola	Soft drinks	1886
Heineken	Beer	1886
Kodak	Photo	1888
Lipton	Tea	1890
Wrigley	Chewing gum	1892
Colgate	Toothpaste	1896
Campbell's	Soup	1898
Marlboro	Tobacco	1902
Pepsi	Soft drinks	1903
Gillette	Shaving products	1908
Camel	Tobacco	1913
Danone	Yogurt	1919
Kellogg's	Cereal	1922
Duracell	Batteries	1930
Nescafé	Coffee	1938
Fanta	Soft drinks	1940
Tropicana	Juices	1952
Friskies	Pet food	1956
Pampers	Nappies (diapers)	1961
Sprite	Soft drinks	1961
Huggies	Nappies (diapers)	1978
Red Bull	Energy drink	1987

Source: Compiled from various company data and annual reports.

product holds. Mindspace and shelfspace are crucial sources of sustainable advantage, not least because they take so long to build.

It was mindspace and shelfspace that prompted Kraft to pay $18.9 billion for Cadbury in January 2010. Kraft already knew how to make and sell quality chocolate: they owned the Suchard business. What they didn't own was the mindspace and shelfspace Cadbury had painstakingly built up over 180 years, especially in emerging markets like India. Cadbury had operated in India since 1948, and have a formidable presence with a 70% share of the rapidly growing chocolate market and a sales coverage that reached over one million stores. The costs and time for Kraft to attempt to replicate this would be unsustainable. Kraft can now use the Cadbury set-up to launch their own brands, and with their superior financial resources are able to add more juice than Cadbury would have been able to. In April 2011, Cadbury India launched Oreo, the Kraft-owned world's number-one cookie brand, using Cadbury contract manufacturing expertise to source the product locally, Cadbury mindspace to brand the product under the Cadbury name and Cadbury shelfspace capabilities to achieve widespread distribution and prominent display. Mindspace and shelfspace are the valuable currencies of FMCG industries.

For the latter half of the twentieth century, mindspace and shelfspace were linked and complementary. A product achieving considerable mindspace (i.e. was liked by many consumers) was a powerful incentive for the distributor to stock it. And shelfspace was also a powerful generator of mindspace. Seeing a product regularly increased its presence in consumers' minds, and improved its image by suggesting it was popular.

Controlling shelfspace

FMCG manufacturers have long been preoccupied with the need to control shelfspace, because in-store presence is critical for low-value purchases, and many companies have invested fortunes over many years to provide themselves with effective and knowledgeable distribution capabilities to achieve such control.

This is because shelfspace is more than just linear inches. It has many qualitative aspects: shelfspace at eye or hand level is worth more than at foot level. The number of facings, depth of inventory, position compared to flow of traffic and the position within the store affect the amount of notice and purchase for the product. Shelfspace can be augmented further by special displays, end-of-aisle features or flagging information ('Star Buy' or '30% off this week'). And these are competitive, as shelfspace is a relatively inelastic commodity: more for your brands means less for the competition.

For decades, large manufacturers had control over shelfspace as it could be planned and bought, rather like advertising or promotions. Small retailers were the willing agents of large manufacturers, taking advice on the optimal management of shelfspace. But those days are over.

Two changes have weakened manufacturers' hold over shelfspace.

- Independent stores, who were heavily influenced by the manufacturers, have declined dramatically in the face of competition from major chains and are now insignificant in most categories
- The large, sophisticated retailers have stopped seeing their shelfspace as a commodity for sale, and now see it as a crucial resource to be used in pursuit of their own objectives. In particular, retailers who are actively marketing their private label brands in competition with manufacturers will use shelfspace to promote their own brands. They have taken back control of 'their' shelfspace.

As a result, gaining shelfspace has become a more strategic challenge for manufacturers. Shelfspace has to be won by planning product offerings to satisfy not just consumers' needs but also the retailers' objectives. Because the retailer is overwhelmed with offerings that claim to have consumer appeal – that is now a given – it is in being seen to best meet the retailers' needs that has become the battleground. Store management wants to increase category sales, improve average margins, provide a good range to shoppers and perhaps offer exclusive products, all the while looking to increase operational efficiency and reduce inventory costs by minimising the number of lines stocked and the workload involved in getting products on the shelf.

Manufacturers now have to win shelfspace by working through these complex and sometimes conflicting needs.

Reducing costs to fund mindspace/shelfspace

Having lost control of shelfspace, the manufacturers' first response was to try to win the war of mindspace, assuming that would lead inexorably to shelfspace, a task made doubly difficult by the shortage of increased marketing budgets to do so. Hence for many years now FMCG manufacturers have been looking to internal efficiencies to free up funds.

As a result of endless efficiency drives, from 1998 to 2008 the average sales per employee across the major FMCG companies increased by 68% (in current dollar terms) (Table 5.2). Even if we adjust for inflation (e.g. the US food inflation for 1998–2008 was slightly over 30%), it is still a significant upsurge. All corporations in our sample, except Coca-Cola, were holding or reducing their headcount in

Table 5.2 Sales per employee in major FMCG and retail companies, US$ in thousands, in 2011 prices

Company	1998	2008	2011	Percentage change, 1998–2011
Diageo	357	804	1050	+194
Philip Morris	368	842	975	+165
Unilever	174	341	395	+127
Nestlé	221	358	429	+94
Procter & Gamble	336	605	639	+90
Colgate-Palmolive	243	419	426	+75
L'Oréal	255	380	409	+60
PepsiCo	148	218	233	+57
Danone	198	278	240	+21
Coca-Cola	432	353	333	−23
Sample average	273	460	513	+88

Source: Compiled from various company data and annual reports.

proportion to sales growth. The most notable examples are Unilever and Diageo, who reduced their staff by 50% and 65% respectively. The main approach to staff cost optimisation has been to outsource functions and operations, such as advertising, market research, sales, trade marketing, IT, HR and others to third-party contractors and agencies.

But this gives no one a real competitive advantage because everyone is doing it. The spread of best-practice outsourcing initiatives ensures that all companies have generated more money to throw at the fixed resource of shelfspace, the inevitable result of which has been its price being inflated. Thus, even the largest companies have seen the percentage of sales they devote to spending on the retailer continue to climb. But the costs that can be cut are finite and beginning to run out, so manufacturers cannot hope to buy their way to shelfspace success in the long run.

Creating mindspace

Many FMCG categories are trivial purchases that excite minimal interest in the consumer. Trying to win mindspace from established brands in low-interest product fields simply by communicating to the consumer is a hit-and-miss affair, to say the least. There may be a better mustard, but most will happily stick with the one they always use. This gives brands that already have mindspace an advantage and is the reason FMCG markets show considerable inertia. If a new brand wants to build mindspace in a low-interest area, it is usually necessary to take a more aggressive approach: by forcing product use, borrowing or buying mindspace.

Forcing use via tactical marketing

Tactical activities that influence consumers at the behavioural level are important for developing mindspace. Promotions such as free gifts and competitions can create impulse purchases. The act of purchase, however prompted, and the use that follows, translates into mindspace.

Many companies use massive sampling at the launch of a product: sampling leads to use, which leads to mindspace. This tool is especially popular among companies that introduce an innovative product to the market. When Starbucks launched its instant coffee brand in Japan in April 2010, they invited customers to participate in a four-day taste challenge to see whether they could taste the different between Starbucks VIA Coffee Essence (known as VIA Ready Brew everywhere else) and their fresh-brewed coffee. Over one million samples were given away at their 870 retail stores, and five months later more than 10 million sticks had been sold, making it one of their most successful new product launches. Starbucks embraced the sampling technique again when they subsequently launched VIA Coffee Essence into 11 000 Japanese grocery and convenience stores; they hired Starbucks baristas to give free VIA samples to shoppers and, to further increase mindspace, gave away one free stick for every three sticks a customer bought, to encourage sharing VIA Coffee Essence with a friend.

Promotion and sampling campaigns are becoming more comprehensive with the purpose not only to distribute samples but also to create a unique brand experience that translates into a much bigger gain in mindspace for target audiences. In February 2011, Doritos launched The End Contest. The contest challenged Canadians to vote for their favourite flavour (Onion Rings N' Ketchup or Buffalo Wings N' Ranch) to decide which one will live and which one will be destroyed. Fans were encouraged to write the end of the unfinished Doritos commercial, and the winner was given 1% of future sales from the remaining flavour and the chance to become part of the Doritos Think Tank. The Marketing VP at PepsiCo Foods Canada said, 'It's the next evolution of consumer engagement where we're handing our brand to Canadians, and giving them a chance to play a role in making Doritos history, [it's] something we've never done before.' The contest was a huge success – it attracted 185 000 votes, 30 000 entries, showcased Doritos as an innovative brand and increased sales.

In October 2011, Heinz UK launched a Facebook promotion where, when someone complained of being ill on their Facebook page, friends could have them sent a tin of either Cream of Chicken or Cream of Tomato soup with a personalised 'get well' message on the label. By such means are lifelong brand associations built.

Buying and renting mindspace

A short-cut to building mindspace is to buy the rights to a brand, or to buy a company that owns established brands. The value that a brand represents is often reflected in the high prices paid for companies that own them. In 2010, Phillips-Van Heusen bought the American Tommy Hilfiger brand for $3 billion to compete with Ralph Lauren and boost their presence in Asia and Europe. In 2010, Unilever bought Sara Lee Personal Care and European Laundry for $1.9 billion to compete in the skin cleansing, baby care and oral care markets – they acquired brand leaders in all three categories, including Radox, Duschdas, Zwitsal, Fissan, Prodent and Zendium. In 2011, Unilever also bought the Alberto Culver Company for $3.7 billion to expand their hair care business, acquiring several leading brands, including TRESemmé, Alberto VO5 and St. Ives. This purchase made Unilever the world's leader in hair conditioner, the second in shampoo and the third in styling.

Companies can also rent or buy equities that exist in consumers' minds. Donald Trump no longer significantly invests in constructing new buildings, instead he rents his name to people who do and want to attach the mindspace associated with the Trump brand to their building.

It is even possible to own mindspace without being able to make a physical product. Franchise operations develop mindspace and then sell it to franchisees, who attach it to their physical output. If you want to open a car repair business, you can build awareness and trust through local advertising and word of mouth, but it will take time: you can kick off faster by renting mindspace from Midas.

Losing mindspace

It is a mistake to think that mindspace is not volatile. Every dominant brand (such as those listed in Table 5.1) has had to reinvest in mindspace every year to keep its position. However, things can go wrong. Mindspace is hard to earn but easy to throw away.

The loss of repeat sales through reducing the quality of the product is a classic failure brought about by management cost-cutting and complacency: taking consumer faith as a given. American brewer Schlitz was a highly successful brand of beer in the United States, but it saw its sales tumble from 18 million barrels in 1974 to one million barrels in 1988 through sheer mismanagement.[1] The American brewer underestimated the effect of reducing quality to gain cost savings. It accelerated its fermentation process, substituted corn syrup for the traditional barley malt and changed stabiliser. The consumer spotted these cost savings, and their perceptions of the brand's quality fell. Heavy advertising expenditures and a return to the previous quality were in vain. The mindspace had been taken by competitors Miller and Anheuser-Busch, and could not easily be retaken. The once strong Schlitz brand was relegated to cheap beer status and became increasingly difficult to find in bars and restaurants, especially after the draft version was discontinued in 2001. A reformulated Sixties style beer was reintroduced in relatively small quantities in 2008 before being rolled out nationally. The re-launch campaign was successful; however, the former popularity and leadership has never been restored.

Perhaps the quickest way to lose mindspace, ironically while a brand name is plastered over the media and social networks, is through a product quality failure. On 17 August 2008, Canada's largest proc-essed meat company, Maple Leaf Foods, issued a voluntary recall for

23 products made in one of its plants. After 22 consumer deaths from listeria and the recall of all 220 products made at the plant, Maple Leaf's total sales across its portfolio of thousands of products plummeted 50%. Two months later, after a widely praised communication strategy, sales were still off by 15%. Another four months later, a survey reported by the Canadian Broadcasting Corporation found that 25% of households that bought Maple Leaf products before the recall still had not done so since.[2]

Mindspace is also fragile when faced with a major technological breakthrough by a competitor if not quickly responded to. Consider the launch of Apple's iPod in 2001. Although it wasn't the first MP3 player on the market (the first was the MPMan-F10 by Eiger Labs in 1999), it was the best pairing of technology and user interface. Apple stunned the competition by selling 125 000 units in the first six weeks and, by 2010, sales had reached $8.4 billion. The previous pioneers of portable music, Sony, were not able to compete with the iPod because they stuck with their own proprietary digital music format, and because of this they lost their music industry mindspace they had been cultivating since the launch of the Walkman in 1979. Mindspace is never permanently won.

Size really does matter

The typical supermarket has doubled, trebled and quadrupled its shelfspace over the last 30 years, yet shelfspace has become harder for manufacturers to hold onto. Over the same period, mindspace has become nearly as difficult to maintain, owing to media fragmentation and a never-ending increase in brands launched onto the market: there are 17 000 new food product launches each year in North America, and AC Nielsen now track over two million brands in the United States.

As we have seen, mindspace and shelfspace can be purchased, but the sale does not increase the overall supply of either. New brands often gain sales through launch promotion, but find that repeat purchases dwindle, not through technical failure but through lack of mindspace and shelfspace. Mindspace and shelfspace are the bottlenecks, and their ownership is often the only critical resource of a brand. To make matters worse, the bottleneck is tightening. As retailers have become competitors of manufacturers in many product categories, they reserve more shelfspace for their private label brands and dominate advertising spending to claim ever-increasing amounts of mindspace.

As the top retailers have become colossal, size has become an issue that affects the negotiating divide: no matter how much mindspace a manufacturer's brands have, their sales represent only a tiny fraction of a large grocery chain's turnover. On the other hand, the large retailers can each account for more than 10% of a brand's sales. Fifty years ago, FMCG manufacturers were the Goliaths and retailers the Davids. Now the situation has reversed, as we can see from Table 5.3.

The top retailers, by becoming so big and growing faster than their suppliers, have made size an issue. The clearest indication of this came on 28 January 2005, when Procter & Gamble, America's largest FMCG company, announced the acquisition of Gillette. Both companies had decades of success developing technologically advanced products and building enviable mindspace positions, yet these were no longer enough to guarantee their desired shelfspace. They realised the only way to compete with the retailers was to become big enough to matter to them.

While absolute size gives a manufacturer more scope for efficiencies, such as in buying, manufacturing and logistics, size also provides clout in dealing with the large retailers. These two factors combine to have a marked impact on the manufacturers' profit margins where there is a positive correlation between the size of a manufacturer and its profitability (Table 5.4).

Today, companies with global sales of less than $5 billion cannot be defined as anything other than weak relative to their larger competitors. A profit margin of 2.8% gives them very little scope to outbid for

Table 5.3 Sales growth of top FMCG manufacturers and retailers

Company	Sales 1998 (US$ billion)	Sales 2011 (US$ billion)	Percentage change
Wal-Mart	118	419	+355%
Carrefour	30	112	+373%
Nestlé	50	109	+218%
Metro Group	33	99	+300%
Tesco	28	98	+350%
Procter & Gamble	37	83	+224%
Kroger	43	90	+209%
Philip Morris	56	76	+136%
Unilever	50	65	+130%
PepsiCo	21	67	+319%
Auchan	19	58	+305%
Sales of retailers		324%	
Sales of manufacturers		186%	

Source: Compiled from various company data, annual reports and specialised financial websites.

Table 5.4 Top 70 branded manufacturers' turnover vs. profitability average for 2009/2010

Sales turnover	Number of companies	Average net margin
> $20 billion	12	11.3%
$10–20 billion	18	7.8%
$5–10 billion	16	7.4%
< $5 billion	24	2.8%

Source: Compiled from various company data, annual reports and specialised financial websites.

precious shelfspace. The 20 most profitable manufacturers generate 86% of the total profits of the top 70 manufacturers in the world, giving them plenty of scope to use their muscle.

The consolidation trend is clear. In 2007, the global cigarette industry, consolidated as Imperial Tobacco, purchased Altadis, and Japan

Tobacco acquired Gallaher. The Mars purchase of Wrigley in 2008 and Kraft's acquisition of Cadbury in 2010 began a process of consolidating the fragmented confectionery market. The same happened in the beer market with the merger of Inbev (itself a product of many mergers and acquisitions) and Anheuser-Busch, followed by the merger of Coors and Molson.

The trend continues: Anheuser-Busch bought one of the fastest-growing micro-breweries in the United States, Goose Island, for $39 million in March 2011, and in June 2011 Molson-Coors acquired a majority stake in Cobra India to increase their presence in emerging markets. The world's second-largest brewery, SABMiller PLC, also followed suit and acquired Australian Foster's Group in September 2011 for $10.2 billion. Rumours suggest Anheuser-Busch or SABMiller may be eyeing Molson-Coors for further expansion in the next few years.

But as companies continue to consolidate, size will soon become another necessary but insufficient factor for manufacturers. It won't give them a competitive advantage because they will all be on the same level. More importantly, retailers' growth rates continue to outstrip those of manufacturers, so the size gap, while closed by the step-change of manufacturers' consolidation, will continue to widen.

Key learnings

- Manufacturers **have lost their ability to dictate** or even substantially influence the allocation of shelfspace in major retailers.
- Manufacturers' allocation of funds between consumer investment and retailer investment continues to swing inexorably towards the retailers, **who attract in excess of 20%** of a typical FMCG manufacturer's net sales value, compared to 5% spent on advertising. Cost-cutting elsewhere in the business is the

(Continued)

only way manufacturers have been able to fund this ever-rising expense.

- Retailers have **consistently outstripped manufacturers in size and average growth rates** over the past 15 years, now making them the physically dominant partner.
- **Manufacturer size has become the crucial determinant** in their ability to deal with the mega-retailers and still make profits. Mergers and acquisitions strategy to maintain a critical mass relative to the retailers is now a necessary facilitator of mind-space and shelfspace strategies for all but the strongest niche brands. If you have less than a $5 billion annual turnover, you need to buy before you are acquired.

Top brands stayed on top because of the continual investment and commitment of the manufacturers during a time when mass media gave them an affordable and highly effective route to the consumers' minds. They were able to defend their positions because they could afford more R & D, more advertising and a bigger sales force than any interlopers. Manufacturers became used to the idea of owning space in the consumer's mind and believed it was theirs by right. But brand mindspace is not a permanently acquired asset that continually delivers profits. Rather, it represents a position that must be continually defended, especially today, where competition from retailers comes as a shock to most manufacturers.

Notes

1. Aaker D (1991) *Managing Brand Equity: Capitalising on the value of a brand name*. New York, Free Press, pp. 78–9.
2. http://www.cbc.ca/news/health/story/2009/03/25/listeria-survey.html? ref=rss. Accessed 25 July 2011.

Chapter 6

M ANUFACTURERS HAVE NOT always had exclusivity over branding rights – they were just advantaged in being able to execute branding better than retailers or distributors during the twentieth century. However, since the turn of the century, retailers have shown that they can procure high-quality goods and deliver them with very effective branding, garnering considerable shelfspace and mindspace. Brand loyalty is not dead; it is just shifting to another player in the value chain as retailers are challenging manufacturers for control of their traditional source of profit: *mindspace.*

Brand management with retail characteristics

Manufacturers have to justify their existence now that retailers are competing for consumer trust. This poses the question to manufacturers as to what they really are. Van Schaik, once chairman of Heineken, described his firm as 'a marketing organisation with production facilities'. What is to stop retailers becoming marketing organisations with retail outlets? This is not far from the current position of Tesco, whose long-term vision was defined by their CEO, Philip Clarke, in their 2011 Annual Report:

> I would like Tesco to be seen as the *most highly valued* business
> in the world. We will continue to pursue growth in all parts of

the business – in the UK, internationally, in services and across general merchandise, clothing and electricals. Our strategy is evolving, [with] important new additions around being a multi-channel retailer, creating highly valued brands and building our team.

Tesco's success depends on their ability to replace manufacturer brands with their brands, which they have already achieved on 50% of their product listings. Retailers want to own mindspace because that is where the higher profits lie. To achieve this, they need to weaken consumer attachments to manufacturer brands and replace with attachments to their brands; hence retailers have become active marketers.

Retailers' advantages for creating mindspace

Retailers have four advantages over manufacturers when it comes to influencing consumers: the cost-effectiveness of their branding model, direct contact with shoppers, control of 'point of purchase' marketing variables and access to data on buying behaviour. Together, these make a potent mix.

Retailers' Branding Model

The most obvious difference between the branding model of a retailer and a manufacturer is that, for the most part, retailers use a master brand model, supporting one brand, the chain, whereas manufacturers primarily use a product brand model supporting a wide portfolio of individual product brands. This gives the retailers an enormous economy of scale advantage because they only have to build and reinforce one brand image that covers billions in sales.

Even in the 1990s, when retailers were just starting to market their brands, they were able to put up advertising spends that matched the biggest manufacturer brands. Since then, a retailer like Tesco has increased its advertising spend more than five-fold and has the United Kingdom's single largest brand advertising budget, yet at the company level it is still a smaller spender than two of its key suppliers, Procter & Gamble and Unilever, who have a huge number of brands to support.

Despite the recession in 2008, Tesco increased their advertising spend by 18.8% to $125 million, and they weren't alone. Asda increased theirs by 52%, Sainsbury's by 21.3% and Morrisons by 15%. But even with recessionary budget cuts from manufacturers, the retailers were still outspent by Unilever, who had an advertising budget of $235 million in 2008 (up $4.8 million from 2007) and Procter & Gamble (P&G), with an advertising budget of $231 million (down $25.5 million from 2007), but spread across many brands. In 2010, only P&G of the United Kingdom's top four FMCG manufacturers increased advertising spend, whereas Tesco and Asda continued to implement double-digit increases (Table 6.1).

The benefit of the retailer master brand model is that $202 million is a colossal amount of advertising for one brand in the UK market, meaning the Tesco brand has terrific awareness and saliency in comparison to any product brand. Retailers have a much larger sales base over which to amortise their advertising costs: Tesco's 2010 UK sales

Table 6.1 Comparison of advertising spending by UK companies in 2009 and 2010

	Media Spend 2009	Media Spend 2010	Change (US$ million)
Procter & Gamble	253	315	+62
Unilever	234	218	−16
Tesco	189	202	+13
Asda	165	178	+13
Reckitt Benckiser	133	121	−12
Kellogg's	131	118	−13

Source: AC Nielsen.

were $70.3 billion compared to P&G's at $16.6 billion and Unilever's at $3.9 billion and yet both manufacturers still had to outspend Tesco on advertising because of the vast range of brands they own. However, there is more to building trust than throwing mountains of cash at design companies, advertising agencies and television stations. There also comes responsibility. Retail brands are just as vulnerable as product brands to a loss of trust based on, for example, a major product quality failure, but the stakes and risks are much higher. A brand such as Tesco Basics has annual sales of £1 billion, so the value that can be lost is huge. Equally, the brand is composed of hundreds of products manufactured by third parties, so the risks of a product quality failure are magnified. Retailers need to have the best systems possible in place to police the quality that is going out under their name.

Direct Consumer Contact

Direct consumer contact is an advantage for retailers, as 70% of shoppers make purchase decisions in stores and are thus open to last-minute persuasion. The physical presence of shops following a uniform design, name, logo and style is equivalent to a permanent poster campaign on premium advertising sites, perfectly targeted. When shoppers enter the stores, they form a strong impression, and each visit provides the retailer with an opportunity to communicate and tangibly demonstrate something about the company and products.

Many retailers are becoming increasingly involved with in-store advertising: interactive touch screens, motion graphics and floor and ceiling displays are common in developed markets. But unlike retailers, who control the store environment, manufacturers have to pay for every opportunity to communicate with their consumers in the minutes prior to the purchase decision: they have to spend money to stop their brands being forgotten. This has encouraged manufacturers to experiment with finding ways to have some kind of interaction with shoppers in-store.

In Germany, P&G are testing radio-frequency tags on products in Metro Group stores. When a customer takes the product off the shelf, a digital screen at eye level customises its message to deliver relevant content. For example, if a customer picks up toothpaste, the screen recommends the best dental floss or toothbrush to go with the toothpaste. They are also testing the effectiveness of displaying messages based on a consumer's appearance detected through cameras in the screens.

In-store scent and sensory marketing is also becoming popular. In June 2011, Schick launched the first scented men's razor, the Xtreme3 Refresh. Scent is embedded in the handle, but they are also using ambient scenting in-store. They want to establish brand loyalty through emotions, as fragrances can create positive experience with brands on the subconscious level by influencing perception, mood and shopping behaviour.

In South Africa, the top in-store media provider, Primedia, is tracking the eye movement and fixation patterns of consumers reading in-store messages; their Tobii Eye Tracking System identifies whether intended core messages are being communicated properly. The solution will help brands improve their shelf presence, which in turn will increase in-store sales. It will be available in 1000 retail outlets if the trial, started in March 2011, is successful.

Although many in-store media innovations are coming from manufacturers, retailers still choose whether they want to allow a manufacturer to use them in their stores, or even if they want to use them themselves. Thus, retailers retain control over most aspects of direct consumer contact.

But manufacturers still control the packaging, which gives them options with, for example, QR codes printed on-pack. When ConAgra Foods launched the new pop-up bowl for their Orville Redenbacher's Gourmet Popping Corn line, they used QR to direct shoppers to a short video that gave them more detail on the pop-up, trying to influence their buying decision at the point-of-purchase.

But the battle is tilted in favour of the retailers, who have continued to build their use of media-type strategies (creating awareness via stores, backed up with communication in-store) at just a time when manufacturers have been finding it harder to reach their consumers.

Control of Marketing-Mix Variables

Retailers control a number of key marketing-mix variables, including in-store presence, price and promotions, and sampling. They can influence the mindspace of their brands and competitors' brands, not just by delisting but also by altering these variables. The more they become interested in competing with manufacturer brands, the more they can benefit from altering the elements of the marketing mix under their control.

The opportunities for retailers are as follows:

- **In-store Presence and Prominence:** In markets where impulse buying is important or variety-seeking the norm, eye-level location or an end-of-gondola feature will be a critical purchase factor, sometimes more than absolute brand preference. Brand preference research often ignores the physical facts of presence in the store: the weight of lifting heavy bottles down from a high shelf or the extra second needed to notice a brand on a low shelf. One retailer told us that, as a rule of thumb, sales of a brand will be reduced by two-thirds if it is moved from an eye-level to a foot-level position. Presence in store is critical for new products, and since retailers can always guarantee prominence for their new products, it gives them an advantage.
- **Prices and Promotions:** Manufacturers used to plan promotions as part of their marketing mix, including 'flagging' ('This week's best buy' or 'Special purchase'). Now retailers, such as Carrefour, use promotions as part of their private label marketing. Carrefour launched private label products in Indonesia in July 2011, and when sales were low (only 7–8% of their total sales) they increased in-store promotions and consequently blocked other brands from using in-store media. Since the control of price setting and promotions lies

with the retailer, manufacturers' pricing and promotion strategy is now dictated or superseded by the retailers' objectives.

Wal-Mart control the pricing and promotional strategy of all the products they sell. Manufacturers who supply Wal-Mart not only pass a rigorous process that includes packaging requirements and quality testing but also agree to Wal-Mart's purchasing price for their product: it's the manufacturer's responsibility to meet that price. Many have been forced to move their production facilities to emerging markets to ensure their cost structure was compatible. One consequence is that more Americans now work in retailing than in manufacturing. Any manufacturer who breaks Wal-Mart's requirements is subject to delisting.

- **Sampling, Merchandising and Special Displays:** Sampling was frequently used by manufacturers to increase trial of their best-selling brands and to gain awareness of their new brands. Retailers would be happy to host them because of the interest it would bring to their shoppers. Not any more. Sophisticated retailers realise the importance of controlling their environment to achieve the ambiance they want for their retail brand. Consequently, there are few major retailers who permit manufacturers to sample extensively, Costco being a notable exception, although they are more likely to sample their own Kirkland Signature brand than manufacturers' brands.

Information

Thirty years ago, stores had to physically count stock to figure out how much they sold, and replenishment was managed at the store level by suppliers' representatives. Today, scanner-equipped checkouts tell the retailer what is being sold, tell replenishment what to deliver and pass the order to the supplier. The savings from the checkout revolution have been tremendous.

But the real value is created when purchase data is married to shopper loyalty cards. These tell the retailer who bought what, when, with what else, how frequently and so on. Enrolling card holders gives a retailer the chance to find out more about its customer base (where they live, family composition, family income). By integrating this information with known purchasing behaviour, retailers are able to target direct marketing activities with a precision and success rate well above that of manufacturers. This gives retailers an information advantage that they have not had since the dawn of modern retailing.

When Tesco introduced the first loyalty cards in the United Kingdom in 1995, they quickly overtook Sainsbury's, who snootily dismissed Tesco's card as 'electronic Green Shield Stamps', as the number-one retailer in part because their cards allowed them to learn about actual buying behaviour at the customer level, which they translated into complex marketing strategies and promotional campaigns. Today, over 20 million people use Tesco's loyalty cards, and the data collected has guided key decisions, including the launch of Tesco.com, entry into non-food categories and their expansion into financial services.

In 2006, the X5 Retail Group launched Club Perekrestok at their retail outlets. Club Perekrestok allows consumers to collect points that can be exchanged for purchases, and additional points are given for shopping in the morning, on customers' birthdays and for buying private label. It has made the X5 Retail Group one of the most competitive and efficient retail trade structures in Russia, and helped them grow their sales from $6.15 billion in 2007 to $11.3 billion in 2010.

Even small retailers are taking advantage of loyalty cards. In Japan, a club of independent retailers, Zen Nippon Shokuhin, help local retailers compete against supermarkets. Initially, Zen Nippon Shokuhin acted as their combined wholesaler, but recently they started collecting consumer data from the retailers and using it to help them improve their stores. In January 2011, Zen Nippon Shokuhin launched a loyalty card that provides electronic discounts for shoppers at all their retail affiliates. They are using the information to bargain with manufacturers for better deals. It is ironic that independent retailers are using loyalty programmes to refine their campaigns; large stores started using them to develop experiences that mimicked the one-to-one service of independent stores, and now local retailers are using them to fight back.

These four advantages (brand model, direct consumer contact, control of marketing-mix variables and information) mean that once retailers decide to challenge the manufacturers' hold on mindspace they are awesome opponents. As retailers become more committed to developing their importance to the consumer, they take tighter control of the in-store marketing variables, which increases their influence on the market. Any mindspace they succeed in capturing is taken from the manufacturers and translates into increased negotiating power against those suppliers. Retailing will never again fit the 'transparent model' assumed in traditional marketing theory, where they merely channel consumer demand information back to manufacturers.

Despite these changes, many manufacturer brands continue to turn impressive profits. This is because they also have sources of efficiency and know-how that remain crucial even in the changing climate.

Manufacturers' mindspace advantages

Unlike retailers, manufacturers find economies and synergy within one or a number of related product fields. This specialisation gives them particular strengths in technology, communication and consumer understanding. No matter how large and enlightened retailers become, they remain generalists, and there are things that are difficult for them to do as well as a manufacturer. In particular, retailers cannot:

- Always get the quality they want.
- Advertise specific functions of a brand.
- Create a strong, emotional brand image.
- Give a sense of wide choice.
- Invest in deep understanding of consumer behaviour in all product fields that they operate.

The more these factors are important in a product field, the less retailers are able to win mindspace from manufacturer brands. Conversely, in categories where these factors play a small or no role, such as eggs, milk, butter, flour etc., manufacturers have been unable to halt the retail juggernaut.

Technology

Everyone, including Gillette, was surprised when their strategy to de-commoditise shaving worked, turning millions of men from Bic disposables back to high-quality, expensive and highly profitable system razors. The fact that it worked is a reminder of manufacturers' power to add value to their markets in a way that retailers cannot. This is because the quality and innovation of retailer brands is limited to what they can negotiate from manufacturers. For products that are technologically sophisticated, like detergents and coffee, there are few top-quality suppliers willing to entertain private label, hence manufacturer brands are in the driver's seat. For example, Procter & Gamble, Unilever, Henkel and Colgate hold all but the cheapest segment of the washing-powder market, and Nestlé, Kraft and Unilever hold onto the instant-coffee market. Their technological leads, backed by communication focused on the functional and taste superiority, has kept private label share below average in most countries.

It is tempting for manufacturers to believe that advertising will protect their brands, but if retailers can match a brand on product quality there is usually no stopping them. This is because a well-tended retail master brand provides a sufficient level of trust for the consumer to at least try the product if prominently presented and well priced in-store.

The difficulty for retailers is getting the product to be as good as or better than leading brands. In many product fields, the number of top-quality suppliers is strictly limited. Retailers who want to compete with the top brands have only the choice of these top suppliers. Any manufacturer who has invested in the technology wants to be paid for the investment made. In addition, these suppliers are usually involved in the branded consumer market and not ready to see the overall price level jeopardised. Hence, technically sophisticated products are weaker areas for retailers because the only people with the technical know-how to match the big-brand owners are other big-brand owners.

However, many supermarket product categories are not high-tech and can be produced to indistinguishable standards by a large number of producers. This divide of technical sophistication is one of the factors that decides who is going to own the brands, or at least who is going to make profits out of them.

Pointed Communication

Retailers follow a policy of umbrella branding across their entire product range. The retail name is seen as one brand with extensions in many fields. There may be a linking theme across products, often a 'good value' positioning, but essentially the name gives reassurance on quality. When awareness and reassurance are all that is required, umbrella branding will be as effective as individual branding, and is cheaper because it requires no additional investment for individual products. This is the case for most low-tech, low-image product categories, such as basic cooking ingredients: rice, tinned fruit and frozen vegetables.

But only manufacturers can pursue a more specific type of branding where they discover new consumer wants, satisfy them with a functionally or emotionally superior product and attach the benefits via advertising to a specific brand name. This is why a retailer has trouble generating the same credibility as a brand like Crest toothpaste, which continually invests in its 'healthy teeth for children' positioning, or Axe deodorant, which targets young males with the fantasy of 'women making the first move.' Even manufacturer master branding is more targeted than retailers, because it is usually category specific: Lean Cuisine has more specific associations in frozen food than, say, Safeway.

To overcome this barrier, retailers sometimes create sub-brands. The largest supermarket in Spain, Mercadona, has created several: 'Hacendado' for their food products, 'Bosque Verde' for their cleaning products and 'Deliplus' for their healthcare and beauty products. The largest supermarket in India, Foodworld, have also launched brands for different lines, using 'Foodworld' for grocery items and 'Nature's Bounty' for herbal beauty products. Following the logic, retailers have to advertise these sub-brands, as presence on the shelf alone is unlikely to give them meaning in the consumer's eyes. This not only erodes the retailer's advertising cost advantage but also gives them a disadvantage over nationally available advertised brands, as their brands are only available in a small percentage of the market, their own stores, and thus tend to be of small volume in comparison. However, advertising is expensive and needs to be amortised over a large market share to be viable.

Many manufacturers use international advertising to spread the cost of advertising development and production; negotiations with media suppliers are also helped by size. Instead of amortising advertising internationally, retailers must amortise over a wider range of goods.

Realistically, retailers are constrained to create an overall image to support all the categories in which they compete with manufacturers or service providers. The name 'Carrefour' is used on food products, financial services, holidays, insurance, car centre, garden centre, petrol, home deliveries of heating oil, hardware, sportswear and more, which creates their next weakness relative to manufacturers: image.

Image

Brand messages are important for functional products, and they are even more important for products chosen for their image or emotional values. This makes image a problem for retailers, owing to the broad positioning they must adopt. To communicate prestige benefits, retailers have to dissociate from their own functional, low-price images.

Hoping to create a little prestige, some retailers develop and advertise premium clothes sub-brands. In 2006, Myer, one of Australia's largest retailers, launched a fashion line by top designer Wayne Cooper, known as 'Wayne by Wayne Cooper Collection'. In 2010, Tesco launched a high-end fashion range, F&F, following Asda, who have created the most successful retail clothing sub-brand, George, by well-known British designer George Davies, which is worth $1.6 billion and is being rolled out in Wal-Marts across North America.

It is debatable whether retailer brands can gain prestige through advertising. The idea of the 'independent' brand was to separate the product line from the store, but the advertising must also re-associate it with the store as that is the only place it can be bought. It's an image oxymoron.

The most successful example of a retailer that has built brands of enduring class and image is perhaps Boots. Their best-selling brand in the United States, Botanics, features aromatherapy products made from pure plant extracts, and in the United Kingdom their best-selling brand, No7, features high-end anti-ageing treatments and cosmetics. They also developed The Sanctuary from Boots, modelled from a famous spa in London's Covent Garden, and Lee Stafford Hair Care from Boots, based on one of the United Kingdom's most influential hairdressers. But Boots do not have a low-price master brand image to contend with.

In some areas, manufacturers are facing the dilemma of legitimising retailer brands by seeking distribution for their own prestige brands in major retail chains. This needs careful planning, as demonstrated by L'Oréal 30 years ago. In 1982, L'Oréal took the plunge with the launch of Plenitude, signed with the L'Oréal name, into supermarkets. Previously, high-tech, high-price face-care products had only been sold through chemists, pharmacies and department stores. Plenitude made these products available to a broader market, and moved some sales from specialist outlets to self-service supermarkets. L'Oréal enjoyed enormous success with Plenitude, creating and dominating a new supermarket category. Ten years later, Carrefour introduced a range of face-care products called Les Cosmetiques, priced at the same level as L'Oréal's Plenitude, and packaged with an equal level of luxury. It is arguable that Carrefour could not have created its brand, demanding the same high prices, without the lead from Plenitude in legitimising the hypermarket as a location for prestige cosmetics. Similarly, Nicole by OPI (a premium brand of nail polish) was launched in Wal-Mart and Target in 2002, and, true to form, Target soon followed up with the launch of their premium brand, Sonia Kashuk.

The incentive for the manufacturer to take such a step is volume, but the risks are significant, both at the consumer and retail levels. For the consumer, once the prestige names are sharing the shopping cart with carrots and floor polish, it is a smaller step to trade down to the private label brand (as with Plenitude). Thus, the prestige brands in a supermarket open the way for the stores to market their own competitor, which they will if they can find a quality supplier. The other danger comes from alienating the specialist retailer by making it more difficult for them to compete with the large discounters and supermarkets. There is no attraction for specialists once a recognised brand is sold in supermarkets. When the specialist retailers turn away from, say, Levi's jeans to try to find more exclusive brands to justify their higher prices, Levi Strauss will lose the influence of these opinion leaders and advisers.

Variety, Choice and Novelty

In many FMCG markets the consumer demands a sense of choice and variety within the category: the process of choosing from many alternatives can become one of the defining characteristics of the category. Chocolate confectionery would be a good example. In most developed markets there can easily be 50 brands available with most coming into multiple product size and packaging format options. Most purchases are made on impulse while perusing the display. Convenience stores have held onto a significant share of this category because they are able and willing to stock most of the manufacturer brands, which supermarkets are not. Supermarkets are even less inclined to develop private label versions of so many offerings as there would not be the sales volume or the shelfspace to justify them. The critical mass and specialisation of manufacturers allows them to service this need for variety and choice more effectively than retailers can.

This feature of the market works best when competing manufacturers all play the same game. For example, in the skin care sector of the supermarket Johnson & Johnson offer nine pedigrees, including Johnson's body care, Aveeno and Lubriderm. Each pedigree offers ranges targeted at slightly different groups, often with virtually identical products. For example, to moisturise dry skin Johnson's body care offers Deep Hydrating lotion, Aveeno offers Positively Nourishing lotion and Lubriderm offers Advanced Moisture Therapy lotion. The different brands allow the consumer to match their image needs or seek variety; a retail brand, even a sub-brand, fails to generate the same sense of choice. More importantly, it allows Johnson & Johnson to have a larger market share than one company with one brand and one non-self-duplicating range could.

In high-value product fields (e.g. computers, washing machines) consumers prefer to feel that at least half a dozen companies are competing for their money. A producer with one brand will have less chance of satisfying the consumer than a producer with three or four brands, unless the prices are so obviously low, as is the case for big-ticket items in Costco.

In other markets (toys, breakfast cereals, soft drinks), there is a significant 'novelty sector' that sells alongside the staples. This is similar to image brands as it is largely animated by paid-for communication. Novelty implies risk and therefore demands high margins, which does not fit with the retailer's value proposition. And in other areas (canned peas, frozen French fries), the consumer does not seek variety, choice or novelty, and retailers that offer their brands and small ranges can win high shares.

Where the shopper's appetite for variety, choice and novelty are greater, the specialisation of manufacturers into product categories gives them the critical mass and know-how to dominate the battle for mindspace.

Consumer Understanding

Successful brand management depends on a continually updated understanding of consumers' needs and wants in a product category. This is more difficult to achieve for a retailer than for a manufacturer because, even though retailers have access to detailed shopping data, it is difficult to use more than a fraction of it effectively. The sheer quantity means that, while it can be mined for patterns and is a great tool for understanding what has happened, it can be difficult to derive new insights into what else may happen, in the future. It is also necessary to have the right expertise to analyse the data, as translating findings into ideas demands marketing specialists. A retailer cannot employ sufficient numbers of specialists to cover all the major product fields of their private labels, whereas specialised manufacturers can.

Understanding consumer attitudes and behaviour in a category is an asset of the manufacturer and a source of power in the battle for mindspace, provided they haven't cost-saved in that area to fund more retailer discounts. Or, to put it another way, if a retailer knows more about a product category than does a manufacturer, then the manufacturer does not deserve the retailer's business.

Pressure on second-tier brands

The critical mass advantages that manufacturers enjoy only apply to strong brands; for smaller brands they are less apparent, or even nonexistent. In all too many product categories, the sad fact for manufacturers is that a portion of their brand portfolio is no longer relevant to the new retailing world.

The power of twentieth-century manufacturer brand-building tools coupled with the weakness of twentieth-century retailers meant there was an explosion in the size of companies' brand portfolios. The heyday of television advertising from the 1960s to the 1980s spawned countless 'brands' that, in truth, had little to commend them in terms of uniqueness or enduring appeal. For example, until 1960 Cadbury in the United Kingdom regularly advertised only four brands. By 1964, they were advertising 17, rising to 25 by 1973. With compliant retailers, these products found their way onto the shelves with ease. The majority of these are now dead or dying. This is because many were never really brands but were products with names that had television advertising behind them.

In other cases, a brand with strong credentials may have been neglected by previous owners and lost its previous premier status, which then moves it into the retailer's cross-hairs, as Britain's Premier Brands discovered to their cost in the first half of 2011. In retaliation for attempting to impose a 14% price increase, Tesco, Premier Brands' biggest customer, delisted a whole raft of once-mighty brands, such as Oxo and Branston Pickle. Premier Brands are one of several companies who have made a success of buying such brands cheaply and then re-energising them with a level of focus and investment the previous owner was no longer willing or able to devote. But it is rare that such brands return to their previous 'must stock' status, as Tesco demonstrated.

Technology, variety where appropriate, advertising muscle and consumer understanding are the key benefits for manufacturer brands, and each is highly sensitive to economies of scale. Once the funding for innovation and advertising is in retreat, a consumer brand weakens. This vicious circle is almost impossible to redress unless there is some special protection through patent or niching.

Second-tier brands are most threatened by the retailer's appetite to create brands themselves, and traditional consumer marketing techniques offer little to hold back the tide. In the battle for mindspace, possessing neither a retailer's contact with the market nor the muscle of a brand leader leads to a negative spiral for most consumer brands.

Key learnings

- In the battle for mindspace, there **is nothing to stop retailers from being the best provider of consumer trust**. Manufacturers do not own this by right. The question is: in what circumstances are they able to do so more efficiently than manufacturers?
- There are **some FMCG categories where retailers are destined to control mindspace**. These are the low-technology, low-image, low-novelty areas. Retailers are likely to be the most efficient suppliers of 'commodity' products because of their umbrella reassurance.
- In areas **where image and/or innovation are important** and brand-specific advertising is crucial, **manufacturers are likely to be more efficient** because of their size and specialisation. High-ubiquity products (impulse items such as drinks and snacks bought for immediate consumption) that need to be very widely distributed are also somewhat protected, but not necessarily for ever.
- From the manufacturer's point of view, the **situation varies according to whether a brand is a leader or a follower**. A brand leader is more likely to hold consumers through investing in brand-building actions and be able to motivate distribution via consumer demand. Less popular brands will be squeezed both by branded competition and retailers' brands.

Today, no matter how strong a brand's mindspace, most manufacturers are denied the freedom to merchandise or take orders in-store as retailers want to control *their* brand environment. Retailers who are marketing private label brands in competition with manufacturer brands will feature their own brands first and foremost, which puts more pressure on the fixed resource of shelfspace. Manufacturers used to battle other manufacturers for shelfspace; now they have to battle the retailer.

Chapter 7

R ETAILERS KNOW THEIR shelfspace is a valuable resource. But this is a recent discovery; in the past, they gave it away, then they thought of selling it. Manufacturers either paid directly, via slotting allowances etc., or paid in materials and labour to make the shelves more attractive and better organised; then they paid both as demand for shelfspace exceeded supply. More recently, for fast turnover items, manufacturers such as Frito-Lay have used a direct delivery and merchandising service where their people will spend pretty much all day in store refilling shelves to their and the store's mutual benefit.

However, today's retailers exploit their shelfspace resource for their own use. When Sainsbury's launched their private label cola, they gave it over 50% of the cola shelfspace and 100% of the best shelfspace. The pressure on shelfspace is further compounded by the manufacturers' actions. From tampons to crispbread, from rice to bleach, hyper-segmentation has taken hold, and every product now comes in at least six varieties, and every year 17 000 new products are added to grocery stores in North America, while shelfspace within each store mostly remains constant. It is estimated that each US grocery store spends an average of nearly $1 million per year to introduce new products that will fail.[1] Little wonder retailers demand slotting and shelf-relaying fees from manufacturers.

The delisting spectre

It is not unnatural for manufacturers to be terrified that their brands may be delisted by a major retailer, but this is more paranoia than reality. In fact, retailers are afraid of delisting manufacturers' brands, or at least the brands they perceive contribute to their store traffic, transaction size or those that contribute large sums in trade spend to the retailer's bottom line. Stocking products is the retailers' business: *not* stocking a product sought by shoppers is a failure to their customers. The downside of a retailer overusing its listing power against manufacturers is the potential of losing assortment appeal against the retail competition. If a retailer doesn't stock the things you want to buy, there aren't any other compelling reasons to go there.

Deciding how many lines to stock is an important strategic choice for retailers as they can, in principle, stock anywhere from several hundred to hundreds of thousands of SKUs. Convenience stores and hard discounters offer the smallest range: in general, Aldi offer about 1000; 7–11, 2000; Lianhua in China, 2000; and Perekrestok, the soft discounter in Russia, 7500 SKUs. Supermarkets provide more: Pak'nSave in New Zealand offer 12 000; Foodworld in India, 15 000 and ParknShop in Hong Kong, 40 000 SKUs. Hypermarkets offer the most, and start at around 50 000 SKUs; Wal-Mart, the largest in the world, offer more than 115 000 SKUs in their largest stores.

But whatever the size, a grocer cannot stock all brands in all sizes and varieties. They have to be selective about what products to stock and what new ones to add. To a greater extent than before, the retailer has to use skill and judgement to allocate scarce shelfspace.

FMCG purchases rank among some of the least important deci-sions we make in our lives. According to one American survey, 69% of people do not use shopping lists, and 66% of purchases are not planned;[2] indeed, many shopping trips are not planned.[3] It is reason-able to assume that when shoppers do not plan, the selection of brands available in-store set the agenda for purchase decisions. Winning presence in-store is now more important for manufacturers compared to their traditional priority, winning consumer preference, which is just the entry price to be considered for shelfspace.

However, even if shopping trips are not planned, most consumers will shop in a habitual fashion. They will predominantly follow a regular route through the store, either diligently travelling every aisle or equally diligently never going down certain aisles. As they meander through the store, key brands in each sector will catch their eye, and, in a microsecond, a decision is made on whether there is need for more shampoo. It is at this point, consideration of need/no need, that there is a maximum opportunity to switch brands; therefore, retailers' reassertion of control over their shelf space gives them more power than ever to influence brand choice; an advantage they fully leverage in positioning their private label.

The decision of which brands to list is of critical importance to both parties. It is a key issue in negotiations, which are underpinned by the perceived costs to both of non-listing. Added to the listing negotiation is the subsequent need for the manufacturer to keep the retailer adequately supplied and for the retailer to have efficient distribution systems to keep the listed products on the shelf.

The cost of non-listing depends on what the customer will do if a brand is not in stock, either because of a supply failure or because it's been delisted.

The possible outcomes of an 'out-of-stock'

Suppose the product that would have been chosen by the shopper is missing. The shopper has four possible options. They can:

- substitute an alternative SKU (brand, flavour or size)
- resolve to seek the missing SKU at another store
- defer purchase until the current store restocks
- drop the purchase altogether.

Research has indicated that around 43% of shoppers will substitute either a different brand or a different SKU within the same brand, 35% will buy the item from another store, 13% will delay purchase and 9% will not purchase at all.[4]

The decision between options is driven by the balance between two factors: the shopper's perceived cost of switching brands or size/flavour compared to their perceived cost of switching stores.

Cost of Switching Brands (CSB)

Loyalty is never absolute. Brand loyalty is a matter of degree, with some brands preferred and others less preferred but acceptable. There is a lot of talk in marketing departments about loyalty; the reality is there is only 'brand preference'. The CSB is the marginal satisfaction lost when the shopper substitutes the next-best SKU or brand for the unavailable favourite. They will still be somewhat satisfied, or they wouldn't have bought it, but not as much as if they had bought their first choice.

The degree of marginal satisfaction lost depends on relative brand preference: the more one brand is preferred over the available alternative, the more satisfaction is given up when forced to switch. Marginal satisfaction also varies depending on the shopper's brand choice behaviour in the product category.

There are three types of brand choice behaviour:

- **Preferred**: where the shopper always tries to buy the same brand.
- **Repertoire**: where the shopper chooses from among a repertoire of accepted brands.
- **Promiscuous**: where the shopper is open to consider any brand on any purchase occasion.

Table 7.1 shows how brand choice behaviour can vary across product fields. It shows the results of a French study that compared loyalty to brands with the importance of brands in forming the purchase choice.[5]

Table 7.1 Importance of brands compared to brand choice (French consumers)

Brand choice behaviour	Importance of brand	Percentage of buyers		
		Preferred	Repertoire	Promiscuous
Champagne	high	24	68	8
Mineral water	high	44	37	19
Coffee	high	52	41	7
Washing-up liquid	medium	54	39	7
Chocolate (tablet)	medium	30	56	14
Washing powder	medium	45	40	15
Jam	low	32	51	17
Yogurt	low	23	49	28
Tights	low	23	29	48
Dress	low	4	33	63

Source: Adapted from Jean-Noel Kapferer and Gilles Laurent, *La Marque*, Ediscience International, Paris, 1989, ch. 3, pp. 96–8.

As one would anticipate, there is a correlation between the importance of brands in a category and brand preference. However, the importance in a category does not always imply that behaviour in that category will be a slavish loyalty to a particular brand.

In some categories brands are very important to consumers, but many consumers are repertoire buyers or even promiscuous ones. For example, 'brand' is of great importance when choosing champagne, but only about one in four shoppers is loyal to *a single* brand. The implication is that the marginal satisfaction of one brand over the others (i.e. its CSB) will be low for 76% of consumers. In other words, for the majority of buyers looking for something to take to a best friend's birthday, any of Dom Pérignon, Krug or Bollinger would do, whereas an unknown brand would not. In contrast, 54% of French consumers always try to buy the same washing-up liquid, hence a lowly washing-up liquid brand may have a stronger case than prestigious champagne when demanding shelfspace: the retailer may decide it can get by with one brand of premium champagne but must have the top three brands of washing-up liquid.

In markets where consumers actively seek variety, the CSB for individual brands will be small or non-existent. With repertoire buying behaviour, where several brands are bought concurrently with varying frequency, the absence of any for a short period should not cause much dissatisfaction. Such is the case with biscuits (cookies), where customers regularly switch between several brands. As long as consumers feel they have a rich choice, the occasional absence of one or two well-liked brands will not cause a loss of satisfaction.

Even where the shopper has an absolute brand preference, the marginal satisfaction may be eliminated by point-of-sale activities, such as promotions; these are important for the retailer in reducing the CSB in the aftermath of delisting a brand.

But there are categories where many consumers have a single preferred brand. In this case, when a consumer is confronted with a stock-out of a brand, they will register dissatisfaction with the store whatever action (options 1 to 4 described above) they decide to take.

Cost of Switching Stores (CSS)

'Store loyalty' is a rather ill-defined notion, as most consumers have patterns of shopping that involve several stores. Different stores may serve different roles, either by shopping occasion (Friday night big shop vs. lunch-hour fill-up) or by 'speciality' (e.g. vegetables, meat, discount). Some shoppers take shopping very seriously and invest time visiting different stores, cherry picking for good value and tracking down preferred items; this is facilitated in some markets by retailers' heavy use of weekly promotional flyers. Some shoppers visit different stores on a regular basis, both to compare prices and because they enjoy a sense of variety, choice and change. Many shoppers regularly visit two or more stores simply because they arrange shopping trips from different geographical bases (e.g. home and work). One snapshot of shopping habits, gathered in a US survey, is displayed in Table 7.2.

Table 7.2 A snapshot of shopping habits

	Household penetration	Annual trips per household
Supermarket	99%	57
Mass merchandisers	76%	13
Warehouse clubs	51%	12

Source: The 78th Annual Report of the grocery industry, *Progressive Grocer*, April 2011.

An earlier survey by the same publication found that 27% of super-market shoppers visited only one supermarket each week, 46% visited two, 22% visited three and 5% visited four or more.

A more objective way to measure the tendency of a shopper to switch stores is the perceived CSS. This is the perceived cost to a consumer of making a visit to a competitive store to find a missing SKU. The cost will include the physical cost of the trip, the psychological cost of not making the purchase immediately and the psychological cost of not making the purchase at this store.

Physical cost of the trip

Shopping behaviour has a significant impact on the physical cost of switching stores. For a repertoire shopper who regularly visits more than one supermarket, the physical cost of visiting an alternative store will be small. Such a shopper may know that one store never stocks a desired item and habitually buys it from another store without inconvenience.

Other shoppers put greater value on time and convenience and gravitate to 'one-stop shopping'. For shoppers who aim to reduce shopping to one trip a fortnight to their preferred store, the perceived physical cost of an extra trip to an alternative store will be significant.

Psychological cost of not making the purchase immediately

This cost is driven by the type of purchase. In a main shopping trip, many purchases would be stocking up, with the shopper's decision being driven by several factors: the products available, the offers on those products and the stock at home. Holding stock at home enables the prudent shopper to benefit from promotions and negate the inconvenience of out-of-stock items. A promotion can increase home inventories; a stock-out in the store may be allowed to deplete them.

However, some items are difficult for the consumer to stock for very long. Depending on food habits, bread, milk, fruit, salad, vegetables, fish and meat may demand purchase several times a week, and so an out-of-stock can be hugely inconvenient and irritating.

In addition, urgent needs arise: missing ingredients for a planned meal, a bottle of wine, a pair of tights, tampons, a cheap away-from-home lunch or insect-killing products. Households also come up with urgent shopping items because the home inventory has failed. Salt, disposable nappies or washing-up liquid are easy to stock, but a shortage lasting one day can be unacceptable.

Psychological cost of not making the purchase at this store

The psychological cost of seeking the preferred SKU in another shop includes frustration and inconvenience. A shopper may resent the original store for being out-of-stock, especially if they have to pay more for the item at another store.

For one-stop shoppers who have a high level of private label purchases, the CSS is greatly increased. If a shopper is in the habit of making a lot of private label purchases in one chain, switching chains will mean those brands will be unavailable to them. This implies that the cost of switching stores (at least for a regular stocking-up trip) will be great.

The risk for the retailer when a shopper switches stores is that a habit will be broken and the shopper will enjoy an emotional benefit (rather than cost) in going elsewhere. Since location plays a dominant role in store choice, it is likely that some people shop where they do because it's the most convenient one, despite it perhaps having a marginal or negative emotional appeal. These shoppers are waiting to be pushed to make the physical effort to go to another store, where they will gain the emotional satisfaction of going to a 'better' shop.

What will happen?

The critical factor in the outcome of an out-of-stock is the ratio between brand loyalty (CSB) and store loyalty (CSS). Let us consider the possible outcomes:

Low CSB, High CSS: The retailer holds the power

Where the marginal satisfaction for the preferred SKU is negligible (or is eliminated by the retailer through in-store promotions), the outcome of being out of stock will be to substitute another item. The retailer holds on to the shopper, and, in addition, the forced trial of an alternative SKU has the potential to reduce even further the CSB by proving to be perfectly acceptable. In this situation the power lies almost exclusively with the retailer rather than the manufacturer, and applies particularly in product categories with little added value and differentiation between brands. For the manufacturer, having a negligible CSB on their brand is never a good situation.

High CSB, Slightly Higher CSS: The retailer is betting the store

If a consciously preferred item is not available and the CSS is high, the shopper will likely defer the purchase until the preferred store restocks. However, deferral is not an option if the store has delisted the item, or if the shopper's need is urgent. Since the CSS only marginally outweighs the CSB, the shopper is better in the short-term accepting the loss of satisfaction and buying the best alternative available. In other words, in this instance switching brands is easier for the shopper than switching stores. Thus, the retailer has 'won', but not without some cost in terms of customer dissatisfaction. In this instance, the retailer has 'forced' the shopper to swap brands, and the shopper consciously feels the pain and dilemma of out-of-stock products.

The long-term outcome once it becomes clear to the shopper that their preferred brand isn't coming back is uncertain. To reduce irritation, shoppers must modify their brand preference or modify their shopping habits. This is a crunch point, with the store pitting its appeal and loyalty against that created by the manufacturer. A retailer may be able to destroy a brand's CSB by forcing a trial of substitutes that are found to be acceptable, but the store risks its CSS in the process. In this situation, a sensible retailer will get the product back in stock before shoppers begin deserting to a competing store.

CSB is High, Higher than CSS: Retail nightmare!

If the shopper feels the CSB is strong and the CSS is small, seeking the desired SKU from another shop becomes appealing for a shopper when faced with a 'stock out'. This is the retailer's nightmare, where a whole basket of shopping may be lost through a failure to deliver just one product the shopper seeks. It doesn't even have to be a top-seller, such as Tide in North America or Ariel in the United Kingdom. A gigantic store such as a Carrefour could lose a shopping cart piled high every week simply by delisting the shopper's favourite type of artisanal cheese. This is a significant factor behind the average conversion rate for grocery retailers being less than 100%, i.e. somewhere between 5 and 10% of their customers leave without buying anything.

If the cost of switching stores is small but not negligible, and the need is non-urgent, the shopper may defer the purchase and avoid an extra visit to another store. The willingness to defer depends on the perceived CSS compared to the urgency of the need. The retailer should rush to restock before the shopper loses patience.

An urgent need raises the stakes, but can be a Pyrrhic victory for the store if the shopper switches brands. On this occasion, the retailer has twisted the consumer's arm successfully, but the shopper is likely to bear a grudge and modify shopping preferences as a result.

Anomalies

There are shopping items that have a high 'presence elasticity' (i.e. if the product is not there then the need disappears or was not stimulated at all). That's why Coca-Cola's goal is to be within a customer's reach at the time of thirst: they know that the more Coke a shopper buys, the more that person will consume; if a person buys less Coke because it's unavailable, they drink less and that sale is gone for ever.

A similar situation exists for impulse categories that are mostly only considered if the consumer notices them. This is often the case for items such as cut flowers, confectionery, treats and novelties. If the product is not seen, the consumer is unaware of dropping the purchase and won't seek to find it elsewhere.

Presence elasticity is higher for new products because manufacturers will be spending fortunes to encourage trial, and the interest and satisfaction that is generated when purchased will be used as negotiating factors when dealing with retailers. Advertising is also used by manufacturers to create dissatisfaction from shoppers if a brand is not stocked. In 2005, Superunie, one of the largest food retail buying organisations in the Netherlands, decided to boycott Fanta and Sprite because of a buying conflict with Coca-Cola. Coca-Cola responded by advertising Fanta using promotions (such as 2-for-1 coupons) in high-population areas to increase customer demand. As a result, Superunie shoppers forced them to restock the brands.[5]

Finally, there are also purchases for which the CSB is not zero but the products are not essential and can be dropped for one shopping trip. If a consumer is set on one brand, its absence may prompt them to do without until the next time. A typical example would be a non-essential like a bath additive. Although the brand will be bought again in the future (the consumer may think they are postponing purchase), it is dropped in the sense that renewed purchases will not make up the lost sales: they will have taken baths without any additive and will not add any more to their next bath or take more baths to make up for it. In this case, potential consumption is lost for ever.

The balance of power

The discussion above suggests that, in most instances, the retailer has the power to force brand switching. However, this underestimates the effect that cumulative frustration and disappointment has on the CSS. Each unwilling brand switch will erode the emotional CSS. Once the shopper has been frustrated by three or four out-of-stock products, store loyalty may be insufficient to prevent a trip to another supermarket. If multiple stock-outs occur on the same shopping trip, the retailer faces Armageddon. This becomes apparent when a chain suffers a poor implementation of a new distribution system.

By 2004, Loblaws had become one of the most successful and profitable grocery retailers in the world, but a disastrous revamping of their buying and distribution systems in 2004–2006 crippled the company.[6] Losing slickness in distribution caused a cascade of problems that lost customers and destroyed margins. Empty shelves and stale produce angered shoppers. Stock for flyer promotions or seasonal products arrived late, causing further upset. Margins were hit by mistimed or misdated product having to be sold off cheaply, which took up valuable shelfspace, meaning that new product launches did not appear in Loblaws stores because they didn't have space. Their CEO at the time remarked, 'When you begin to take for granted that you can just execute, you become a little bit careless.' Becoming a little bit careless wiped out $8 billion from Loblaws' share value and caused shoppers to permanently defect to their rivals.

Fighting for shelfspace

The greatest ally for brands is the uncertainty in retailers' minds. The costs to retailers in lowering the satisfaction of their shoppers are less visible than those to manufacturers. CSB accumulates both across brands and through time, so retailers, given the number of SKUs they stock, are very vulnerable to an undercurrent of shopper dissatisfaction growing without them knowing about it until it is too late, so they are prone to overcompensate the other way. The solution to this dilemma for retailers has been to invest in and build their CSS through building up the CSB of their private label brands.

The cost to a retailer of losing a sale is not the potential loss from that item: it is the fear that being out of stock of one key item may lead the shopper to make a whole basket of purchases elsewhere, or that the accumulation of being out of stock of several brands will lead to a level of dissatisfaction that will change the customer's long-term shopping pattern. A strong private label range gives the retailer confidence that the shopper will not desert their store, thus losing the opportunity to buy that store's private labels, because one or two manufacturer brands have disappeared.

Because the issue is complex, the retailer is wary of mistakes, either overestimating a store's power to influence brand choice or overestimating the shopper's loyalty to brands. Manufacturers of strong brands need to have the confidence to exploit these uncertainties in situations where they are still preferred over the retailer's private label offerings.

During the crucial listing negotiation between manufacturer and retailer, the outcomes of delisting are weighed by the two parties. Thinking about CSB and CSS helps both parties in their two major challenges.

The first task is to understand the balance of power. Understanding the balance of power implies knowing how much satisfaction is given up on switching brand compared to how easy it is for a consumer to switch store. To whom will the cost fall? How strong is the consumer's attachment to the brand? How does the cost of switching brands differ for impulse-purchase items such as confectionery? How much out-of-stock will the consumer tolerate?

The second task is to influence the CSB and CSS: retailers and manufacturers are free to alter the balance in their favour. What strategies would influence the outcome in favour of manufacturers and what in favour of the retailers? Let us consider some possibilities.

- It is clear that manufacturers should encourage consumers to shop around, as that is the retailer's Achilles heel. A good way of achieving this is to constantly nurture new outlets and channels of distribution. Manufacturers should also reflect on the effect of promotions, which are mostly designed to encourage brand switching and thus actually aid the retailer as they reduce the CSB.
- Retailers with strongly branded private label brands create additional loyalty to their stores by adding the CSB they are able to build around their own brands to their existing CSS. Foodworld's 'Foodworld,' Costco's 'Kirkland Signature,' and Trader Joe's 'Trader's' brands are good examples of where both brand and chain are exerting a positive pressure on the shopper not to defect elsewhere. Manufacturer brands in this environment have a tough task convincing a retailer that their shoppers will go elsewhere if one brand is not stocked.
- A retailer contemplating delisting a manufacturer's product should do everything possible to reduce the potential loss of satisfaction from shoppers. This means stocking other SKUs that lower the CSB of the brand on the chopping block, and then planning promotions, merchandising, layout and pricing to compensate disappointed shoppers. They can also mention the duration of out-of-stock items (put up signs apologising for the inconvenience and promising resumed supplies within a specific time), which may encourage consumers to defer buying the product until next time instead of switching stores. But not all delistings go according to plan. In 2004, the Dutch food retailer Edah delisted hundreds of national brands because they wanted to create more shelfspace for their private label brands. However, they had thousands of customer complaints and after six months, when sales were dropping owing to poor transition planning, they reintroduced virtually all the brands they had dropped.

- Thanks to loyalty card data, retailers have a massive advantage with information on shopping habits and in-store decision behaviour. Manufacturers cannot hope to match this directly, so they must focus on what they can do best: understand their category and brand behaviour to the same level of sophistication.

- Urgent purchases are special. Urgent needs play into the hands of the retailer if the shopper is not brand loyal. This gives retailers more power over items like fresh produce. However, the tables are turned when shoppers are brand loyal and urgent need can initiate a special trip to a competitor's store, resulting in the loss of a basket of sales, perhaps permanently. Retailers need to understand this dynamic in detail.

- A store specialising in fresh perishable items that the shopper cannot stock up on at home will generate more frequent visits and a higher store loyalty. This has been behind the remarkable growth of Morrisons in the United Kingdom, whose average growth rate over the past two decades has been higher than that of Tesco. Retailers very much have the upper hand with produce because suppliers find it hard to create fresh 'brands': bananas being the exception, where Chiquita, Dole, Del Monte, Fyffes and Noboa account for nearly 90% of sales. The fact that bananas are usually the single fastest-selling SKU in a grocery store and that they are so difficult to get to the store in perfect condition gives the brand owners leverage they otherwise would not have. However, it is debateable whether any of the major banana brands have a significant CSB, creating something of a 'brands of equal value' commodity market not unlike champagne brands.

- There are certain product fields where the retailer is destined to have considerable control (i.e. where shoppers are happy whatever brands are in stock). However, these are likely to be the 'dead' categories, e.g. table salt or canned vegetables, where the retailer also has little chance of differentiating from local retail competition other than on price. These products are most efficiently marketed under the retailer's umbrella brand.

Key learnings

- Retailers will always magnify the spectre of delisting a line, but in practice will **rarely use it punitively**. They have too much to lose in keeping their shoppers happy.
- A manufacturer's goal is to **develop a high cost of switching brands** for their products. Weak brands are doomed.
- Similarly, a retailer must always seek to find ways of **increasing, or at least not decreasing, the perceived cost of switching stores**.
- Manufacturers must seek to widen their distribution and **proactively embrace new customers and distribution channels**, be it hard discounters such as Aldi, club stores such as Costco, Dollar or Pound chains, and even less traditional outlets like vending machines. Such new opportunities can be substantial; in 2010, Dollar stores opened up more new retail space in the United States than did Wal-Mart.[7] These actions reduce the CSS for brands, which gives manufacturers more leverage.
- The theatre of battle for shelfspace is preference, which can be owned either by the manufacturer or by the store. In other words, the **best weapon for winning shelfspace is a strong** *mindspace*.

While the battle between retailers and manufacturers can sometimes dominate the thinking of manufacturers, retailers spend much more of their time and effort evaluating their competitive situation versus other retailers. This is because retailing brands are far more homogeneous than are manufacturer brands, and miniscule differences can be important. Any manufacturer hoping to gain influence with a retailer needs to thoroughly understand the retailers' never-ending battle for differential advantage.

Notes

1. http://www.allbusiness.com/marketing/market-research/631186–1.html. Accessed 7 November 2011.
2. Sansolo M (1989) 'Rethinking the shopper': Reporting on Coca-Cola Retailing Research Council Survey: 'Merchandising in the 1990s'. *Progressive Grocer* May: 63–6.
3. Leahy T (1992) Tesco: 'The retailers' viewpoint'. In: *Branding: A key marketing tool*, (ed.) JM Murphy. Macmillan, London, p. 116.
4. Grocery Manufacturers of America/Food Marketing Institute/ CIES (2002) Retail Out-of-Stocks: A worldwide examination of extent, causes, and consumer responses. GMA, Washington, http://www.theconsumergoodsforum.com/pfiles/publications/CIES-FMI-GMA-retail_out_of_stock-study_2002.pdf. Accessed 26 March 2012.
5. http://repub.eur.nl/res/pub/7438/EPS20060874MKT_9058921026_SLOOT.pdf. Accessed 21 August 2011.
6. Strauss M (2007) Memories of Excellence. *The Globe and Mail*, 26 January, http://www.theglobeandmail.com/report-on-business/memories-of-excellence/article737906/singlepage/#articlecontent. Accessed 7 August 2011.
7. http://www.acgchicago.com/assets/10/documents/Opportunities_and_Threats_in_a_Consolidating_Retail_Environment_Layout_1.pdf. Accessed 18 November 2011.

Chapter 8

RETAILERS NEED TO differentiate their offering. Location used to be the deciding advantage, but as retail saturation and consumer mobility increases, it provides less protection; the only stores that can still use location as their differential advantage are convenience stores. Other retailers, like manufacturers, must differentiate their offering to create customer loyalty and improve profits.

What counts as a differential advantage?

In every market there are key success factors that a company must be proficient at in order to survive. In retailing, good locations and competitive prices are essential, and achieving them can be a challenge. But to win, retailers need to create a differential advantage on top of these key factors.

A differential advantage is obtained when a product or service is perceived as different in a positive way in the minds of consumers, so that it is no longer easily substitutable with competitive products or services. A differential advantage must have three attributes. It must be:

- **Perceived as unique:** A differential advantage sets the retailer apart from the competition in the eyes of the consumer, so the offer must be distinct. Although uniqueness will not necessarily motivate a purchase, it is a prerequisite.

- **Important to the target market:** Since the target market of a store is broad, the differential advantage must motivate a range of shoppers. Retailers have a habit of assuming that price is important to all buyers: it is important for some, but less important for others. Since retailers have to go for all segments, they must find benefits that motivate each type of shopper to become loyal to the store.
- **Sustainable:** If a retailer finds a differential advantage that attracts shoppers, competitors will immediately try to match it. To be successful, an advantage has to be sustainable against the competition, which means it must be unique to the company and difficult to copy. In general, services (such as smiling checkout staff) are easy to copy, and worth copying if they are profitable. Low prices on manufacturer brands are also easy to copy, unless the store has a structural and sustainable lead in efficiency, as do Wal-Mart.

There are several potential sources of retail differential advantage.

Differential Advantage via Fresh Produce

Perishables have become an increasingly used area by retailers to differentiate their chains because they control the handling and presentation and because of the paucity of supplier brands. The retailer specifies what they want, how they want it packed and they send it back if it fails their quality checks. Some supermarkets have developed this area as a strong differential advantage, creating in-store bakeries, delicatessen, fishmongers and butchers. The French chain Casino boast that fish reach their stores less than 24 hours after being purchased on the docks, while the average retailer gets the same fish two days later. Shoppers used to go to greengrocers and markets to buy high-quality vegetables, but now those sources cannot get the best produce because it goes straight to the supermarket chains.

Developing fresh foods as a differential advantage is important for two reasons. First, fresh products increase the frequency of store visits, as fresh food is bought more frequently than dried groceries. Second, since specialist greengrocers, markets and bakers still have a significant market share even in the most developed markets, it creates an opportunity for chain retailers to grow sales into a premium price area rather than just compete in a zero-sum game with their direct competitors. Chain retailers also have a distinct advantage over independent specialists in being able to provide pre-packed products, such as chopped lettuce or baby carrots, by leveraging their refrigerated transportation and display capabilities.

Morrisons, until recently a regional UK supermarket, are a compelling example of a retailer who uses fresh produce as a differential advantage. As a chain they appear at first glance to have several disadvantages versus the likes of Tesco and Sainsbury's. They sell at the lower end of the price range, have shown little interest in loyalty cards, do not offer significant online shopping and yet have consistently beaten or matched their larger competitors on growth rate, profitability levels and return on capital. Their success is due to a focus on, and more importantly a business model structured around, superior fresh produce. At the heart of their offering is their 'Market Street', designed to replicate the High Street with a real fishmonger, a butcher and a greengrocer. But this is no gimmick of dressing the nearest employee in a striped apron.

Morrisons have, through vertical integration, a greater control over their fresh produce supply chain than their competitors do. They butcher their own meat, prepare their own sausages, bacon and cheese, and pack their fruit and vegetables. Instead of providing the same produce year-round from across the globe, they provide the best local produce when in season, including 15 varieties of English apples across the year.

They also have structured their stores to be able to prepare in-store fresh products to be sold on the same day. Sandwiches are made in the store, as are apple pies, stuffed joints of meat along with over 1700 other produce lines. This entails a commitment to supply chain owner-ship, systems, staff selection and training and in-store production facilities that are almost impossible for competitors such as Tesco, Sainsbury's and Asda to copy. Hence, there is little sign of Morrisons' growth stopping soon.

In India, Big Bazaar employ a similar strategy but it is executed very differently. The main challenge Big Bazaar face is not from other sophisticated retailers but from millions of local retailers together with the reality that Indian food shoppers' love to see, feel and handle produce before buying. Thus, while employing modern retailing tech-niques and selling over 200000 SKUs, Big Bazaar present the Food Bazaar section of the store like an Indian street market. It is a unique concept and difficult for competitors to copy now that they have the scale to execute at low cost. Launched in 2001, there are already over 150 Big Bazaars in 80 cities across India.

Differential Advantage via Multi-segmentation

Retailers have great difficulty cost-efficiently segmenting shoppers with a range of different retail brands, so a more effective way to segment shoppers is by the type of shopping trip, for example via either a 'regular stock-up shop' or an 'emergency top-up shop'. Some super-markets have organised themselves so that top-up shoppers can enter part of the store for bread and newspapers without having to go round the main store. Fast checkouts for people with fewer than 10 items are also an attempt to satisfy the top-up shopper segment.

The expansion of supermarkets back to the High Street with smaller stores that focus on top-up items and pre-prepared meals is a more dramatic and successful example. It is harder to copy because the first mover, for example, Tesco in the United Kingdom and Wal-Mart Express in the United States, have an advantage as these locations can only economically support a low density of such stores. Other retailers wanting to expand have a difficult time finding space, and many have to buy existing outlets at premium prices, such as when Asda bought Netto to expand into the smaller retail market in Europe. Also, for retailers like Wal-Mart who have found local legislative barriers to expanding with their large-format stores into major metropolitan areas such as New York City and Chicago, having a range of smaller formats becomes an essential component of a growth strategy. Wal-Mart's expansion plans in Chicago are being spearheaded by their Market and Express banners, and they are even testing a banner, Wal-Mart on Campus, which at 3500 ft² is less than 5% the size of their out-of-town locations.

But even within such segmented stores, each shopper type attracted to the store needs to be understood and offered a shopping experience that satisfies their needs. For example, in the fruit and vegetable sections, pre-packing offers convenience and speed, but some shoppers prefer the choice and flexibility offered by 'choose your own' vegetable sections. The 'multi-segment' solution is to provide both options to serve the different segments (convenience and quality), although the balance between pre-packaged and loose will be very different in the large grocery store format compared to the convenience format.

Differential Advantage via Loyalty Cards

Loyalty cards create several opportunities for retailers. At their most basic level they create differential advantage by tying the shopper to the store. One way of cost-effectively achieving this is by price discriminating between shoppers so that the most price-sensitive can be satisfied, while also achieving a higher margin from quality- or service-sensitive shoppers. Cards make this possible as discounts and offers can be targeted at different customers according to the store's objectives and the customers' preferences. In Europe and India, the Payback programme helps retailers create customised offerings based on price-sensitivity levels. Customers receive a targeted selection of offerings, including discounts, exclusive offers, bonus points, prizes and other benefits, all designed to increase customer retention and sales by improving customer satisfaction across different shopper segments.

The reward system that many supermarkets run, giving a blanket discount of, for example, 1%, is a sorry misuse of the possibilities as this system does little to price discriminate between customers. A 1% discount is expensive for the store, which may be operating off a margin as low as 2%, and may be of marginal interest to wealthy shoppers. A 'service card' offering extra services such as a faster checkout (similar to the first-class airline check-in) may be more appealing to price-insensitive customers than reward points are.

These blanket schemes also encourage shoppers to use cards from other stores, as the rewards are linear. Rewards should *always* be 'raked', increasing with expenditure, and preferably demand a minimum threshold expenditure. The raking needs to be calculated so that most people cannot reach maximum benefits with more than one retailer. Safeway Canada recently launched a raked loyalty programme to acknowledge their best Club Card holders. Shoppers who spend more than $125/week gain special perks, including discounts on petrol (gas), roses and deli sandwiches, cash back of up to $300 and refunds without receipts. They are also given the store manager's cell phone number, which they are encouraged to use if service doesn't meet their expectations. Other programmes, such as Club Perekrestok, also offer a progressive accumulation of rewards, giving more points for elite customer segments.

Loyalty schemes that are raked, so that shoppers have to commit to one chain to gain the top benefits, can create so-called orderly retail competition. In contrast, cards that offer a 1% discount are quickly matched by competitors and raise costs for all; they are thus correctly derided as 'electronic Green Shield stamps'. In many of the emerging markets, there are card schemes that are effectively discount schemes ranging from 3 to 10% off. These undoubtedly lose the retailer money and miss the whole point, which is to gather real customer/consumer data that can be used to refine the retail offering at both the macro- and the micro-level. When a retailer knows what the consumer is buying and in what patterns, it can develop win–win consumer offers that are attractive to the consumer and make money for the retailer.

Finding a device for segmenting customers at a one-to-one level has been a massive breakthrough in retail marketing. The amount someone shops at a store is the first level of segmentation that most retailers use: customers who are major spenders ('gold' shoppers), light spenders ('silver' shoppers) or occasional spenders ('bronze' shoppers). Although most people regularly shop at several stores, they usually focus their spending at one.

Every retailer needs to develop their marketing strategy to maintain and grow their gold shoppers, and try to convert silver shoppers into gold ones. In terms of demographic and social measures, gold and silver shoppers may differ very little, which is why customer identification via purchasing habits is vital.

Safeway developed a successful campaign in the United States to grow sales from light shoppers and increase sales from heavy shoppers. They sent a monthly newsletter to 1.2 million card holders. Those whom they identified as secondary shoppers (people who mainly shop somewhere else) received a coupon for departments they didn't use, like the meat or produce section. Primary shoppers (people who mainly shop at Safeway) were also given coupons, but to less common areas, like the cookie aisle, as they already visited the main departments. The campaign was a huge success, increasing same-store sales and sales from secondary shoppers, plus it changed customer behaviour by converting secondary shoppers into primary ones. The campaign also improved Safeway's image by going beyond a general discount to create targeted deals. They sent out 451 800 versions of their offering.

Differential Advantage via Price

There is always a position in every market for the *hard discount retailer*. They are the one type of grocer that can and do clearly segment the market: they have a pointed image that is attractive to some shoppers but alienates others. For one player in any market, price can be their differential advantage. Aldi are the classic example. They promise an exceptional ratio between low price and good or sometimes excellent quality, made possible by low store values, a small assortment and cutting costs hard; so hard that for many years its stores did not even have telephones. The impressive thing about Aldi is that they have stayed lean enough to occupy this advantage for over 40 years. Although they are rarely the dominant force in the market, Germany being the only example, they are now established across Europe and are continuing to expand. Discount no longer automatically equates to poor quality. The quality of Aldi products is regularly rated higher than well-known manufacturer brands.

Mercadona in Spain is another great example of a hard price retailer, promising 'always low prices'. Like Aldi, they only have products in the economy price range, the majority of their products are private label and they keep prices low by having one exclusive supplier for each major category. They've grown to over 1300 stores in Spain, and continue to gain share with their unbeatable offering.

As Table 8.1 shows, hard discounters have increased their total share of European grocery sales since the early 1990s and are forecast to keep on gaining, with a 20% total share now being realistic by 2020. Yet you don't have to shop in a hard discounter to benefit from them. No mainstream, high-volume store can allow the price gap between themselves and the bottom of the market to become significant, so hard discounters keep everyone's prices low, for some products at least. But the trouble for those competing with hard discounters is that they cannot make price their differential advantage and yet they still have to invest an enormous amount of time and effort into managing their price perception.

Shoppers often have only a vague feel for the actual price differences between stores, and are incapable of making accurate assessments of different prices. Table 8.2 shows how perceptions of price are different from actual prices; a price image more than 100 means

Table 8.1 Share of hard discounters in Western Europe, % of total grocery sales

Year	Percentage of total grocery sales
1991	5.1%
1993	6.5%
1995	8.0%
1997	8.6%
2000	9.1%
2002	10.4%
2004	11.7%
2006	11.6%
2007	11.9%
2008	13.3%
2009	14.4%
2010	14.7%

Source: AC Nielsen.

Table 8.2 Comparison of objective and perceived prices of French supermarkets

Store chain	Price image index	Actual price index
Leclerc	183	94
Intermarché	161	94
Continent	138	92
Rallye	116	97
Euromarché	112	99
Auchan	112	93
Franprix	109	105
Mammouth	104	98
Carrefour	97	95
Lion	81	104
Cora	78	101
Super U	76	100
Champion	74	97
Geant Casino	33	103
Suma	26	108

Source: Denis Stoclet, 'Quelle Politique de Prix pour les Grandes Surfaces Alimentaires', Points de Vente, No. 380, 15 February 1990, p. 34.

that the store is viewed as being cheaper than average, whereas a price less than 100 means that the store is more expensive than average.

According to the survey, Carrefour is price-competitive: its index of 95 means it has cheaper-than-average prices. But consumers failed to perceive this position, as Carrefour's price image is worse than average. In contrast, Leclerc charge the same (94 against Carrefour's 95) but have the best price image in the market, far better than that of Carrefour. Monsieur Leclerc frequently appeared in the media arguing pro-consumer issues, such as price maintenance and 'right to sell' legislation: his store's price image is a tribute to his charisma and entrepreneurship.

It is interesting to note how little variation there is in prices among the large supermarket chains. Yet the differences in terms of perception are huge, showing that consumers are inclined to exaggerate price differences. Surveys consistently show that a substantial proportion of shoppers cannot quote a price for an item they have just purchased, and those who give a price are usually well wide of the mark.

Consumers form their impression of a retailer's price position in five main ways:

- **Direct price comparisons across certain products (known value items, or KVIs):** Products can be in this subset because of high unit costs, frequency of purchase, frequent retail promotions or an idiosyncrasy of the shopper. The problem for retailers is that these products vary for different shoppers and may be magnified by word of mouth.
- **Promotional activity:** Buying one item at a noticeably lower price may register more than getting 10 items at slightly more competitive prices. A shopper experiencing two stores with the same net prices may feel that the one signalling more reductions and special offers is giving better deals.
- **Store presentation:** A 'no frills' atmosphere improves price perceptions, which is why discount stores have developed conventions, like walls of stacked product and cheaply made signs. Conversely, efforts

made to improve the store experience (tidiness, spaciousness) may have a negative effect on price perceptions.

- **Direct communication:** Flyers that advertise price claims reassure shoppers that the store does everything possible to be price-competitive. Public relations campaigns where retailers support the consumer (such as those run in the past by M. Leclerc for Leclerc or Sam Walton for Wal-Mart) can also improve perceptions.

- **Price offers tailored to the individual:** It is now possible to direct pricing efforts towards individual shoppers. Offers made via loyalty cards can improve the price image the customer perceives compared to stores that do not bother with a card. It also limits price comparisons, as the consumer can't compare the price they paid because the advantages, like air miles, will modify the real price. Similarly, it is difficult for retailers competing against Club stores such as Costco to get shoppers to factor their membership fees into the low prices.

Maintaining the right balance of image between quality, value, convenience and price perception to attract the largest proportion of shopper segments is a delicate operation; it takes a long time and is costly to re-establish an image for any chain that loses their credibility. Every communication and action on each attribute will have an impact on other attributes, and past actions and image will persist and affect current perceptions. Positioning a retail chain is much more of a balancing act than positioning a brand.

Subhiksha was the first hard discounter in India and won customers with their message 'Why pay more when you can get it for less at Subhiksha?' With a strong EDLP (every day low prices) model, including no air-conditioning or fancy lighting and only 1200 SKUs, they grew rapidly. But in 2008, they started losing customers. They had problems with logistics and inefficient inventory as a result of expanding quickly, which created massive stock-outs; they couldn't do what they promised (sell products at the lowest prices). Unable to recover from their loss in image, they closed down all 1600 stores on 9 February 2011 and said they would need $65 million to re-open them.

Pricing tactics

A non-hard discounter has three options to manage its pricing strategy: Every Day Low Prices (EDLP), High–Low and Premium.

Every Day Low Prices

EDLP has moved from being marketing jargon to gaining currency in normal language, and in the process it has lost its precise meaning. Instead of complex pricing schemes, coupons and exceptional promotions, EDLP means the store maintains a uniform policy on mark-ups, giving permanently competitive prices. This has an honest ring and is guaranteed to garner favourable media coverage, which is why organisations loudly adopt it, sometimes adding the weasel phrase 'on a limited range of products'. In reality, EDLP is relevant to, and can only be practised by, a small proportion of retailers.

EDLP fits when the philosophy of the store is value, Wal-Mart being the perfect example. The most compelling argument for EDLP is that it is the most cost-efficient pricing strategy for retailers and manufacturers. EDLP cuts the costs of special promotions (materials, staff time) and those associated with continually changing prices; fewer promotions smoothes demand and reduces inventory costs and stock-outs. In addition, less advertising is needed because good value wins trust, builds consumer loyalty and appeals to one-stop shoppers; although EDLP reduces the need for advertising and door-to-door brochures, Wal-Mart still use flyers to reinforce their pricing message.

The second reason for a retailer to loudly adopt EDLP is that it tells the competition they are following a price orientation, and competitors can take the stable and predictable prices as a baseline. Retailers are ill-advised to try to win on price against any chain with a serious EDLP positioning.

Because EDLP is efficient and warns off competition, it is the best pricing policy for hard discounters whose only advantage is price. They have the cost structure to support it, as EDLP is the main factor in their cost structure. The question for other retailers is how to compete. How can they cultivate the best price image without detracting from their quality rating and destroying profitability?

A retailer facing competition from hard discounters or Wal-Mart cannot afford to lose their price-sensitive shoppers, because, as we saw in Chapter 2, retailers are sensitive to small changes in sales, and price-sensitive shoppers are a significant segment of shoppers. Dropping prices on a wide range of lines (i.e. approaching EDLP) is often perceived as the only strategy when faced with a serious EDLP-er, as management feel they need to retain shoppers and maintain volume. The larger stores run price advertising and try to match or beat the discounter's prices. Bearing in mind that price perceptions are subjective and unscientific (Table 8.2), it may not even work. A store following this solution usually only increases its problems, for three reasons:

- **Plausibility:** It is difficult for a large assortment retailer to earn the same price image as an EDLP competitor, even with comparable prices on comparable goods. It may be impossible to bring perceptions in line with reality, simply because the store looks more expensive.
- **Profitability:** The store may gain sales on the discounted lines, but it will lose money on sales from less-price-sensitive customers who would have bought at the previous price; the volume gained on the discounted lines is unlikely to compensate for their lower prices. Profitability will be preserved only if the discounted prices protect volume on non-discounted lines (i.e. stop their shoppers deserting to the EDLP store). To maintain EDLP the store must develop the cost structure necessary to offer discount prices, which may be impossible for legacy reasons.
- **Competitive reaction:** If mainstream stores advertise their intention to join the discount game, it can reinforce price sensitivity. A large store is admitting that quality and low price can exist together, and is endorsing the belief that shoppers should be more price-sensitive. Thus, the number of price-sensitive shoppers will increase,

and the group seeking quality irrespective of price will diminish. Most sinister of all, if a store attacks a discounter on price, the discounter has only one weapon of defence: it must preserve its differential advantage by further cutting prices. Faced with retaliation, the store cannot quickly withdraw (having advertised its intention to compete). This can lead retailers into a price war, where the total cost of the price cuts will increase well beyond initial estimates.

Low prices across all products is an appealing consumer proposition if you are a discount retailer with cost structures to match. Any retailer with higher costs (and hopefully quality) will shoot itself in the foot trying to support claims that it offers low prices across the board.

High–Low

A non-EDLP retailer who wants to maintain a good value image has to develop its price image through a strategy of continual, but unpredictable, promotions. The point of high–low pricing is to discriminate, both across consumers and product lines. The high part of high–low creates the opportunity to improve margins by selling to less-price-sensitive consumers at higher margins, and providing higher margins on key lines, while the low half is used on lines that are known to be price-sensitive and are easy to use for comparisons. Promotions and the occasional real bargains are used to impress the shopper, supported by competitive prices on easy-to-compare items.

Kroger, one of the largest supermarket chains in the United States, use high–low pricing. For example, during the run-up to 2011 Thanksgiving, Kroger sold turkey cheaper than other retailers, at $0.98/pound. By providing the lowest price on the most compared product they got people to shop at their stores, and made their profit on potatoes, yams and other holiday items that were priced higher than at other retailers.

For products costing more than $50, you wait to buy until a discount is offered on those products. | 15% | 31% | 45%

If there is a big discount on a product you often buy, you buy more of it than you usually would. | 18% | 34% | 40%

You decide where to shop based on prices or discounts you learn about in advertisements and flyers. | 18% | 30% | 37%

Sale items bring you to a store, but you end up buying more than just the sale items. | 22% | 29% | 26%

■ Never   Almost never   ■ Sometimes   ■ Often   ■ Extremely often

Base: 999 consumers in the United States

Figure 8.1 High–low pricing as a viable strategy with consumers.
Source: GartnerGS, January 2004.

High–low pricing appeals to price-sensitive consumers because it gives them the chance to find genuine bargains. Thus, it gives a price-based appeal to a store competing against a price-oriented EDLP operator; EDLP may even seem boring for some price-sensitive consumers because they enjoy special offers. Figure 8.1, taken from a 2004 study by Gartner, illustrates the enduring appeal of a high–low strategy very well – a significant percentage of shoppers love a bargain and will alter their behaviour to get one. It is not that EDLP will always triumph over high–low, or vice versa, but how well each is executed.

One could argue that a high–low pricing policy is higher-minded than EDLP: every consumer gets what they want (or need) and the rich help the poor, Robin Hood style. South Africa's Pick 'n Pay adopted a high–low pricing strategy to attract the maximum number of shoppers from their diverse population, ensuring everyone can shop at Pick 'n Pay and buy items within their price range.

High–low pricing needs more data (local competitors' prices) plus a management system to operate an efficient discrimination strategy, as prices have to be fine-tuned locally. Tesco have a sophisticated system for 'area pricing'; Safeway have a team dedicated to local pricing; and Morrisons have made it a cornerstone of their strategy. However, the overall price image still has to be managed centrally. Many high–low retailers achieve this by having inexpensive private label brands. For example, Kroger have 'For Maximum Value', which offers staples like sugar, flour and canned goods at the lowest prices. 'For Maximum Value' helps Kroger showcase their 'lowest price for the highest quality' message.

Premium

A third alternative, albeit a niche one, is to not play the price game at all. This was the strategy of Marks & Spencer in the United Kingdom for decades. They were successful because virtually everything they sold was under their 'St Michael' private label brand, so there was no direct price comparison. Modelled after Marks & Spencer, Woolworths in South Africa also chose a premium pricing strategy, succeeding with an extensive portfolio of high-quality apparel, contemporary home products and organic produce. In the United States, Whole Foods followed a similar path, being able to hide or justify their increased prices through their focus on organic and a robust private label strategy.

Price guarantees

Retail pricing is a dynamic area, and any change by one player forces the others to consider if or how to respond. Price guarantees (like John Lewis's 'Never knowingly undersold' in the United Kingdom and Darty's 'Le Contrat de Confiance' in France) are a way of creating a good price image and discriminating between price-sensitive and non-price-sensitive customers, as they allow price increases without losing price image. The stores reassure customers that if they find the same goods on sale at lower prices elsewhere they will be refunded the difference. In practice, only the price-sensitive customers claim the guarantees, while the less diligent ones pay the higher price, believing that the store is doing their best to be at the lowest current price.

Price-matching tactics can also curb the price-cutting zeal of the competition and restore order and profits. In one example, Big Star, a large supermarket in the United States, were suffering from price attacks by another supermarket, Food Lion. Big Star announced that they would 'match to the cent and for all time' Food Lion's prices on a named set of competitive lines, listed in their *Price Finder* magazine. The results of the price matching are shown in Tables 8.3 and 8.4.

The study found that the prices of the products that were matched by Big Star rose by an average of 11%. Food Lion recognised that any price cut would be matched, making cuts on these lines futile, but also that any price rises would be matched, making price increases

Table 8.3 The effect of Big Star's promise to match prices on items subjected to price matching and included in their *Price Finder* magazine

Product lines subject to matching	First week		Last week	
	Food Lion	Big Star	Food Lion	Big Star
Hellman's Mayonnaise	1.49	1.49	1.69	1.69
Chef Boyardee Pizza	1.39	1.39	1.44	1.44
Hunt's Whole Tomatoes	0.60	0.60	0.50	0.50
Pillsbury Flour	0.79	0.79	0.79	0.79
Mazola Oil	1.99	1.99	1.73	1.73
Maxwell House Coffee	2.19	2.33	2.89	2.89
Comet cleanser	0.69	0.69	0.74	0.74
Nabisco Oreo Cookies	1.89	1.85	2.46	2.46
Mrs Smith's Apple Pie	2.94	2.94	3.35	3.35
Average price	**1.55**	**1.56**	**1.73**	**1.73**

Source: Reproduced, with permission, from J. D. Hess and E. Gerstner, 'Price matching policies: An empirical case', *Managerial and Decision Economics*, August 1991, p. 307.

Table 8.4 The effect of the price matching on products not listed in *Price Finder* magazine

Products not subject to rigorous matching	First week		Last week	
	Food Lion	Big Star	Food Lion	Big Star
Cut green beans	0.35	0.35	0.33	0.33
Thin sliced bread	0.59	0.55	0.55	0.69
Head lettuce	0.89	0.69	0.89	0.99
Pork loin chops	3.69	2.49	3.49	2.99
Ground beef	1.69	1.69	1.49	1.69
Swift hostess ham	8.99	8.99	9.99	9.99
Coke	0.99	1.29	1.09	0.89
Pepsi	1.47	1.19	1.29	1.39
Large grade A eggs	1.33	1.37	0.78	0.49
Miller beer	2.71	2.71	2.84	2.84
Average price	**2.27**	**2.13**	**2.27**	**2.23**

Source: Reproduced, with permission, from J. D. Hess and E. Gerstner, 'Price matching policies: An empirical case', *Managerial and Decision Economics*, August 1991, p. 307.

attractive. Both retailers did better on products that were matched, as the average price of non-matched lines was stable in Food Lion and only increased by 4.7% in Big Star.

Price discrimination

Manufacturers discriminate on price by developing and positioning their brands on a price/quality axis. This is clear in cars, where the luxury model can cost double the basic model, and each intermediate price point is filled by a model with more functions. The different models ask the consumer: 'How much do you want to spend?'

Retailers have to create a pricing structure that allows each price segment of the market to be satisfied. This may mean developing a predictable set of price levels within each category. For example, having a policy that sets the relative price levels for generic (unbranded) brands, cheap brands, quality private label brands and premium brands. Stores can mark certain brands as offering the rock-bottom price position: by flagging 400 basic lines, a store can guide a shopper to a subset of lines that add up to a 'hard discount' experience. The need to do so because of the rise of the likes of Aldi has led to the revival of the cheap, generic private label offering, which we shall discuss in the next chapter. Stores can also arrange themselves into separate sections or boutiques, which operate different pricing rules.

The aim is to find socially and legally acceptable ways of allowing price-sensitive shoppers to pay less, while leaving the less-price-sensitive customers to pay more, which is what manufacturers achieve with their portfolios of brands. Retailers can use their own quality brands, cheap and false brands and manufacturer brands to price discriminate. Coupons, price guarantees and convenience can also be used creatively.

Key learnings

- **Location** used to be the major differential advantage for retailers, but increasing mobility and saturation have reduced its impact. It is still important but is only a differential advantage for 'convenience stores'. However, the trend into multilevel formats from hypermarkets to convenience within one chain may eventually result in a small number of retailers providing their brand and image at every retail type, with very small differences other than location between the actual offering.
- **Fresh produce** and other 'destination' products can create a sustainable differential advantage, as they have the potential for deciding the destination of the shopper.
- **Multi-segmentation**, **loyalty cards** and **pricing** can also create differential advantages.

(Continued)

- There are **three price points** in retailing: EDLP, high–low and premium. Only the committed discounter can go for EDLP.
- **EDLP** can only provide a differential advantage for one player in any one market. But their presence means that all retailers must keep their prices low; every retailer has to be competitive on easily compared lines and must manage their competitive price image. An emerging future retail positioning may be high quality/high value always at low prices, coupled with fresh, local and organic.

Brands are not dying, but the manufacturers' stranglehold on them is weakening. We saw in Chapter 1 how power and profits have historically moved up and down the value chain; that battle has been re-energised by the retailer. In the next chapter, we consider the most powerful tool in the retailers' armoury for developing consumer loyalty and price discriminating between customers: private label.

Chapter 9

PRIVATE LABEL IS booming. In Europe and the United States during the period 2000–2010, *private label* was responsible for the majority of the growth in packaged foods, cosmetics and home care. Its share of global FMCG sales is approaching 20%, and its growth rate has surpassed that of manufacturers' brands in 9 of the last 10 years (Figure 9.1).

The root of this stunning success is that private label has become the dominant strategy in the retailers' move from a selling to a marketing orientation. Everyone in FMCG retailing and manufacturing needs to understand private label intimately in order to succeed.

Private label started over 100 years ago as generics in basic product categories like detergent and flour, but now features in over 95% of grocery categories. There is barely a product category that remains immune, even previous untouchables such as cosmetics and baby food are being breached (Table 9.1).

The size and growth rate of the private label grocery category is astounding. In 2005, the best-selling brand in the US grocery market became Wal-Mart's Great Value brand, and other retailer brands, like Tesco Value, Carrefour's '1' and President's Choice are achieving huge success. Private label is predicted to keep gaining share in all grocery markets, as shown by Table 9.2.

Just as the penetration of private label varies widely by country, so it does by retailer. In 2009, Costco had a relatively small portfolio of

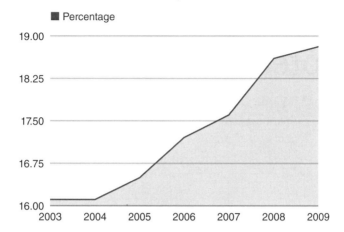

Figure 9.1 Private label's market share, 2003–2009.
Source: Private Label Manufacturers Association and AC Nielsen.[1]

Table 9.1 Percentage share of consumers buying private label by category (2007)

Food category	Sweden	United Kingdom	United States
Dairy	33	60	52
Frozen food	40	51	43
Cakes and biscuits	16	44	28
Breakfast cereals	20	30	34
Confectionery	13	20	22
Clothes	11	25	17
Beer, wine, spirits	8	15	9
Cosmetics	12	7	9
Baby food	3	4	4

Source: Saatchi & Saatchi X.

private label, with sales at 18% of their turnover; Carrefour at 36%; Wal-Mart at 39%; Tesco at 50%; and Aldi way out in front at 94%. Private label is also playing a role in smaller, more specialised retailers such as Trader Joe's and Whole Foods. It is also becoming prevalent in emerging markets like Brazil and South Africa. Grupo Pão de Açúcar became one of Brazil's most successful retailers by popularising their private label brands. Pick 'n Pay also experienced tremendous success with their private label portfolio, and are using it to compete

Table 9.2 Share of private label in total grocery retail turnover by country

Country	2008 (%)	2013F (%)
Switzerland	46	47
United Kingdom	39	43
Germany	34	37
Spain	29	32
France	27	29
Netherlands	24	27
Canada	21	24
United States	19	22
India	10	14
Brazil	6	8
China	3	5
Russia	3	4

Source: Planet Retail.

with Wal-Mart by increasing their product ranges and repackaging current offerings.

Evolution of private label

As we saw in Chapter 1, private label is not a new phenomenon; it was the cornerstone of A&P becoming the largest retailer in the world. A&P started roasting coffee and packaging tea after the American Civil War. By 1930, they were the planet's largest coffee merchant. A&P were managing their own plantations and, in addition, running a vast enterprise across dozens of product categories, packing 72000 jars of jam a day and baking half a billion loaves a year.[2] Having a large private label operation was the reason A&P consistently delivered returns on capital of over 20%. A&P's competitors were not slow to catch on to the benefits of such a strategy. In 1932, Kroger, the second-most-popular retailer at the time, also chose to develop private label to gain power over the emerging national brand manufacturers.

At the time, the opportunity for chains like A&P and Kroger was to grow at the expense of independent grocers. Private label made sense because most independents sold generic products of dubious quality, and private labels were seen as a way to build a retail brand on a solid grounding of quality and reliability. So why did private label not go from strength to strength and dominate the twentieth-century retail landscape?

Because of the emergence of the 100% branded retailing concept developed by Michael Cullen. In addition to selling only nationally available, advertised items at miniscule margins, Cullen's stores were larger and needed 10 times the turnover of a typical A&P store for the concept to pay off. It was only due to the emergence of radio advertising driving demand for the national brands that such sales volumes were possible. As manufacturers' brands had the scale to better leverage mass media than any one retailer's private label, they gained better awareness and reputations for unimpeachable quality. Given that Cullen was prepared to sell the big, national brands essentially at cost, the retailers who relied on private label had lost their previous advantages in relative quality and value, meaning that the manufacturer brands triumphed.

Despite the dominance of the manufacturer brand during the latter two-thirds of the twentieth century, the strategic reasons for private label never went away; they were just submerged by the big brand culture of the post-WWII era. Plus, it was not until the emergence of the really large, highly professional retailers in the latter part of the twentieth century that there existed the management and logistical infrastructures capable of developing and managing a complex private label portfolio.

Re-emergence of private label

Once large, discount-focused retail chains had to compete with other large discounters rather than Mom and Pop stores, it became difficult for them to make acceptable margins. Cullen's model of selling top brands at cost then morphed into their being sold as loss-leaders, owing to the inexorable need to attract shoppers into grocery stores. This is why private label brands eventually reappeared: to counter the power of national brands upon which retailers were actually making a loss. The increased size of retailers meant that many had become large enough to commission private labels sold exclusively through their outlets. They could see the economic attractiveness of being able to strip out the burgeoning brand-related costs from manufacturer brands and make a very good margin, even if the volumes were going to be low. There is a lot of profit available if you do not spend 5–10% of retail selling price (RSP) on marketing, 2% on product development, 10% on high management costs and 8% on a sales force.

As we have seen in the previous chapter, no retailer can afford to ignore price-sensitive shoppers, and since top brands were being sold at or slightly below cost, the selling price was being determined by the manufacturers' list price. Retailers knew if list prices could be encouraged to creep up there would be room for a cheaper but still profitable private label offering in categories where branding was relatively weak. The most obvious categories were food staples such as flour, baking soda and dairy.

At first, private label reflected the philosophy of its inventor: the discount-focused retailer, who could source them cheaply and, even after taking a healthy margin, could offer them to their shoppers at a lower price than the branded equivalents. Such private label offerings had to stand out on-shelf as the lowest-cost option, which was reflected in their basic, almost shoddy appearance. They adopted a 'commodity-style' presentation, using minimalist white packs with black print stating contents. The retailer often didn't use their brand name on the packaging, so they became known as *generics*.

Generics would only come in one size and variant, never be promoted through price or displays and thus would not account for much volume. But they did set a marker for how low a price could be and still generate decent margins. For example, a supermarket may sell a branded version of a commodity like milk at a 2–3% margin but, by buying competitively and minimising packaging and marketing costs, could offer lower prices for generic milk and make margins five times higher.

Generics were not created to be a differential advantage against other retailers but to help the retailer control the manufacturer, and they became an important negotiating tool against national brands. By taking up shelfspace with generics, the retailer increased the competition for the remaining space between the national brands, which helped ratchet up listing fees. The retailer could now feel better about selling major brands at a tiny margin as they were making larger margins on generics and squeezing more money out of the manufacturers, thus making the category more profitable for themselves. However, everyone still knew that the major brands were the reason people came into the store.

Copycat private label

The sales potential of generics was always going to be limited by their poor quality – imagined or real – when compared to major brands. Since the bottom of the market is limited in size (most people seek average or premium quality), generics can take only a limited share. Retailers realised there was a greater opportunity to compete directly with national brands for some of their volume, and, by not incurring the brands' advertising and sales force costs, be more profitable. Hence *copycat* brands, close copies of manufacturer brands, were a natural progression and have become entrenched in the market.

The success of copycat brands depends on the retailer offering being as close as possible to the quality, packaging and presentation of national brands, but cheaper. They are also marketed in the store in the same manner as the manufacturer brands, with price promotions, flyers and displays. Many retailers support their copycat brands with extravagant quality guarantees, such as Kroger's 'Try it, Like it, or

Get the National Brand Free' promise, where if the customer does not believe the Kroger brand is as good as the national brand they can exchange the unused portion of the product for the equivalent national brand free of charge.

Copycats target the biggest brands. Unilever's Lipton Yellow Label tea is the most popular brand in the world, with a 15% market share, which is almost three times larger than their nearest rival. Consequently, many retailers have created copycats using the yellow label brand, as the colour itself is so well established as to communicate quality on the tea fixture. Brand manufacturers have had mixed results in trademarking their brand colours; Cadbury tried and failed to trademark the colour purple in Australia but succeeded in the United Kingdom.

The copycat strategy depends on the consumer having no doubt which brand leader is being copied, which can sometimes lead the retailer into overstepping the trademark. Belgian retailer GB chose the colours of 'J & B' whisky for their own whisky, naturally called 'GB' whisky. Asda developed 'You'd Butter Believe It' margarine packs, which are almost identical to Unilever's 'I Can't Believe It's Not Butter' and the popular biscuit 'Jammie Dodgers' have been copied by Lidl with their 'Jammy Rings' and Aldi with their 'Jammy Devils'.

Some retailers even put a twist on the packaging, 'This is *not* Johnson & Johnson© Baby Oil'. Arguably, that is unfair and borderline illegal. In the United Kingdom, manufacturers have lobbied for years to tighten trademark legislation, and it is not uncommon for a brand manufacturer to launch legal proceedings against their retail customers when a copycat brand steps over the line.

In 2009, the world's most powerful drinks company, Diageo, sued Sainsbury's. They claimed Sainsbury's gin-based drink, Pitchers, was breaching the copyright of their Pimm's brand. Diageo won, forcing Sainsbury's to modify the packaging. Despite the lawsuit, Diageo claimed that 'Sainsbury's is a valued customer and we hope will continue to be so for many years.' United Biscuits also launched legal action against Asda over their Puffin mimic of Penguin biscuits. They won, proving Asda was 'passing off' their brand; Asda was allowed to keep the brand but forced to change the packaging.

Despite thousands of copycat brands, few other cases have been won. Copycat packaging is not well addressed by trademark law, and since consumers don't complain about it, regulatory bodies are more focused on health and food-safety issues. Retailers argue that their intention is not to confuse their shoppers into picking up a copycat thinking it is the real brand but to signal to the shopper the comparison that should be made.

Most manufacturers resented the re-emergence of private labels once copycats became the prevalent form. However, manufacturers of quality brands were confident that the skills that protected their brands from cheaper alternatives, advertising and innovation would work against the new competition. Premium brands remained the most profitable, and manufacturers dominated the FMCG sector, but weaker manufacturers broke ranks and manufactured private label to keep up their volumes.

In markets where consumers are sensitive to quality differences (e.g. washing powder, instant coffee, sanitary protection) the share for generics and copycats usually plateaus below 20%. In segments where differences are marginal (such as paper products or basic cooking ingredients), generics and copycats sometimes take 50% or more of the share. In most markets, private label got off to a good start, but ended stable or declining after its first decade. Branded manufacturers felt they had seen them off for good. But such confidence was misplaced: private label came back in a more deadly form.

Today's private labels

Return of the Generics

Just when it seemed generics had passed their sell-by date, they have come back in fashion at major retailers in response to the emergence of the hard discounters. With Aldi's private label sales topping $40 billion, almost entirely from products that sell for less than manufacturer brands and retailers' copycat private labels, European retailers were in danger of being seen as too expensive. So they brought back a range of private label products that represent the lowest selling price in each category.

However, the old model of cheap-looking, low-quality products was not going to work any more because of the prestige brand images that retailer's built when they adopted marketing strategies. Thus, they developed quality products, equivalent to the major brands, sold at rock-bottom prices supported by one of three branding strategies: store sub-brand, e.g. Safeway Select and Perekrestok; stand-alone brands, e.g. Mercadona's 'Hacendado' or Foodworld's 'Nature's Bounty'; or a consortium brand where several retailers band together to develop a single brand, such as Euro Shopper.

Each branding concept works and the one chosen is driven more by fit with the store's preferred marketing strategy than by any perception of one being intrinsically stronger than the other. This is because the strength lies in the strategic role of generic private labels rather than how they are communicated. They are not there to attract shoppers into the store or to take share from branded products but to protect the store's appeal to price-conscious shoppers and prevent them defecting to hard discounters. The underlying message of any generic private label is, 'If you are attracted by Aldi's prices and are not bothered about buying national brands, you can still shop here.'

Copycats Are Here to Stay

The copycat private label brand is strong and represents the bulk of private label volume. The proposition is so established in the consumers' minds that any major retailer would be foolish to pass on the opportunity to take market share from the #3 and #4 manufacturer brands, who are the helpless victims of this strategy. In February 2010, Ad Age reported that Wal-Mart had consolidated its stocked range of food bags from three brands, Ziploc, Glad and Hefty, down to the market leader, Ziploc, and their own Great Value private label offering.[3] Pactiv, the makers of Hefty, gained the consolation prize of the contract to manufacture the Great Value products, whereas the owners of Glad lost their entire food bag business in Wal-Mart.

Wal-Mart could do this easily as, unlike many other retailers, they consolidate all manufacturer payments into the buying price and pass on most of the benefit to the shopper in lower prices. Retailers who take manufacturer payments to their bottom line are sometimes unwilling to give up the short-term benefit of such payments for the longer-term return of better margins from their private label. The secondary brands that are targeted by private label are usually big payers of trade spend to make up for their lower level of consumer appeal versus the top brands.

However, as weak manufacturer brands vanish from the shelves, the role of the copycat brand changes from capturing a manufacturer's volume to demanding higher margins from the brand leader and in restricting manufacturer price increases. A manufacturer cannot unthinkingly increase prices when its main competitor could be a copycat who would have no inclination to follow, as the bigger the price gap, the more the copycat would sell.

Copycat brands are a tool for vertical competition with manufacturers; they do relatively little in the horizontal competition with other retailers to attract more shoppers. A retailer's direct competitors have their own copycat versions, and since they are copycats of the same national brands and most likely coming from the same supplier, the horizontal competitive effect between retailers is neutral. Although retailers need copycat brands for profitability reasons, they cannot build differentiation for their chain brand through them. Copycats also play no role in increasing the average basket size, as they replace the sale of a branded product. So in order to win more shoppers and boost their takings per shopper, retailers have been investing in store brands that are better than anything else on the market.

Premium on the Up

Premium private labels have emerged with three objectives: to escape the commoditisation and price competition of copycat brands, to be differentiated from the best-selling manufacturer brands and to contribute to a distinct store image. The strength of a retailer's image usually dictates how they will execute this strategy. If they have not built a strong image for quality, their premium offerings will usually be of a higher quality than the leading brand's, but will still need to be sold at competitive prices.

The premium private label strategy is only possible when manufacturers have allowed a quality–value gap to open. This happens when manufacturers' either price their brands too high or reduce input costs too much. Both give scope to a retailer to develop an offering of superior value: either same quality at a lower price or higher quality at the same price.

Premium private labels in the United Kingdom have been led by Sainsbury's and Tesco. Their premium labels – Sainsbury's Taste the Difference (TTD) and Tesco's Finest – are successful because shoppers value their exceptional quality. In 2010, Sainsbury's re-launched their premium range to ensure customers still saw them as premium products, and not a post-recession 'budget food'.

Loblaws in Canada launched their first premium private label, President's Choice, to provide the best value and quality offering relative to the branded competition; it is now their main advertising effort because it defines what makes them unique. Costco followed suit with Kirkland Signature. Kirkland Signature doesn't get brand-specific advertising like President's Choice, but its presence in the in-store and member communication has defined the Costco brand. Pick 'n Pay also recently developed PnP to improve their image by providing higher-quality products at decent prices. It's already one of the most recognised and trusted brands in South Africa, and has improved Pick 'n Pay's quality image.

In 2009, German-based Rewe launched their premium private label 'Feine Welt'. Like Pick 'n Pay, they wanted to create a 'new indulgence brand' to capitalise on premium products and improve profit margins. Private labels now account for more than 40% of the market share in Germany, and German retailers spend several hundred million euros on brand management. Not surprisingly, Trader Joe's also rely heavily on private label products, which account for 85% of their SKUs. As a result of the higher selling prices, their sales per square foot are double most of their competitors'.

Retailers have also discovered that, provided they consistently deliver better quality, the top manufacturer brand doesn't have to represent the maximum achievable price for private label products. A Costco executive explained the opportunity:

> For years supermarkets demanded price points. You take something as basic as a can of tuna: throughout the '80s and '90s every time the cost went up [the manufacturer would] make it a 5.1 oz can instead of a 5.2 oz can. [Grocers said] 'Let's do less fillet and more chunk because we've got to sell something 3-for-$5 on a special.' We upped the quality, upped the price above the branded item and we're selling more units. Because it's the best tuna you can buy.[4]

So, if a private label brand can be priced above the branded equivalent, can retailers develop new brands, or sub-brands, that are price/quality leaders in their categories?

The Emergence of Premium-Plus

The premium-plus private label emerged in the United Kingdom primarily through Marks & Spencer. Marks & Spencer had long cultivated premium imagery on their clothing; their reputation stood for the best quality in the mainstream market, and for decades they were Britain's largest underwear retailer. In the 1980s, Marks & Spencer successfully extended their brand into foods, particularly pre-prepared meals, sold at premium prices and earning attractive margins. Other retailers were jealous of the new category owned by Marks & Spencer, but getting into it required an established image for high quality. The first British grocer to successfully compete with Marks & Spencer was Waitrose, with their Essentials private label. In the United States, Wal-Mart's Sam's Choice and Kroger's Private Selection were close behind.

Premium-plus private labels are used to differentiate chains. The closer the brand can be associated with the parent chain, the more it can differentiate from its competitors and attract loyal shoppers. A strong premium-plus private label range can also lift the quality perception of the chain's entire private label offerings, which is why Tesco use the sub-brand approach.

Premium-plus private labels also increase the average transaction size and profit margins. They are profitable because the retailers are getting premium prices without incurring the costs of equivalent manufacturer brands, such as advertising, consumer promotions and sales force.

Benefit-based

In tandem with premium and premium-plus private labels, retailers have seen the opportunity to develop private label offerings that focus on one consumer benefit, such as organic, healthy-eating, environmentally conscious, low-calorie and so on. Thus, we now see such offerings in virtually all major grocery retailers.

One of the biggest benefit-based trends of this century has been the emergence of gluten-free products. The global market grew to $2.3 billion in 2009, and is predicted to reach $5 billion by 2015. The biggest retailers, Tesco, Wal-Mart, Carrefour, Foodworld and Mercadona, now have gluten-free sections and many, like Trader Joe's and Safeway, have developed private label brands; over 3% of gluten-free sales are now private label.

Private label brand portfolios

Private label brands and sub-brands that build loyalty are a singularly powerful tool for creating a sustainable differential retail advantage. These are sometimes called 'destination' products, as they have the potential for deciding the destination of the shopper. A retailer with 'destination' private label brands can build loyalty, differentiate itself from its retail competition, enhance its margins and hold a sustainable position against price rivals.

The outcome of the multiplicity of private label opportunities is that leading retailers now have complex brand portfolios, and need to adopt the skills of a branded manufacturer's marketing department. Consider the portfolio of one of the best private label retailers, Tesco:

Generics: Tesco Value
Copycat: Discount Brands at Tesco
Premium: Tesco Standard
Super-premium: Tesco's Finest
Benefit-based: Healthy Living, Light Choices, Organic, Kids, Free From, Wholefoods

Just like a manufacturer's brand portfolio, these ranges compete for internal resources and, more importantly, shelfspace. Not only is the retailer competing with other retailers and manufacturers, there is also internal competition, especially for shelfspace, which remains finite. It will only continue to get more complex. In May 2011, Tesco's new CEO, Philip Clarke, announced plans to develop more brands as a new strategic pillar, ensuring Tesco would be 'a creator of highly valued brands'.[5] This signals the shifting of skillsets and competencies that has taken place since the 1980s: manufacturers have begun learning to think like retailers, while retailers now must think like manufacturers, managing complex brand portfolios and infusing their brands with imagery, emotion and consumer appeal.

Risks for the retailer

There are downsides for a retailer developing premium and premium-plus private labels. With generics and copycats, there is virtually no risk: generics protect the bottom of the market and copycats only copy successful offerings. However, retailers need to execute premium and premium-plus concepts consistently well for them to work.

Increased Costs

With premium and premium-plus offerings, the retailer is entering uncharted waters, so there will be extra R & D costs, plus costs associated with a higher failure rate. These are fixed irrespective of volume, which means retailers then suffer from the defining feature of private labels: they are only sold in their own stores, which limits the volume that costs can be amortised over. While much private label manufacturing is concentrated across a relatively small number of manufacturers who supply several retailers, and thus amortise fixed costs across all of them, if a retailer develops genuinely unique products solely for their own private label, which is usually the goal for premium-plus offerings, they assume all these costs across just their own volume.

Reduced Manufacturer Leverage

Another drawback for retailers developing strong premium and premium-plus private label brands is that they reduce sales of branded goods, which lessens their negotiating strength with manufacturers.

On the other hand, major brands can be used to play a different role for the retailer. In a price-driven store, national brands are discounted to create a good price image and generate traffic; in a quality store they are there to satisfy shoppers who are brand-loyal and so do not need to have their prices cut to the bone. Manufacturers need to understand with each retailer what role their brand actually plays in the retailer's strategy.

Going Too Far

Private label seems like a dream come true for the modern retailer. It attracts customers, makes them more loyal and increases profitability. What chain wouldn't want that? The temptation is to keep increasing the private label range and cutting back on brands. But historically, there has seemed to be a limit. When Sainsbury's was the dominant UK retailer in the 1980s, their private label sales were 60% of their turnover. This ratio or greater has been proven to be sustainable by a hard-discounter model, but there have always been risks for the mainstream retailer as manufacturer brands still command substantial consumer loyalty. Sainsbury's launched their Classic Cola in 1994, giving it a huge prominence on the shelf and in promotional slots at the expense of Coca-Cola and Pepsi. The private label won a 60% share within Sainsbury's, but Sainsbury's total volume of cola sold declined. Retailers are in the business of selling the products that their shoppers want to buy, and this still includes strong manufacturer brands. What has not yet been tested is how far a retailer can push their private label strategy when using a multi-layered one. Many are keen to find out.

Implications for manufacturers

Tesco and many other retailers now sell as much private label as they do manufacturer brands. In most categories, their brand is the leader. Many of their shoppers are loyal to brands that can only be obtained from Tesco. It would be awkward for Tesco shoppers to stock up elsewhere, as another store would not have 50% of the brands the shopper usually buys. Manufacturers used to hold power over retailers because of the effect on shopper loyalty that would be felt if their brands were not stocked. But manufacturers have lost the main support for that stance as private label has overcome its low-quality stigma: more than 77% of consumers agree that store brands are as good as, if not better than, manufacturer brands.[6] Retailers like Tesco now create loyalty to their chain because competitor stores do not stock Tesco's private label. Private label has become the main vehicle for building loyalty.

The interesting thing about building loyalty with private labels is that it can provide a differential advantage for more than one player in the market. Just as loyalty to different brands of coffee increases the value of the coffee market and creates profitable coffee brands, loyalty to retail brands increases the value of the retail market, and makes retailers more profitable. Sainsbury's and Tesco's instant coffee may be of equal quality, but as long as shoppers develop a preference for one or the other, both are protected from substitutability and its evil twin: price competition.

Private label is not going away, so how can manufacturers respond?

Total System Profitability

Owing to the ever-increasing pressure on space, as retailers continue to extend private label ranges, there is a risk of branded products being moved to less-optimal locations, having fewer promotional slots and facings or being delisted. Manufacturers cannot wait for this to happen before reacting; they must be proactive in making the case for their brands. While the absolute cash and margins on private labels may be higher for the retailer, the manufacturer has to shift the focus to total system profitability. Many factors favour manufacturer brands when total profitability is considered, including:

- **Sales velocity:** Shelfspace turnover is often higher for manufacturer brands. The velocity of leading manufacturer brands is often 10% higher.
- **Profit per linear inch of shelfspace.**
- **Discounts and off-invoice allowances:** Includes slotting allowances, listing fees, promotional deals, advertising and merchandising allowances, and credit for return of unsold merchandise.
- **Promotional and advertising fees.**

- **Provision of 'free' logistics services:** Includes transportation, warehouse and store labour, and merchandising help for the retailer.
- Manufacturer brands usually retail at higher-than-average prices: Even when the net margin on manufacturer brands is lower, the absolute cash profit per unit may be higher.

Proactively Managing Their Product Ranges

The most vulnerable brands to private label are not the strongest but the weakest. Such brands are usually cash cows for the manufacturer, generating very high profit margins. Manufacturers want to keep them around, hoping they'll continue to deliver profits while not incurring costs. But it is better for the manufacturer to rediscover the art of repositioning established brand equities to breathe new life and vigour into them. A good example is the job done on Old Spice by P&G. Old Spice was introduced in 1938 and, by the time the brand was bought by P&G in 1990, its consumer base was even older than the brand. The reinvention of Old Spice for young males made what was a sure-fire candidate for being delisted into a must-stock brand. P&G excel at proactively managing their product ranges, as they have a history of divesting commodity-type brands, like Crisco and Oxydol, brands they owned for a century, while purchasing ones that are larger, have greater scope for innovation and a proven ability to sustain price premiums, such as Gillette, Clairol and Duracell.

Keep Building Brand Imagery

Although private label shoppers benefit from not having to pay for flashy advertising, private labels miss out on a key brand role: being vehicles for self-expression. It's difficult to keep manufacturer brands in the must-stock category based on the price/quality spectrum, so they rely on creating desirable imagery that cannot be found in a retailer's portfolio.

Of the Top Most Valued Brands in 2011, Coca-Cola and Marlboro were 6th and 8th, with their brands valued at $73.8 billion and $67.5 billion. Although retailers have developed private label cola and cigarettes, they can't position them like these brands, using anything like the Open Happiness campaign and the Marlboro Man, because the private label imagery is intimately tied to the store's imagery, which by definition will always have to be very broad and bland in comparison.

Innovation

Manufacturers have one advantage that can never be overcome if used with focus, vigour and investment, and that is innovation. Yogurt, seemingly an ideal category for private label to take the lion's share, has seen private label share decline. The top-five leaders, Danone, Yoplait/Sodiaal, Yakult Honsha, Nestlé and Müller, represent half of all yogurt sales. Their innovation has been developing premium products, like pro-biotic yogurt and yogurt enhanced with fruit, and they launch continually; between 2006 and 2010 Danone introduced nine new products. Although retailers have developed brands, Aldi has Fit & Active non-fat yogurt and Kroger has Carb Master Yogurt, they haven't won over consumers, owing to their lack of innovation. Both are seeing sales decline.

But copycats are almost inevitable and manufacturers must plan for them appearing soon after the launch of their innovation. Copycatting raises the bar for manufacturers because their innovations need to be real breakthroughs, and since the only barriers are intellectual property and speed, they need to be brought to market faster and in greater numbers than before.

Unfortunately, the power of radio and then television advertising made life too easy for manufacturers. They became complacent

Table 9.3 Major FMCG manufacturers' R & D spending (2009)

FMCG manufacturers	Percentage of sales
P&G	2.7
Nestlé	1.8
Unilever	2.3
L'Oréal	3.3
Kraft Foods	1.2
PepsiCo	0.9
Philip Morris	0.5
Danone	1.3
Colgate-Palmolive	1.7
Kellogg's	1.4
Diageo	0.2

Source: Compiled from various company data and annual reports.

and grew comfortable with little turnover in their portfolios and small R & D budgets, as shown by Table 9.3. They need to rediscover what made them successful in the first place: consumer insight, customer knowledge, innovation and brand-building. The adoption of open-innovation strategies by majors such as Nestlé and P&G is a reflection of their need to ramp up innovation speed and capabilities.

To supply or not to supply?

Retailers pressure the top-branded manufacturers to supply them with private label products, a request that usually creates an intensely emotional internal debate. Private label production may threaten the company's long-term interests, which is often the case for successful branded manufacturers, but it can be a vital source of revenue. This creates a dilemma: do they supply the retailers or do they let their competitors? Some reject the notion outright and feel that everyone would be better off if nobody provided private label at all. Thus P&G, Mars, Kellogg's, Gillette and Coca-Cola all refuse private label contracts, while, on the other hand, Unilever, PepsiCo, Nestlé, Heinz, Playtex, Ralston Purina, Hershey, RJR Nabisco and McCain embrace them.

For premium-brand manufacturers with spare capacity, private label offers increased volume and revenue. However, it can lead to difficulties if the branded business picks up and the spare capacity is no longer spare. Private label ends up competing with brands for production capacity or necessitating unbudgeted extra shifts. In addition, the costing of short-term, opportunistic private label is sometimes lax and may not take into account subsequent demands from the retailer, including formula modifications and new packaging sizes. Manufacturers have to take a *strategic* decision on the matter.

For manufacturers who can no longer create sufficient consumer pull to sell their brands, private label production can be an attractive option. Competing for mindspace against larger and wealthier brands involves enormous investment and expertise, but the rise of market-oriented retailers has opened up a more efficient source of consumer reassurance and mindspace: the retailer's brand. Teaming up with a retailer who can provide low-cost umbrella branding is a way of avoiding brand-building costs and having to arm-wrestle other retailers for profits.

Producing for private label involves a commitment to low-cost production and to satisfying the retailers' demands in terms of service, quality and innovation. This is a very different culture from a brand-building one, and the two are often incompatible within the same business unit.

The market to supply private label is competitive – private label sales were more than $60 billion in 2011 – and no manufacturer can expect to succeed if their approach is half-hearted. There are 3200 members of the private label Manufacturers Association, most being unknown to the public either because they specialise in private label and invest nothing in building their awareness or they produce private label in addition to their own brands and have no wish to publicise this.

Clearly, making the commitment to devote significant resources to an activity that at some levels competes with the main activity of the company is an enormous and far-reaching decision.

Producing for private label

A company aiming to operate in the private label market has to approach it as rigorously and strategically as the consumer market; the decision means major, irreversible investments. To give value (which is the only way to succeed) implies developing low-cost production (capital investment) and a highly efficient supply chain. Lead times have to be fast: in some cases six weeks between the retailer request for a new line and its arrival on the shelf, complete with packaging and launch displays. Previous success in brand marketing does not guarantee that a company will be able to make a success in this new discipline.

Private label strategy is a different game from consumer marketing. Many companies (e.g. Danone, Unilever) feel that it should be dealt with by a separate organisation with separate profit centres to avoid conflicts over allocating overheads. Even production should be separated, as common facilities can lead retailers to question the costs of producing the branded version, based on their knowledge of the production of their private label. It also helps avoid conflict that can arise over the use of production capacity or technology: should the private label get the new developments, if so, when?

In addition, successful private label and brand strategies need different core competencies. A manager who excels in the low-cost, efficient operations may not excel at mindspace management and consumer marketing. Management needs to specialise in different skills, which reinforces the idea that they should be managed separately.

For companies with successful premium brands, the greatest risk is that in going down the private label route they end up competing with themselves. They need to ensure that they will be able to retain a superior technical quality for their brands. If the quality gap between their brands and those produced for private label narrows, so does the price that can be charged.

A purely industrial company (or division of a consumer company) can focus on efficient production and logistics and become a low-cost producer of generics and copycats. These companies only aim to understand trade marketing and the needs of their retail customers, and leave consumer marketing to their retail partners. In countries or distribution channels where retailers are less sophisticated, there is room for industrial manufacturers who can provide consumer understanding and brand management skills as well as efficient production. Partnering with a retailer who can provide umbrella branding, shelf-space and in-store support, but who needs help in product innovation and managing these assets, is an opportunity for some 'squeezed-out' manufacturers.

Private label is a strategic issue that needs to be faced. It is not an easy market compared to the branded one, but for a company with the right resources and philosophy, it can be an opportunity. On the other hand, to make a success of it demands commitment and investment – it is not a solution for a failing manufacturer. For companies that are strong in their technological delivery or operate in markets where manufacturers have mindspace advantages over retailers, the right decision may be to concentrate on building their consumer franchise. However, even for the strongest brands, co-existence with private label is a reality that will not go away, and brand strategies have to reflect this. In emerging markets, such as China, consumers still have a lower level of acceptance for private label, not dissimilar to developed markets in the 1970s, so retailers cannot rush to impose their highly evolved private label strategies too quickly.

Key learnings

- Private label has shown **consistent, above-average growth** rates and has become the most dynamic factor in the FMCG industry.
- It is **now established** in all major retailers, product sectors and with all shopper types.
- **Premium and premium-plus private labels** are the retailers' main focus as they provide the strongest means of differentiation. Leading retailers now offer a minimum of three levels of Private Label, and usually more.
- To be successful in private label, retailers need to be **competent in most of the branded manufacturer's core skills**. (Retailers now manage complex portfolios segmented by price, value and user-perceived benefits.)
- **No brand is totally safe from private labels.** Manufacturer brands can only survive by being unique, well branded and backed with real, fast innovations.
- Every manufacturer needs to have a **clearly articulated and aggressively implemented strategy** on supplying private label.

(See Appendix 1 for details of major private label suppliers.)

Private label is a thorny issue for branded manufacturers, not just in should they provide it but also in how to position their brands against it. As such, it is a microcosm of an issue that has bedevilled manufacturers ever since the rise of the marketing-orientated retailer: how to manage the disparate interests of retail customers, consumers and their own bottom line. That struggle has manifested itself in the emergence of the trade marketing discipline.

Notes

1. http://www.foodprocessing.com/articles/2010/processor-of-the-year. html. Accessed 14 November 2011.
2. Tedlow RS (1990) *New and Improved*. Basic Books Inc., New York, pp. 210–211.
3. http://adage.com/article/news/walmart-food-bag-consolidation-leaves-glad-hefty/141918/. Accessed 14 November 2011.
4. PLMA Consumer Research Report, http://plma.com/PLMA_Store_ Brands_and_the_Recession.pdf. Accessed 18 August 2011.
5. http://www.thisismoney.co.uk/money/markets/article-1722830/Tesco-boss-unveils-a-brand-new-vision.html. Accessed 17 August 2011.
6. *Supermarketing Magazine*, 29 April 1994, p. 28.

Chapter 10

Since the 1980s, manufacturers have evolved through three different attitudes to 'the trade':

- Most manufacturers spent the vast majority of the twentieth century
  believing that the retail trade needed them badly; without strong
  brands, consumer markets would not exist and shops would be
  mostly empty, therefore retailers should be grateful. Manufacturers
  resented the increasing aggressiveness of retailers, finding it outra-
  geous if their brands were not given shelfspace commensurate with
  their share of the market. These manufacturers rejected out of hand
  the possibility of making private label.
- Over time, many manufacturers became increasingly impressed
  with the retailers' tough stance in negotiations. They believed this
  was an enduring phenomenon, and the answer was to fight fire with
  fire and learn how to negotiate more effectively. Hence, the rise of
  the tough and fast-talking salespeople in FMCG companies who
  could slug it out toe-to-toe with hard-bitten buyers.
- This position evolved into a recognition that a fundamental shift
  in power had taken place. The more perceptive manufacturers
  saw that the concentration within the retail industry had left the
  survivors with increased power. Their response was to adapt their

organisations and business approaches to have a wider relationship with the retailers, and the tough salespeople were gradually replaced by business managers with broader skillsets. Another manifestation of this change was a concentration of resources and effort on trade marketing.

Manufacturers who believe that it all comes down to negotiations are doomed. Negotiations are not the real fight, and 'cooperation' or 'partnership' is not a solution; they are the tip of the iceberg. The outcome depends to a small degree on the negotiating skills of the parties but to a larger degree on their understanding of the balance of power between them. Once negotiations begin, nine-tenths of the battle is over. The balance of power is dictated by brand loyalty, store loyalty, shopping habits, retail structure and manufacturer size, and the extent to which the two parties understand these parameters.

Cooperation can be part of the equation where there are efficiencies to be derived from it, but manufacturers and retailers are inevitably competing with each other for the spoils of the value chain, so cooperation only goes so far. The market-oriented approach of the biggest retailers has further intensified the situation by making the competition between manufacturers and retailers more overt. Cooperation is not a means in itself, much less a solution to a weak position: it is the outcome of particular circumstances. Most sophisticated manufacturers now recognise the terms 'cooperation' and 'partnership' as mere codes for competition by another name.

FMCG companies have been wrestling with trade marketing in some form or other for a couple of decades. But it has been, and continues to be, a struggle to integrate seamlessly into brand-driven structures, processes and reporting. The trade marketing function, often developed from sales or account management, has grown up parallel to and independent from the consumer marketing side, and these functions have often been in conflict. A special effort has to be made to harmonise and integrate the two.

From selling to trade marketing

For a long time, in both the United States and Europe, retailing was a controlled market with various 'price maintenance' laws and 'right to sell' legislation. Once this legislation disappeared in most countries, suppliers had a free-trade market.

Manufacturers, who had already been finding various ways to get around price controls, responded with strategies that hustled the retailer. They depended on giving the retailer money (discounts, subsidies, advertising moneys, etc.) for something in return, such as more shelfspace, displays in the aisle, additional refrigerators etc. These strategies were effective for large manufacturers because retailers provided effective merchandising opportunities at a nominal cost. Hustle strategies were also profitable as they were usually funded from across-the-board price increases, but the discounts were only given to a few retailers. This is the point when gross sales and net sales began to diverge for manufacturers.

During the 1970s and 1980s, retailers developed new merchandising vehicles, such as weekly newspaper ads, in-store sampling programmes, store magazines listing offers of the week/month/season, all of which cost the manufacturer money to access. Added to these were charges for the retailer's services, such as slotting fees for new products, cut-in fees to actually create a space in the shelves, communication cost to all internal store managers and so on. The outcome was that trade promotion investment escalated for manufacturers.

Manufacturers sought to retain control of this rapidly growing cost through developing performance-based bill-back allowances. But retailers realised that, if they negotiated hard enough, they could get the allowances off the invoice up front with a promise to perform to 'earn' the allowance. As this happened, manufacturers began to look for more ways to put pressure on retailers to perform for these allowances, counteracted by the retailers' development of deductions off the invoice for real or perceived failures by the manufacturers.

In the 1990s, it became clear to manufacturers that trade promotion management required a more detailed, analytical approach. They needed help to manage the growing expense, often using specialist consulting firms who promised to 'get at' the substantial sums of trade spend that were being 'wasted'. Retailers invented more buckets of manufacturer expenditure, such as Promotional Trigger Funding, Over-riding Discount, Over and Above, to keep the topic as opaque as possible. The trend to off-invoice payments continued such that, by the mid-1990s, more than 90% of trade promotions involved off-invoice allowances: straightforward reductions in price below the manufacturer's listed wholesale price.

Although hustle strategies cost manufacturers more and more money, they helped them stay in control. When the incentives were tied to quantity discounts and in-store marketing-mix variables, hustle strategies inhibited retailers from manipulating sales-mix and in-store variables to meet their own objectives. Although retailers felt powerful when they were bribed and hustled by their suppliers, and some still do, these strategies did not serve their best interests.

Retailers were led to operate their stores in a way that satisfied the manufacturers' objectives, which often conflicted with those of market-oriented retailers. By encouraging a price orientation among retailers through offering price-based promotions, manufacturers were making shoppers more price-sensitive and more likely to switch stores to cherry pick promotions. This weakens store loyalty while promoting brand loyalty.

However, in most developed markets, retailers now reject manufacturers' hustle strategies, although not the funds that accompany them. Wal-Mart simply ask their suppliers to consolidate all the payments and discounts into one lower price. In return, they get to have their products sold in Wal-Mart. Retailers, who once sold their assets for money, are now only willing to grant them to manufacturers who have something unique to offer, or who show a willingness to help them satisfy their own objectives.

Shelfspace, number of facings, position, local promotion, advertising, information from scanning data and choice of new products are all key assets for retailers. Selling them used to be the simplest way of dealing with them. But allocating these resources optimally from a retail business perspective increases sales volumes, margins, the satisfaction and comfort of their shoppers, their image and, ultimately, store loyalty. A number of retailers will not supply data on their stock/sales to AC Nielsen as this has real commercial value, and makes it easier for a manufacturer to negotiate.

In countries where retailers have adopted marketing-oriented strategies, there is less scope for hustling. Manufacturers now see the need to focus on the retailers' needs and create value for them. However, doing so effectively across a range of retailers, while integrating with their own objectives, has not been easy, or cheap.

Total global trade spend is now estimated to be over $125 billion, well above the total profits of the major retailers, and McKinsey estimate it to be typically 30% of an FMCG manufacturer's cost base, second only to the cost of goods at 40%.[1] Most manufacturers now spend more on trade marketing than brand/consumer marketing; a typical allocation for an FMCG manufacturer who is dependent on the big grocery chains would be in the region of 67% on trade promotions, 22% on brand advertising and 11% on coupons. Even the very biggest players cannot escape the trade-spend burden. For example, in 2009, with revenue of nearly $10 billion, Unilever spent $2 billion on trade-marketing activities compared to $1 billion on consumer marketing. The previous year, P&G spent $3.5 billion on trade marketing in North America alone!

A sometimes hidden further cost is the thousands of people employed by manufacturers, either directly or indirectly, to work in the retailers' stores filling the shelves, rotating the stock, applying shelf labels etc. Some retailers demand that, if a manufacturer wants to have their people merchandise in-store, they must spend half the time doing whatever the retailer asks. In many countries, PepsiCo's Frito-Lay potato chip brands are only touched once by the retailer's staff – at the checkout, and even that is diminishing thanks to the spread of self-service checkouts.

But is trade spend paying back? The evidence suggests not. One AC Nielsen study suggested that 90% of trade-marketing initiatives do not produce a positive ROI,[2] while a staggering 40% of items sold in US supermarkets were on promotion.[3] Obviously this is highly unsatisfactory for manufacturers: over 80% think trade spend is too high.[4]

Getting a handle on spending with the trade has become the crucial area of profitability for manufacturers, and many major consulting firms are rushing in to provide assistance (e.g. Accenture,[5] Bain,[6] BCG,[7] IBM,[8] McKinsey,[9] SAP[10]). Indeed, SAP estimate that nearly 50% of trade spend is never evaluated at all for effectiveness.[11]

The strategic triangle of trade marketing

Trade marketing is business-to-business marketing, which is very different from marketing to consumers. To succeed, you need to balance three issues:

- **Maximising the value offered to retailers:** Retailers are buying with the objective of reselling the product and making a profit, so their buying decision is ultimately assessed in terms of economic criteria. Although price is important, it may not be the most important variable with respect to the overall value provided. A company wishing to sell to another business needs to become expert in analysing and manipulating the *value* delivered to its clients.
- **Ensuring profitability to the manufacturer of individual accounts:** Offering greater value has cost implications that vary between customers. Successful trade marketing implies managing the balance between giving value and making profits. Hence, the trade marketer must determine how profitable each account is, and how that profitability is affected by different value-creating actions.

- **Avoiding dependence:** Since the client base is concentrated more in industrial markets than consumer markets, the danger of dependence is more dramatic. One or two large retail customers may represent make-or-break for the manufacturer. Having gained this fortunate position, a retailer will exploit it in future negotiations, so the manufacturer must diversify its portfolio in order to divide and rule, or it will be ruled. The retail industry is volatile, with frequent mergers and not infrequent bankruptcies. Thus, when a retailer is a profitable account, the manufacturer has to calculate the account risk and dependence in a way that is unfamiliar to consumer marketers.

These three elements are the heart of trade marketing. The company has to maximise the value offered, while earning acceptable profits and guarding against overdependence on any client.

Customer value

The first objective of trade marketing is to create superior value for retailers compared to that achieved by other manufacturers. Since retailers will assess an offer on its economic worth using tools such as direct product profitability (DPP), the manufacturer should assess value in the same way. To win, manufacturers must offer more value, *in the eyes of the retail customer*, than their competitors do. To measure value, we need to break it down into its components. Defining the components means identifying all the aspects that influence customers when making their choice (Box 10.1).

Box 10.1 Direct product profitability equation

$$\text{Value} = \frac{\text{Product benefits} + \text{Non-Product Benefits}}{\text{Price} + \text{Associated Costs}}$$

The more benefits and costs are broken into their components, the easier it is to assess how separate aspects affect the overall value.

Total benefits

It is useful to consider product-related and non-product benefits separately. Typical product-related benefits include:

- **Profitability:** Retailers buy products to make money on them, not because the products wash whiter or smell nicer. The primary benefit to a retailer is the product's profitability on being resold, which translates into a certain gross margin on a certain volume moved. Thus, margin and rotation are likely to figure prominently in a list of benefits.
- **Consumer pull:** In the chapter on mindspace we went into great detail about the cost of switching brands to a shopper, and how this compared to the cost of switching stores. If the manufacturer can convince the retailer that delisting will hurt consumer satisfaction and possibly lead to store switching, then that will be second in importance to direct profits. As stores now segment their shoppers into groups relevant to their marketing effort (e.g. irregular stock-up shopper), manufacturers need to show how their presence, or their marketing activity, might matter to key shopper segments.
- **Marketing support:** Marketing targeted at the consumer is likely to improve rotation, and may affect margins. This is why promotional support directed at the consumer can be counted as an incentive to the retailer. However, at the strategic level, good promotions are designed to increase the brand's CSB, and thus the cost to the store of delisting, which retailers may not accept as being beneficial to them in the long term. In contrast, retailers often try to drive manufacturers' marketing support to areas where the benefit accrues mostly to the retailer (e.g. store magazines or generic campaigns that are not brand-specific).

- **Exclusivity:** If a brand is sold exclusively to one retailer, its CSB will add directly to the store's CSS. In addition, a product that is sold exclusively to one retailer is also likely to generate higher margins.
- **Category considerations:** Retailers try to present shoppers with a complete but streamlined range of products: a category. The ideal category offers alternatives in all major segments, covers a range of price points and optimises impulse buying. Since retailers focus on categories, manufacturers need to view their brand as being part of a category, and should aim to create (or invest in) brands that have a category-strategic, rather than simply a brand-strategic, role.
- **Marketing aims/image:** A retailer that has positioning aims (e.g. trying to improve its image with respect to healthy food or trying to upstage wholesaler clubs with huge packs) will value products that strengthen those positions. Similarly, a market-oriented retailer will have a strategy with respect to price structure, promotions, range and private label. By understanding the retailer's objectives, the right offerings can be presented.
- **Retailers' profit margin:** In categories with high consumer-marketing and trade-marketing spend, retailers can benefit in two ways: first, from the higher levels of discounts that can be squeezed and, second, such brands usually provide a high price umbrella under which above-average margins can be earned on private label offerings.

Non-product benefits are those that the supplying company attaches to its offer but are not tied to the product itself. Typical examples include:

- **Administration, ECR (efficient customer response) and EDI (electronic data interchange:** The supply chain has to respond efficiently to the consumer's behaviour. The key to efficiency is the flow of information. The information is used to predict what will be sold where, and the prediction is continually adjusted once consumers reveal what they are going to do. Information has to flow smoothly so that the right goods can arrive at their destination without delay.

Any manufacturer who cannot seamlessly comply with every retailer requirement in these areas is doomed.

- **'Advice and help'**: Many manufacturers offer shelfspace allocation models, or category management advice should they be favoured with *category captain* status. Manufacturers specialising in a category may advise the retailer on optimising sales of the whole category through their specialist knowledge of the consumer and their experience with other retailers. Unfortunately, even today such 'advice' is often a thinly disguised sales pitch that retailers treat with scepticism. When it is not, manufacturers often fail to see any benefit from promoting their competitors' brands ahead of their own. For smaller chains and independent retailers, or retailers in emerging markets, space allocation is a serious concern, and help may gratefully be accepted. Retailers with their own marketing objectives will have space allocation models developed for their needs.

Total costs

The total cost to the retailer of selling the product to the consumer must be broken down in a parallel way to benefits.

In addition to price and terms of payment, the retailer faces a number of non-price costs. All the actions from loading delivery trucks, unpacking cases, mixing the right assortment of SKUs, labelling prices and arranging displays add up to a significant part of the cost. Tesco now have 70% of their stock delivered in shelf-ready packaging that requires minimum effort from their staff. Choices made by the supplier will affect these costs. Separating the elements that create costs help identify the most efficient way of reducing overall cost. A typical list of costs could include:

- **Price:** The price, taking into account quantity discounts and various direct subsidies or allowances, forms the most visible component of cost.

- **Terms of payment:** The terms of payment are an element of cost and will vary in their value between retailers, who will each have different costs of capital.

- **Shelfspace:** Shelfspace demands vary among products depending on their form and packaging. Compactness or efficient forms of display can favourably affect the total cost of selling a product. Also, some manufacturers may require multiple locations, including highly specialised merchandising vehicles (e.g. carbonated soft drinks demand cooler locations in addition to the ambient fixture).

- **Transportation:** By understanding how a particular retailer organises distribution, warehousing, transport, etc., a supplier can offer more suitable delivery arrangements, day or night, faster response times (JIT, or just-in-time) and so on. Usually, however, major retailers will dictate their transportation needs.

- **Handling costs:** The product design, including individual and case packaging, can be economical to transport in terms of size/weight, withstand rough treatment and be easy to unpack. The packaging may be easy to stack and presented directly to the consumer. The store's prices, or store-specific information, like category codes, can be printed in advance. The combination of SKUs in a delivery can be suited to the assortment needed on the shelf. Since labour forms a large part of retail costs, the idea of saving two minutes per case is exciting! This is why Wal-Mart require their suppliers to follow strict label and packaging requirements, so they have the lowest cost structure and can pass on the savings to their shoppers.

- **Inventory costs:** A retailer holding inventory suffers financial risks, financial costs, physical risks and physical costs. In inflationary times, the costs of holding goods are concealed because the value of the goods appreciates and the retailer may show a profit on the act of holding. However, in deflationary times, the opposite can happen. An untimely price cut can mean a warehouse manager wakes up on Monday morning with a warehouse full of goods worth less than on the previous Friday. The retailer also has the responsibility of looking after the physical products, which means warehouse space, and may involve keeping it warm or cold. There are other risks: flood, fire, frost, mice, insects and bacteria damage products, and employees or burglars may steal them. Clearly, there are savings in cutting inventory to a minimum.

- **Obsolete goods:** Longer-lasting fresh produce, greater shelf stability or, where relevant, greater consistency, can reduce the cost of obsolete or returned goods.

Deciding which aspects of value count as benefits and which count as costs can be arbitrary. For example, is a more efficient package a benefit or a reduction in costs? Are terms of payment a benefit or a cost saving? The best answer is how they are perceived by the client. Although counting something as an additional benefit rather than a reduction in cost will not affect the outcome of the analysis, understanding how each customer evaluates them will. Assessing the benefits and costs to the customer is an essential part of trade marketing, and must be performed in every presentation to the retail buyer.

Customer profitability

Customer profitability is the second element of trade marketing. When considering whether the value offered to a retailer should be improved, the manufacturer must know how profitable that retailer is to its business, so analysing customer profitability is an essential discipline for manufacturers.

The logic of direct customer profitability is that the costs of selling to each retailer should be allocated as nearly as possible to the activities that generate those costs. The costs are influenced by more than product and price: volumes (ordered and per delivery), discounts, bonuses, sales force attention, storage, merchandising support, promotions, returns, order processing and disputes also affect net profit.

Customer profitability analysis implies finding out the cost of customer servicing. For example, what is the cost of supplying different product mixes, delays in payment, discounts related to size of order, unique products/packaging for specific customers or different delivery requirements? Centralising this information with trade marketers, who decide how to allocate these resources, is a significant challenge in accounting practices for many companies.

Once the information is available to the people responsible for account profitability, they can determine which accounts are more or less profitable and why. This influences how future trade marketing investments are allocated across accounts. It can lead to a more precise discount policy, a more effective use of sales force time and a more effective use of marketing investment.

Understanding the profitability of individual accounts can create new bases for negotiation. If an account *is* unprofitable, what changes are needed to make it profitable? Account-based profitability also reveals the impact of losing the account. In negotiations, it is helpful to know the cost impact of not reaching an agreement.

Client profitability analysis has two weaknesses. First, many of the costs allocated across customers are fixed, so dropping unprofitable accounts has the effect of making the remaining accounts less profitable as they have to pick up some of the costs. Second, seeking only the most profitable activities or accounts may lead to an unacceptable degree of dependence.

Category management

Category *management* is something of a misnomer; category *understanding* may be a better goal. Category understanding should be an effort to see the market from the retail point of view, and offer brands/SKUs that retailers want to stock. The idea is not to sell to retailers what you want to produce, but produce what they want to sell and their shoppers want to buy.

A manufacturer taking a category-based view understands the role of the category within different chains and store formats, as different retailers have different category objectives. Retailers' price positioning, quality positioning, growth objectives and margin objectives will affect their 'ideal' category, and the role of private label, their technical sophistication, size and the size of their stores will affect category objectives. Thus, the category objectives of Sainsbury's in the United Kingdom will be different from a Costco in the United States and Carrefour in Brazil.

Retailers' objectives

Category planning implies understanding the role of the category within the store, and the brands within the category. For example, at the store level, how important is the category in forming the store image: how price-sensitive and range-sensitive are shoppers with respect to this category? What are the effects of greater shelfspace, position in store, promotions, merchandising on this category? How can it be managed to improve profits?

Within the category, what is the optimal combination of brands and formats to cover the maximum buying intentions, and what is the optimal price structure for discriminating without losing sales? Retailers want to know the most efficient way to keep SKUs and inventory to a minimum. At the brand level, what is the most common price reference point and how price-sensitive are consumers within the category? What is the effect of destocking brands, and how can the impact of reducing the range be minimised?

The retailer has three objectives when deciding categories, and the products to create the category:

• **Provide a satisfactory shopping experience for shoppers:** A store must offer the right categories in the right places in the store. It must define its categories in a way that seems natural and helpful to the shopper. A category (such as a staffed delicatessen) could be less profitable than normal on a per-square-metre basis, but justify its space on shopper satisfaction and store ambiance.

- **Maximise satisfaction, revenue and profits from each category:** A well-planned category will satisfy the largest proportion of shoppers, actualise every potential sale and prompt unplanned purchases. Profits will be affected by the mix of sales: the range should price-discriminate, satisfying price-sensitive customers while earning higher margins from quality-sensitive shoppers. For many retailers, category planning also involves promoting their private label brands.
- **Maximise efficiency by limiting and simplifying the range of products handled:** This objective usually works against the other objectives, but limiting customers to a smaller range reduces handling, inventory and shelfspace costs. Profits per square foot will usually be increased by reducing the space taken by a category.

Achieving these objectives depends on the store. Even within a chain, stores can vary enormously in size and type of area (poor/affluent, old/young, retail competition). The category has to vary accordingly: there can be no catch-all solution to the question of category planning.

Manufacturers' advantage: Specialisation

Category management is a priority for retailers, and manufacturers have to recognise retailers' expertise and right to organise their stores based on their understanding of their shoppers. Shoppers' desires may differ from those imagined by manufacturers. Manufacturers are organised by product area, whereas consumers may shop by meal, which is why you find mushrooms next to the steak section as well as in the produce section.

However, manufacturers do play a role in category planning because they can synthesise their experiences across the different chains they serve, both nationally and internationally. They have the critical mass to make it worthwhile to conduct research on different segments and in-store buying behaviour. In particular, it is worthwhile for a manufacturer to analyse the retailer's scanner data for the category, even when it is not economic for the retailer to do so for each of its many categories.

The retailer is interested in the consumers' behaviour in each of the two or three hundred categories it offers, but owing to a lack of critical mass in each category, the retailer does not have the budget or the personnel to discover the information. However, for a manufacturer, concentrating on a small set of categories, it is worthwhile. The manufacturer can relate in-store data with the information collected from consumer research: how consumers choose in this category, which consumers choose what, which brands compete most closely with each other and which command the greatest brand loyalty. Since the retailers have the data, and since both benefit from its analysis, but only the manufacturer has the specialisation to make it worthwhile, cooperation is necessary.

Category management and smaller manufacturers

Category captains are recognised by retailers as having the greatest knowledge of consumer behaviour and mechanics in a category, and usually will have the most comprehensive range. Retailers believe that stocking this manufacturer's range, backed with their understanding of positioning, merchandising, shelf allocation etc., should optimise sales. This opportunity usually goes by default to the dominant manufacturers, like Gillette in shaving, Kellogg's in cereal, L'Oréal in hair colour (in Europe), Cadbury in confectionery (in Australia), Wrigley in gum, Pampers in disposable nappies (diapers) and Coca-Cola/Pepsi in soft drinks. Manufacturers thus compete to be perceived as the best and most appropriate category managers. For example, in 2005,

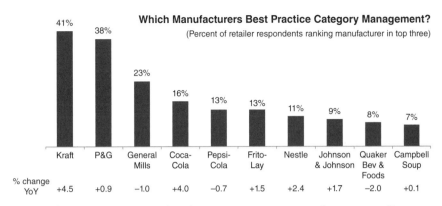

Figure 10.1 Best practices in category management by company.[13]

Category / Retailer	Home Care	Food Bags, Wraps, Cntrs	Trash Bags	Water Filtration	Cat Litter	Laundry Additives	Charcoal	Salad Dressing	BBQ & Marinades	Auto Care
Brand	Clorox	Glad	Glad	Brita	Fresh Step, Scoop Away, EverClean	Clorox	Kingsford	Hidden Valley	KC Masterpiece	Armor All, STP
Wal-mart		X	X	X	X	X	X	X		
Target	X	X	X	X	X					X
Dollar General	X	X	X		X	X	X			X
Family Dollar	X	X	X		X	X				X
Safeway	X	X	X			X	X			X
SuperValu	X		X		X	X	X			

X: Clorox designated as category captain.

Figure 10.2 Clorox is a category captain.[14]

according to the Manufacturing Benchmark Survey,[12] Kraft had the best category management practices (Figure 10.1).

A tightly focused manufacturer operating in categories that have a limited number of competitors can accumulate quite a number of category captaincies, which can introduce some internal management complexities. One such example is Clorox, which has 37 category captain positions in six retailers (Figure 10.2).

Of course, being rated the best by retailers may not necessarily always be in the manufacturer's best interests as it could mean most compliant, most generous with allowances and so on.

Smaller players, who recognise they cannot call themselves category captains, have to take a different approach. Some of them aim to have preferred supplier status, which means they select a retailer or group of retailers that they invest disproportionately in, and thus provide the retailers with services that increase the value of the brands to them over the retailers' competitors. However, this also implies deselecting retailers, which could reduce overall distribution.

Another approach is to become *category lieutenants*. This is where a smaller supplier looks to complement the category captain by providing niche brands where the captain is weak or absent, and perhaps offering me-toos to reduce the dominance of the category captain. For example, Method[15] act like a category lieutenant in Safeway by providing niche high-end cleaning products that supplement the category captain Clorox's portfolio. An alternative view of the category, and alternative brands that pressure the category leader, are always welcomed by retailers. No retailer wants to be dependent on its largest supplier.

Conflicts between trade marketing and consumer marketing

Trade marketing and consumer marketing frequently overlap and potentially conflict, as both have an opinion on pricing, allocation of marketing budgets, packaging and product positioning. When trade and consumer marketing conflict, trade will often 'win' (especially towards the end of the financial year) because its effects are immediate, whereas consumer marketing is more concerned with objectives that pay back over time, like building the brand image and maintaining premium prices. Hence, a balance between the two needs to be achieved. Below we look at the areas of potential conflict.

- **Competition for resources:** In many companies, the marketing budget is set as a fixed amount, and has to be divided between trade marketing and consumer marketing. Thus, investments into marketing directed at the retailer reduce the resources available for brand-building campaigns aimed at the consumer.

- **Producing for private label:** Trade marketers see private label as something that the retailer values and they can satisfy, often profitably. Trade marketing has a point: Jacques Vabre, a French coffee manufacturer, built a strong position for their brands through a complex trading arrangement with Carrefour. Jacques agreed to produce Carrefour's private label coffee and in return Carrefour supported Jacques' branded range with premium shelfspace; the arrangement benefited both parties.

  The trade marketer, keen to offer clients the most competitive value it can provide, has a different view on the quality and technology that should be supplied in comparison to the consumer market. Consumer marketers view private label as a threat and believe higher-quality private label should be resisted at all costs. Even old-product development (reformulating, repackaging) presents the same dilemma: should the private label get the latest novelty? Private label can easily become an emotional issue, creating warring factions in a company.

- **Pricing:** Trade marketers can always boost the value they give to retailers by dropping their prices or adding bonuses. This can lead the trade marketer to ignore the needs and objectives of consumer marketing. For example, from the consumer point of view, the product should form a defined part of a range with the correct price relative to other products in the line-up. Consumer marketers spend their careers justifying higher prices for their brands. Price is not simply money received but also perception, positioning and the possibility to invest in brand-building activities for a profitable future.

- **New Products and Category Management:** There are trade-marketing and consumer-marketing reasons for wanting to launch new products and brand extensions; they will not necessarily point to the same new products/extensions. Since a new product has to be accepted by both groups, a new product development group should represent both sides.

- **Packaging:** Packaging is another variable of great interest to retailers and consumers alike, but from different perspectives. Packaging affects the retailer's handling costs and the amount of space taken on the shelves. For the consumer, packaging is a strong element of communication and often important to product use. The interests are sometimes aligned, as in the case of ultra-compact disposable nappies. However, in many cases the tastes of the retailer and the shopper are contradictory. Perrier owe a large part of their consumer appreciation to their elegant and unique glass bottle. On the other hand, this same glass bottle can break, is heavy and has a fat waist that pushes the bottles apart on the shelf, wasting valuable space. For handling and close packing, a square plastic bottle is better. Consumer appeal is an important element of the value that a product delivers to a retailer, and integrating this into the trade marketing's strategic triangle is a delicate challenge.
- **Targeting Retailers:** Trade marketers will view the retail trade as a market with segments, and view some customers as more desirable than others. Desirability is based on criteria like size, volume and ease of servicing. More sophisticated retailers, with modern logistics systems, will be seen as excellent customers. They reorder by EDI, operate from their own centralised warehouses and have a triple-A credit rating. However, looking at retailers as mindspace competitors, these top retailers are precisely the ones that pose the most long-term threat to manufacturers' brands. A consumer marketing executive may not choose to give this group the most favoured trading partner status. Less sophisticated retailers may be given relatively greater priority, following a policy of developing alternative distribution channels.

Managing actions

The goal of trade marketing is to understand and influence shopping behaviour. For different shopper segments and different product categories, several questions need to be asked: what is the level of planned purchases and what is the level of planning (brand, product category)? How do consumers choose in front of the shelf, what is the value of different shelf positions, and the position within the store? What happens when the brand is out of stock? Who are the shoppers? How do young shoppers differ from older ones, richer from poorer, men from women? Once this has been gathered, manufacturers can use it to influence shopping behaviour. But the difficulty lies in balancing the opportunities in retailers with the needs of the manufacturer. For example:

- **Promotions:** Promotions may be perceived by the consumer as coming from the retailer or from the manufacturer. The retailer prefers the consumer to feel that bargains are offered thanks to the store and are less available in other stores. A common form of promotion is free product 'three for the price of two', which has now segued into the BOGOF: buy one get one free. This promotion, although funded by the manufacturer, is presented to the consumer as an act of amazing generosity made by the store.

  Trade marketing is naturally attracted to activities desired by the retailer – their job is to understand and meet where possible the retailer's needs – even though such promotions can easily erode brand loyalty in the long run. For example, trade promotions that showcase retailers as offering basic items on sale encourage brand switching and stock piling, which lowers brand loyalty, increases shoppers' price sensitivity and erodes long-term brand equity.

- **Support weak retailers:** In sophisticated markets, it is not unusual for 20% of retail accounts to take 80% of a manufacturer's business. Manufacturers are inclined to see these large retailers as their best customers, as well as being their worst competition. There has to be a balance between encouraging the concentration in retailing that offers manufacturers economies of scale in logistics, and accepting the cost inefficiencies of a broader customer base to strengthen their strategic position by reducing dependence. For strategic reasons, retailers who are weak and losing customers should be encouraged and supported by manufacturers. Manufacturers should be hesitant to pursue actions that encourage greater retail concentration, even though they may help logistics and administration costs.

- **Favour brand sellers:** One strategy followed by discount chains is to develop their credibility with a bigger-than-average focus on well-known manufacturer brands. Such retailers work in the manufacturers' long-term interests and should be nurtured. Family-owned Mercadona, Spain's largest discount retailer, started with popular brands to attract shoppers. Once they built a following, they developed their brand, 'Hacendado', to ensure they could continue to offer great products at a low price; this strategy strengthened their discounter position and made them competitive with bigger discounters like Dia and Lidl. Wegmans in the United States used a similar strategy to lure shoppers, and once they had established 'Consistent Low Prices' with branded products, they also started a private label range. Finally, Rhino Cash and Carry, one of the most successful independently owned discount retailers in South Africa, realised success with their 'low price and high quality strategy' by offering branded goods to shoppers in local communities.

  Similarly, large chains (such as Auchan in France and Asda in the United Kingdom) have, at certain periods, adopted strategies of stocking a wider-than-average range of national brands. It makes sense for manufacturers to support such store propositions, rewarding their loyalty to brands. The availability of competitively priced national brands and a wide choice may influence the consumer's demand for national brands in other parts of the retail trade.

One of the hardest challenges in trade marketing is to take significant actions with one customer or channel that do not evoke negative repercussions in the others. A ground-breaking study[16] looked at what happens to retailer–manufacturer relationships when one party executes an act the other party considers against their interests. Such a reaction is almost inevitable in customer-marketing strategies, and can cause huge conflict and cost time devoted to attempting to manage the fallout. The study showed four main responses from the aggrieved party: Passive Acceptance (loyalty to the relationship), Constructive Discussion ('Let's work this through'), Venting (an uncomfortable meeting that ends reasonably amicably) or Disengagement (a threat or move to 'punish'). Which response occurs is driven by three main factors:

- **Past efforts at nurturing trust and goodwill** that can be drawn upon as evidence of overall good intentions. Obviously, this cannot be relied upon too often or the well becomes dry.
- **Managing the offended party's perception** of the intention and intensity of the action: the earlier and more honest the communication, the better.
- **Interdependence:** The more interdependent the relationship, the more likely will be an acceptable outcome to a dispute.

The fear of a negative reaction from other retailers can sometimes inhibit a manufacturer's willingness to make bold moves in trade marketing. Indeed, it could be argued that the skillset to avoid or smooth negative reactions from retailers is at least as important within manufacturing companies today as the ability to design customer strategies is.

Organisational implications for manufacturers

Retailers and consumers do not always want the same things; sometimes they want conflicting things. The 'route to market' manager cannot be left to consider the trade in isolation from the consumer manager. An integrated decision process is required, both nationally and internationally.

The Route to Market

Integrating the trade-marketing view and the consumer-marketing view affects many elements of the marketing mix. Packaging has to be designed for supermarket handling as well as consumer appeal and in home use. Merchandising has to appeal to the shopper passing by quickly and to the store manager assessing it in the context of the store's marketing objectives. Pricing has to be planned in terms of a trade price objective and a retail price objective. Consequently, the organisational structure must foster communication and harmony between the executives dealing with trade and consumer demands.

The company must have an overall category strategy. This means defining and implementing the chosen category role: captain, lieutenant or preferred supplier, and assessing and planning the brand portfolio from the retail perspective. It may be that the route to market structure should become a parallel function to brand management, with both structures reporting to an overall authority, perhaps by category. Decisions balancing strategy towards the trade and brand strategies must be made at a level where both are integrated.

The route to market function must ensure customer value at retail level. Logically, this would imply having responsibility for all the functions involved in bringing the products to the customer (physical distribution, wholesale and retail trade, logistics, administration) for a particular product category, because these functions create value for retail customers. This makes the route to market function broad and more sophisticated than that of current sales and national accounts managers. New skills and know-how are necessary to manage the strategic triangle (customer value, profitability and dependence), to represent the needs of the trade within the company and to cooperate with the consumer franchise management.

The route to market function is the company's main contact with the trade. It should develop an expertise on its market comparable to that of brand management's understanding of consumers. It should be able to predict which retailers will survive and thrive, which will provide profits in the long term and which ones are growing. If more favoured deals or exclusivity are to be given, what is the relative worth of each retailer? The function must balance the importance given to the 'non-large accounts' and alternative distribution channels. These routes can provide opportunities for future development and a strategic balance against the constantly increasing power of the largest retailers.

The route to market function also has to connect internationally, both to share information and respond to retailers at an international level.

Key learnings

- **Understanding trade marketing is essential** for manufacturers to succeed. Manufacturers have to maximise the value, earn acceptable profits and guard against overdependence on any retailer.
- **Category management** (understanding how a brand fits in a category) is essential in order to create superior value for the retailer.
- It is necessary to **assess the importance of the two markets** (consumer and retailer) for each brand. Some brands will fulfil different roles: some stay mostly consumer; some mostly are for the retailer's benefit; some have a strategic role for the manufacturer; and some a tactical one.
- Trade marketing and consumer marketing **inherently conflict** because they serve different groups who have different interests.
- **Controlling the increasing costs** of trade marketing is a major challenge for manufacturers. Once a discount is given, it is rarely won back.

(Continued)

- Learning to **straddle both approaches** is hard. It is not enough for a manufacturer to have a trade-marketing function and a consumer-marketing function; companies need to integrate their marketing to retailers with their marketing to consumers and be able to effectively manage the conflicts and trade-offs.
- Understanding and integrating trade and consumer marketing, and **being able to respond to two layers of customers**, is the new paradigm. It took companies a generation to develop marketing expertise to the level found today. No doubt it will take another generation to develop the techniques that will raise trade marketing to its highest level. It is also essential to understand the position of the private label in the category, and how this affects the dynamics of the section.

Trade marketing is a local market activity, meeting the needs of the in-market strategies of individual retailers. But, increasingly, manufacturer–retailer relationships are being played out on the global stage, which creates some very different dynamics and opportunities.

Notes

1. http://www.mckinseyquarterly.com/Stop_wasting_promotional_money_824. Accessed 17 November 2011.
2. http://www.nfbuildingtradescouncil.com/harnessing-the-real-power-of-trade-marketing.html. Accessed 7 September 2011.
3. http://www.promaxtpo.com/trade-promotion-effectiveness/. Accessed 8 September 2011.
4. http://www1.ebiquity.com/media/92751/trade%20promotions%20report%202011.pdf. Accessed 8 September 2011.
5. http://www.accenture.com/SiteCollectionDocuments/PDF/Accenture_CGS_Trade_Promotion_Management.pdf. Accessed 18 November 2011.

6. http://www.bain.com/Images/GMAF_Trade_promotion_management_crash_diets.pdf. Accessed 18 November 2011.

7. http://www.bcg.com/documents/file14480.pdf. Accessed 6 August 2011.

8. http://www.globalscorecard.net/live/download/G510_9137_03f_play_big_1.pdf. Accessed 12 November 2011.

9. http://www.globalscorecard.net/live/download/G510_9137_03f_play_big_1.pdf. Accessed 12 November 2011.

10. http://www.sdn.sap.com/irj/scn/go/portal/prtroot/docs/library/uuid/003b83fe-2fb1–2a10-b08a97a4eac6607?QuickLink=index&overridelayout=true. Accessed 21 November 2011.

11. http://www.sdn.sap.com/irj/scn/go/portal/prtroot/docs/library/uuid/003b83fe-2fb1–2a10-b085-a97a4eac6607?QuickLink=index&overridelayout=true. Accessed 20 November 2011.

12. http://groups.haas.berkeley.edu/marketing/marketing_old/sics/pdf/Dhar/pdf. Accessed 16 September 2011.

13. http://groups.haas.berkeley.edu/marketing/marketing_old/sics/pdf/Dhar.pdf. Accessed 30 November 2011.

14. http://onlinelibrary.wiley.com/doi/10.1111/j.1937–5956.2010.01141.x/pdf. Accessed 18 November 2011.

15. http://business.highbeam.com/412156/article-1G1–240912931/competitive-consequences-using-category-captain. Accessed 10 November 2011.

16. Hibbard JD, Kumar N, Stern LB (2001) Examining the impact of destructive acts in marketing channel relationships. *Journal of Marketing Research* 38: 45–61.

Chapter 11

FMCG INTERNATIONALISATION IS not new. Manufacturers have long realised the benefits of expanding beyond national borders, facilitated by the fact that packaged goods were easily exported. Many desired the virtuous circle of opening up new markets for their key products and thus creating incremental economies of scale in their home-based factories. As long ago as the late nineteenth century, Swiss manufacturers Lindt, Suchard, Nestlé and Cailler were attracted by the size of Europe's biggest consumer market – industrialised Britain – which dwarfed their homeland in market size. They entered as importers with aggressive advertising and distribution strategies, and all developed a strong presence for their Swiss-made cocoa beverages.

Some manufacturers grew their exporting business so successfully that it became more cost-effective to establish factories overseas. Henry J. Heinz first sold his Tomato Ketchup and Distilled White Vinegar into London's Fortnum & Mason in 1886 and, by 1906, the Heinz UK factory was churning out mountains of Heinz Baked Beans with a recipe modified for the British palate. Early-twentieth-century America was a huge attraction to British and European manufacturers, but few were able to overcome the daunting logistical challenges of doing business there, a notable exception being Lever Brothers, who were going toe-to-toe with Procter & Gamble by the 1920s.

Retailers were not as keen or able to expand internationally. They were often family businesses with limited access to finance and were operating in a very capital-hungry business. Retail margins were also so thin that only the richest could fund the building of dozens of stores and setting up an overseas management infrastructure. So most focused on becoming established in their home markets and saw little point in going beyond their national boundaries as there were few economies of scale to be had in international retailing.

However, two American retailers managed to overcome these obstacles. Harry Gordon Selfridge, the brains behind Chicago's Marshall Field, opened his famous London store in 1909. By 1925, he had expanded into France to become Europe's largest retailer. Another to cross the Atlantic was Frank Woolworth, the richest American retailer at the time. He also opened his first store in 1909 and lived to see hundreds of British Woolworth's stores generating more profit than his American Five-and-Ten-Cent store empire.

International expansion for both manufacturers and retailers took place when a company had something new and better to offer to another market. Brand owners like Heinz brought new products to Britain, and Selfridge and Woolworth brought the best of leading-edge American retailing. But these companies only thrived abroad by going local. They were run virtually autonomously from their parent organisations and evolved distinct personas, so much so that it still comes as a shock to many British shoppers to discover that Heinz, Selfridges, Woolworths, Kellogg's and others originated in America.

The widening international gap

For most of the twentieth century, manufacturers were more proactive than retailers in expanding internationally. Why?

- **Uniqueness:** There are thousands of unique branded products that could be taken to new markets, but only a handful of unique retailing concepts. Many brands were protected by a combination of patent, secret recipe and manufacturing complexity, making them very difficult for manufacturers in other countries to copy. Also, in the case of luxury products, another country of origin – such as the United States for computers, Switzerland or Belgium for chocolate and France for perfumes – added to the appeal, whereas there is little appeal in the fact that a retailer is established in another country. On the other hand, retailing concepts are almost impossible to protect from being widely copied. Michael Cullen could do nothing to stop his idea being taken by ambitious retailers, which naturally diminished any opportunities he had to go international should he have so desired.

- **Profitability:** As manufacturers took most of the profits from the value chain, they were better able than the relatively cash-poor retailers to fund international start-ups. Cadbury opened their first overseas factory in Australia in 1920 and did not turn a profit there for 26 years. They had the resources to keep investing throughout that period and are now one of the strongest consumer brands in Australia. No retailer can run an operation at a loss for 26 years.
- **Scale:** For most of the twentieth century, manufacturers were larger than retailers and had the financial and personnel resources to expand internationally, a resource gap that only widened as more manufacturers internationalised.

The outcome was that it became the norm for manufacturers to operate internationally, whereas it was the norm for retailers to operate nationally. Thus, manufacturers have become more adept at internationalisation because they have had more practice: their managers are more likely to have international experience and their operations have long been managed on a global basis. By 1918, Coca-Cola was present in eight countries; 53 by 1940; 163 by 1980; and over 200 today. No grocery retailer has yet operated in more than 38 countries.

While the balance of power was swinging towards retailers in local markets, it remained with manufacturers at the global level as no one retailer accounted for a significant proportion of their global sales. Any retailer could wield a big stick in a local market, but it was hard for them to get access to the top management of globalised manufacturers.

This became more significant when retailers started expanding internationally. A new market for a retailer was almost always an established market for their main suppliers, which tilts the balance of power back to the manufacturer. A retailer hoping to break into a new market could not do so without the presence and support of that country's favourite brands, which gave manufacturers more leverage than perhaps they had become used to in the retailer's homeland.

The rise of the international retailer

Carrefour pioneered the internationalisation of modern retailing with their invention of the hypermarket. They opened the first one in 1963, only four years after they opened their first store. With something unique to export, they expanded successfully to Spain in 1973, followed by Brazil in 1975, Argentina in 1982 and Greece in 1991. Carrefour succeeded because they chose specific markets: countries that didn't have powerful local players who could stifle them. Indeed, their ventures into highly developed, competitive markets such as the United Kingdom and the United States failed. Thus, the selection of markets that offered the greatest chance of winning, not the greatest size, has been key to their success. Carrefour have now expanded into 38 countries, more than any retailer, and are the world's second-largest retailer in size, but third-largest in profitability, owing to their presence being dissipated across many small markets.

Carrefour were not the only European retailer to look abroad. Many had to look at international expansion because of the combination of small home markets and government planning restrictions that limited their domestic growth. The proximity of similar markets on the European continent meant that retailers such as Metro Group, Ahold,

Table 11.1 Top global retailers by the number of countries they operate in (2011)

Company	Number of countries
Carrefour	38*
Metro Group	33
Wal-Mart	27
Schwarz	25
Aldi	18
Rewe	14
Tesco	14
Auchan	12
Ahold	9
ITM	8

Source: Planet Retail; authors' calculations.
Note: 29 owned and 9 franchisees.

Schwartz, Aldi, Auchan, Intermarché (ITM) and Rewe could easily expand into adjacent countries. Thus, it is no coincidence that 7 of the top 10 retailers that have expanded to the most markets are based in continental Europe. For example, 8 of Auchan's 14 markets are European. Table 11.1 lists the top global retailers in 2011.

Perhaps more surprising is the presence of only one American retailer in that list, Wal-Mart. In fact, US retailers are under more attack from European ones breaching the once impregnable US market than the other way round. Aldi with Trader Joe's, Tesco with Fresh & Easy and especially Ahold, who generate over half of their total sales through their Stop & Shop and Giant banners in the United States, are all making inroads. Even the once-mighty icon of American retailing, A&P, is now owned by a European retailer, Tengelmann.

American retailers have not proved to be as adept as Europeans at internationalisation. Safeway extended into the United Kingdom, Australia and Germany in the 1960s, but without a significantly different offering from local players other than higher prices. It failed in all three countries. Their 1980s ventures into Mexico and the Middle East also came to an end, leaving Safeway's last remaining foreign outpost in

Canada. Neither Kroger nor Publix has ventured abroad, perhaps because they were put off by Wal-Mart's early experiences.

Wal-Mart's international expansion started well with their first store in Mexico in 1991, as did their second venture in Canada in 1994 with the purchase of Woolco. However, they had disastrous experiences in Germany, Korea, Indonesia, Hong Kong and, to a lesser extent, Argentina. When they failed, they failed for three reasons, all of which applied to their German operation:

- **Purchasing a local chain that did not have enough mass:** The German retailers they bought in 1998, the Wertkauf chain and a collection of hypermarkets from Interspar, left Wal-Mart short of stores and market share. Even with 85 stores, they were less than one-fifth the size of their nearest rival, Kaufland. Eighty per cent of Germans did not live within a realistic travelling distance of a Wal-Mart.
- **Failing to adapt to local conditions:** Wal-Mart could not have acted less locally in Germany if they had tried. English was decreed the official language at their German Head Office; unions, which are strong in Germany, were ignored, which prompted a strike, and local suppliers were treated as though they needed Wal-Mart Germany more than Wal-Mart Germany needed them. When the suppliers demurred, Wal-Mart relied heavily on its US product mix, which was not well received by the *hausfraus* of Düsseldorf.
- **Facing a crushing response from strong local competition:** Wal-Mart's main German competitors made sure Wal-Mart was unable to offer the cornerstone of its strategy: every day low prices (EDLP). German retailing has some of the thinnest profit margins in the world – 1% or less – and Wal-Mart were competing against the kings of low prices, Aldi and Lidl, who made sure that Wal-Mart never beat their prices on anything.

With not enough stores (and many in the wrong parts of town), a product range not suited to German tastes and prices higher than the country's two leading retailers, Wal-Mart never stood a chance and pulled the plug in 2006, losing over $1.6 billion after selling their stores to Metro Group.

The fact that, globally, Wal-Mart was more than double the size of its closest four competitors combined was no guarantee of success, because retailing is a local business. It doesn't matter how big you are globally, you have to be big locally and/or have a very unique shopping format to stand a chance. Wal-Mart applied this lesson when they entered the United Kingdom with the purchase of Asda, which already had a strong presence that Wal-Mart grew by making Asda even better, rather than turning it into Wal-Mart.

To support or not support?

The decision to support a new retailer is one of the biggest a brand manufacturer faces. Existing retail customers will pressure their suppliers to have little to do with any newcomer, particularly one who demands unique products, formats or price points, such as Aldi, Costco or Dollar stores. But withholding support, while preventing the short-term pain that comes from enraging existing customers, can often be a long-term mistake.

FMCG brands cannot hope to thrive without wide access to shoppers, so if a new retail entrant is going to attract shoppers in the long term, big brands have to be there sooner or later. Many large companies, like Kodak, initially shunned Costco, who demanded large multipacks that set a new low in the price per unit, but ended up having to do business with them as Costco became a major player. It is tempting to see only the problem of uproar from existing customers and not the benefit of long-term sales potential from a successful newcomer.

Manufacturers who offer support from the beginning tend to be rewarded with favourable treatment for a long time, while those who shun and eventually support tend to be at the back of the line for scarce promotional slots. Of course, manufacturers should not mindlessly support every newcomer, for example one who sets up to disrupt the market with ludicrous pricing; the trick is to spot which new entrant has something unique to offer and will succeed.

The emergence of emerging markets

In the twentieth century many of the attempts by retailers to extend internationally were into other developed markets, facing well-established, sophisticated competitors who served marketing-savvy consumers. But only 15% of the world's population live in rich, marketing-saturated societies.

Manufacturers have been much faster in moving into emerging markets, and many of the pioneers have benefited from significant first-mover advantages. The first brands to use advertising when it became available in a country, especially via television, often gained a unique advantage as television ownership spread. In China, 93% of the population now watch television, to the benefit of the brands that have been there from the start. Television is the dominant advertising medium in many other emerging markets; in Brazil, television advertising was worth 15 times as much as Internet advertising in 2010. The influence of television advertising in emerging markets, unlike in developed markets, is expected to continue growing. In emerging markets there are fewer rules and regulations for advertisers to contend with; for example it is still socially acceptable to target children – a boon to categories such as breakfast cereals, soft drinks, savoury snacks, confectionery and fast food.

Many companies believe that countries recently opened to modern marketing – such as Hungary, Poland, India, Vietnam, the Philippines and Indonesia – provide unique opportunities. Diets in these regions are becoming richer as income levels rise, and people are consuming more milk, meat and processed foods. From 2004 to 2008, milk consumption in India grew from 68.9 litres to 75.6 litres per person. Local retailers, like Hero Supermarket in Indonesia and

Reliance Retail in India, have been rapidly expanding to accommodate richer diets.

Changing lifestyles in Asia are, for example, making household and personal-hygiene products more popular. In 2003, Unilever Indonesia executed a local campaign by supplying 12 000 wholesalers with products to distribute to 800 000 market vendors. They supported their campaign with advertising aimed at increasing the use of their products, like Pepsodent, by encouraging them to brush twice a day instead of once.

Expanding into countries with fast-growing consumer markets provides manufacturers with the chance to exploit their expertise in building mindspace (even among those currently unable to buy) in a way that has been virtually exhausted in more developed countries. Hindustan Unilever are one of the best examples of manufacturers building a consumer franchise in a less-developed market.

Hindustan Unilever Limited (HUL) are India's largest FMCG company. Their brands are familiar with two out of three Indians across more than 20 distinct categories in home and personal care products and foods and beverages. The company's turnover from January 2008 to March 2009 was $4 billion, slightly less than 10% of Unilever's global revenue.

HUL's heritage dates back to 1888, when the first Unilever product, Sunlight soap, was introduced in India and local manufacturing began in 1931. HUL's brands – like Lifebuoy, Lux, Surf Excel, Rin, Wheel, Fair & Lovely, Sunsilk, Clinic Plus, Closeup, Pepsodent, Lakmé, Brooke Bond, Kissan and Knorr – are now manufactured in over 35 factories and involve over 2000 suppliers and associates. Their distribution network covers 6.3 million retail outlets, including direct reach to over 1 million, so it is clear that any retailer eyeing the Indian market needs to keep in HUL's good books.

Emerging markets also have very strong local manufacturers with powerful local brands, such as Britannia, India's largest manufacturer of branded biscuits, who international retailers will have had no experience of dealing with and who already have a very extensive retail presence. This places some major challenges on retailers hoping to enter markets such as India, where they have to quickly build new relationships and learn new rules of operating.

In China, the household care product sector is dominated by local brands: Diao (manufactured by Zhejiang Nice Daily Use Chemical Co. Ltd) is the market leader with a 14% share; Keon (Shanxi Nafine Chemical Co. Ltd) comes second with 7%; and Liby (Guangzhou Liby Co. Ltd) just behind with 6.6%. The same situation applies in packaged foods, where all top producers, such as Inner Mongolia Yilli Industrial Group, are local.

It is a mistake for global manufacturers to think that their local rivals in emerging markets are easy pickings. Some are now breaking into the world's top 250 companies, including Mexico's Grupo Bimbo (bakery products) and Taiwan's Uni-President Enterprises (the largest Asian food conglomerate producing dairies, food snacks and beverages). These companies tend to be closely related to the local agricultural and food-processing industries, but in the last few years have been diversifying to a more branded portfolio. Perhaps the best example is the merger of the two largest Brazilian food manufacturers – Sadia and Perdigão – in May 2009. The new company, BRF Brazil Foods, has estimated sales of $13 billion and became the largest global food producer headquartered in the emerging markets; they export 45% of their production, including poultry, meat products and frozen foods (pizzas, lasagnes and chicken nuggets). They are also the largest poultry producer in the world, and have a strong position in Western Europe, Russia and other developing countries as well as being in an even stronger position in their home market, where total retail sales grew by an impressive 10.9% in 2010.

The emerging market phenomenon

The biggest change to the global FMCG landscape has been the shift in growth away from the developed markets responsible for the

Table 11.2 Real GDP growth 2001–2012 (%)

Countries	2001	2002	2003	2004	2005	2006	2007	2008	2009	2010	2011	2012F
Advanced economies	1.4	1.7	1.9	3.2	2.5	3.0	2.7	0.6	−3.4	3.2	1.6	1.2
Emerging markets	3.8	4.8	6.2	7.5	7.1	7.9	8.3	6.0	1.7	7.3	6.2	5.4

Source: IMF World Economic Outlook (WEO), January 2012.

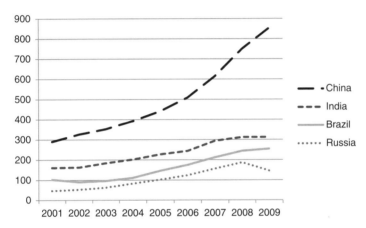

Figure 11.1 Grocery retail trade turnover ($ billion).
Source: National statistics; Planet Retail; authors' calculations.

fortunes of manufacturers and retailers during the last century. The trends are so compelling that no one can ignore them. From 2001 to 2008, the world's emerging economies were growing at an average rate of 6.5% (in real GDP terms), while the advanced economies (including those of the United States, Western Europe and Japan) only grew at 2.1% (Table 11.2).

The size and growth rates of grocery sales in the BRICs nations (Brazil, Russia, India, China) makes the need for major manufacturing and retail companies to join the game compelling (Figure 11.1).

Even after a prolonged period of growth, the emerging markets are far from the saturation and concentration levels of the West. Sales of food in Asia are expected to increase by 70% from $2.7 trillion in 2010 to $4.6 trillion in 2014 while barely growing at all in the West. The emerging markets are populated by passionate consumers whose incomes are growing fast, although from a very low base. In India, the average income per person has increased rapidly from $423 per year in 2002 to $1210 per year in 2011, averaging an annual rate of 14.5%. However, 75.6% of the population still live on less than $2 per day. The average income per capita in China is significantly higher – $7600 in 2011 – but 33.5 million still live on or below the poverty line. In Brazil, the average income per capita is $9390 and in Russia it's $9910.

The needs and requirements of people in emerging countries are expanding quickly. These consumers are not heavily burdened by mortgages, utility bills, huge taxes, insurance and the costs of other amenities of the more developed world, thus a greater percentage of their money finds its way to retailers. At the same time, the rapid development of these economies creates problems for prospective market entrants, including poor infrastructure, logistics and transportation inefficiencies.

Many assume India and China to be seamless and homogenous markets, whereas both consist of multi-local markets in both urban and rural communities. Chinese consumption culture differs markedly not just between urban and rural but also regionally. Carrefour China have established 10 regional procurement centres to better understand and meet local shopper preferences. In China, 240 million people (18% of the population) live in million-plus cities, and 140 million (12%) do in India; it is these cities where the expansion of new retail formats (hypermarkets and supermarkets) has almost exclusively taken place. But despite the rapid development of modern retail formats, they still only account for 10% of a total Chinese retail trade that had reached $2.45 trillion in 2010, making it the second-largest market in the world behind the United States.

Strategies for manufacturers entering emerging markets

Expanding to the emerging markets is an expensive, time-consuming and sophisticated process for any company. A common entry and development strategy for a company (a famous or second-tier global FMCG brand) is as follows:

- **Importing:** A local importer and distributor begin selling the company's products in the market, either after being appointed or sometimes even on their own initiative. The sales volumes can be surprisingly high (even without any marketing support) and the company usually supports the importer with a representative office and spends money on advertising and promotions. The successful distributor gets a special status (exclusivity, franchise etc.) but the manufacturer may also look around to find better partners. In some cases (e.g. if the market is not a priority), this stage may be the only step taken: the company continues importing until its distributor decides to switch to another brand.
- **Full-scale representation:** In legal terms, this means having a commercial vehicle under the jurisdiction of the country it operates in. The company hires a team, usually headed by an expatriate, and continues advertising locally but key decisions are still taken by the head office overseas. The most important element at this stage is the development of effective distribution and sales. The company may focus on major cities, such as Moscow, Mumbai and Shanghai; however, if they are not present in the regional cities, they will become a niche brand. Most leading brands operating in emerging markets work with wholesale distributors to extend beyond the major cities.
- **Step changes:** To increase market share and achieve the benefits of local scale, a foreign company may consider mergers and acquisitions, which is now the main growth strategy of international

retailers in China. The logic is simple: global companies, both manufacturers and retailers, have access to cheap finance from international stock and debt markets that they can use to add strong local brands to their portfolios, while enhancing their local capabilities. For example, in 2010 in India, Reckitt Benckiser acquired Paras Pharmaceuticals Ltd, an over-the-counter health and personal care manufacturer, for $460 million. One of the largest transactions in the emerging markets was in March 2008 by PepsiCo, who paid $1.4 billion for a 76% stake in the leader of the Russian juice market, Lebedyansky. The converse is also happening: Indian companies are buying abroad. Dabur, one of India's largest FMCG manufacturers, made their first overseas acquisition in 2010 as part of their North African and Middle East expansion strategy; they purchased Turkish personal care manufacturer Hobi Kozmetik Group for $69 million. However, the acquired companies often perform poorly after the merger as the integration takes more time and effort than expected. The companies will have different culture and management practices from those of the acquirer, and can be too dependent on charismatic leaders and majority shareholders, who are often eliminated after the merger.

Retailers in emerging markets

In the emerging markets, major international retailers compete with similar competitors as well as traditional retailers and street vendors, who retain a very significant presence in most developing economies. But the retail revolution in the BRICs and other emerging markets is different from the one that took place in Europe and America during the twentieth century. First, it's faster: the Russian and Chinese retail landscapes transformed dramatically within 10 years of opening. Second, the market conditions of today's developing economies are not the same as those of developed markets 40 or 50 years ago: consumers, suppliers, media, investment climate and institutional frameworks have evolved, some beyond recognition.

However, the share of organised retail in emerging markets remains relatively low. In the BRIC nations, Russia has the highest penetration of self-service formats, accounting for 36% of total grocery retail turnover, with discounters being the fastest-growing format, while Brazil is second, with 28%. In China, the share of hypermarkets, supermarkets and modern stores is even lower. India is the least developed retail market, with the penetration of chains accounting for a 6% share in 2008; this is not surprising, as the country's regulators have been restraining foreign investments in domestic retail. However, in 2011, an Indian Government committee did recommend that they should allow foreign companies to own up to 51% of local retail chains, provided the investment was above $100 million.

Another good indicator of retail concentration is the total share controlled by modern retailers, and within that by the five leading retailers, both of which remain low by Western standards (Table 11.3).

However, the situation differs enormously between urban and rural communities. In China's top 15 cities, the share of modern grocery retail approached 50% in 2007, split evenly between hypermarkets and supermarkets. As of mid-2007, hypermarkets had made their biggest impact in Shanghai, and controlled more than 45% of grocery retail sales. China has twice as many hypermarkets as the other BRIC countries combined, mainly because Wal-Mart, Tesco,

Table 11.3 Retail concentration in the BRICs

Country	Share of modern retail chains	Share of top-five retailers
Brazil	28%	11%
Russia	36%	13%
China	20%	4%
India	6%	1%

Source: Authors' estimates based on data from Planet Retail and AT Kearney.

Table 11.4 Major retailers' operations in key emerging markets

	Wal-Mart	Carrefour	Tesco	Metro Group
China	• Entered: 1996 • Hypermarkets and joint ventures with a local player	• Entered: 1995 • Hypermarkets and joint ventures with majority stakes	• Entered: 2004 • 70 stores, 0.1% share (2008) • Hypermarkets, 90% are joint ventures	• Entered: 1999 • $2.1bn in sales • 38 stores, 0.2% share (2008)
India	• Entered: 2009 • 50/50 joint venture	• None	• Plan to set up a wholesale, cash and carry business	• Entered: 2003 • $186m in sales • 5 stores, 0.1% share (2008) • Own stores
Russia	• Not yet • Several attempts to buy a local retailer	• Entered: 2009 but closed down operations in 2010	• None	• Entered: 2001 • $6.5bn in sales • 74 stores, 4.6% share (2008) • Own stores
Brazil	• Entered: 1995 • $9.3bn in sales • 344 stores, 6.1% share (2008) • Own stores and 2 acquisitions	• Entered: 1975 • $12.2bn in sales • 536 stores • Own stores and acquisitions	• None	• None
Turkey	• None	• Entered: 1993 • $2.6bn in sales • 760 stores, 3.3% share (2008) • Own stores, acquisitions and joint ventures	• Entered: 2003 • $1.2bn in sales • 96 stores, 1.6% share (2008) • Acquisition	• Entered: 1990 • $2.2bn in sales • 32 stores, 2.8% share (2008) • Own stores
Czech Republic	• None	• Entered: 1998 • Exited: 2005 • Sold hypermarkets to Tesco	• Entered: 1996 • $2.7bn in sales • 113 stores, 8.6% share (2008) • Own stores and acquisitions	• Entered: 1996 • $2.4 billion in sales • 13 stores, 2.5% share (2008) • Own stores

Table 11.5 Top-five emerging markets operations as percentage of total sales (2010)

Company	Percentage
Metro Group	20
Auchan	19
Carrefour	17
Tesco	15
Schwartz	13
Rewe	11
Wal-Mart	9

Source: Authors' calculations.

Auchan and Carrefour have been focusing on this format in the Chinese market.

According to our analysis and calculations, the combined sales of modern retail formats in the BRIC countries exceeded US$300 billion in 2008. By 2015, this figure may reach US$800 billion.

If we look at a snapshot of the major retailers' operations in the key emerging markets, it is clear that all are very active, although not in the same markets (Table 11.4).

No player has established a dominant position across all emerging markets, but achieving one is the major focus for all of them (Table 11.5).

The most successful emerging market retailer

Metro Group are the third-largest global retail and wholesale corporation, and one of the most successful in emerging markets – they have the highest percentage of sales from emerging markets in comparison to their global competitors, including Wal-Mart, Tesco and Carrefour. Metro Group's biggest success has been Russia, where they built an extensive network of stores in five years, at one point chartering a plane to fly management from site to site so quickly were they opening new stores. They are now a market leader, managing over 100 stores and employing nearly 25 000 people; they are one of the main foreign employers in Russia.

Metro Group opened their first wholesale outlet in Russia in 2001, Metro Cash & Carry. At this time, the market was fragmented, both retailers and manufacturers sourced products from open markets, which led to high prices and few quality controls; the seller's market also meant suppliers determined what was offered and shoppers were happy with whatever they could find. Metro Group entered the chaos and achieved high growth rates owing to their being the first to bring proper disciplines and rigorous controls into the sector. They now dominate the market with 58 Metro Cash & Carry stores.

In 2005, Metro Group introduced their first retail outlet in Russia, Real Hypermarkets, which were supermarkets fitted with self-service checkouts. Real Hypermarkets became famous in Russia because of self-service checkouts, and 76% of shoppers now use them. Real Hypermarkets also succeeded because their stores had convenient locations, large trading areas, well-defined ranges and a wide variety of goods at affordable prices. Today, there are 16 Real Hypermarkets in Moscow, St Petersburg, Lipetsk, Volgograd, Kazan, Yaroslavl and Togliatti.

Metro Group also have a lean cost structure (common service companies that provide unified services, including procurement, logistics and information technology, which help create synergies and reduce costs). A private label range has recently been launched. However, although it accounts for around 15% of sales, it is yet to play a major role in increasing store loyalty and margins.

Having said that, in retailing, nothing is forever. Metro Group face some significant challenges in maintaining their growth record in Russia. Average living standards have stopped growing and are in decline in many cities. Metro Group also face a constant battle to hold onto their qualified personnel. But as the emerging markets quickly mature, the retail battlefield will shift from speed to market towards one more familiar to the Western retail giants: land.

Property acquisition in emerging markets[1,2,3,4,5,6,7]

Property portfolios are now becoming a critical component of major retailers' expansion strategies. The global recession has made prime real estate locations increasingly available and affordable in many developing markets. Property investment for retail has climbed to $6.9 billion, according to CB Richard Ellis – the main focus being in Poland, the Czech Republic and Russia.

Wal-Mart and IKEA Group have been the first to abandon their strategy of leasing in emerging markets, owing to increasing rents. 'It's becoming more and more difficult to get extraordinary leasing terms because Chinese landlords are becoming more sophisticated,' said Michael Klibaner, head of China research at Jones Lang LaSalle Inc. in Shanghai. Wal-Mart and IKEA Group have become the top foreign retailers to buy land: in 2010, Wal-Mart bought real estate in Dalian for the first time, and Ikea Group invested $1.2 billion to build 5.5 million ft^2 of retail space; in March 2011, Tesco also formed a $280 million joint venture to secure land in China to develop three malls.

Magnit, the largest Russian food retailer, is turning inexpensive land into profits. When Russia was hit hard by the financial and economic crises in 2009, they took advantage of low rental and property values and opened over 600 stores.

Foreign investment in Indonesia and other Asian countries has led to a rapid increase in property prices. Many believe the increase is unsustainable: if the bubble bursts, it could create stress in Asian financial markets and hurt retailers pursuing development strategies in Indonesia.

The success of foreign retailers in Vietnam will also depend on real-estate prices, which are being affected by manufacturers, including even some from China, relocating production facilities there, with both having to contend with issues such as protection of private property rights. It may be difficult for retailers to secure property in other emerging markets. This has already proved to be the case with India, because of government restrictions on foreign investment.

Despite the issues, property acquisition in emerging markets is on the rise and will become a key determinant of eventual success. Location always has been a critical success factor for retailers.

Key learnings

- **Manufacturers are more international** than are retailers, which creates two possible benefits for them:
  - Greater negotiating leverage at the corporate level.
  - Gain the upper hand in emerging markets, where, in general, the international manufacturer is strong and the international retailer is weak.
- For retailers to succeed in international markets, they need **local scale, local product mix and a local differential advantage.**
- Manufacturers in emerging markets are **breaking onto the global stage faster** than are retailers from those markets. However, these manufacturers are entering the strong markets of international retailers and will not have the negotiating leverage they are accustomed to.
- For aspiring top-20 global manufacturers and retailers, **entering emerging markets is no longer an 'if' but a 'when and how'.**
- Retail **consolidation in emerging markets has barely begun,** but is proceeding quickly. Manufacturers need to decide who they are going to make special efforts to support.
- Retailers are also investing in property in emerging markets because of increasing rent prices and more amenable government policies; Wal-Mart and IKEA Group are leading the way, followed by Tesco and Carrefour.

(See Appendix 2 for details on the BRIC markets.)

While location always has been a critical success factor in retailing, the Internet is freeing innovative retailers from their earthly shackles. And it is to the infinitely large shopping mall of the Internet we now turn.

Notes

1. http://www.deloitte.com/assets/Dcom-Greece/Local%20Assets/ Documents/Attachments/gfsi/hiddenheroes 2010.pdf. Accessed 21 November 2011.
2. http://www.pie-mag.com/articles/1337/cee-property-investment-nearly doubles-to-euro-4-4bn-cbre/. Accessed 25 November 2011.
3. http://investment-in-turkey.com/page2.html. Accessed 22 November 2011.
4. http://www.bloomberg.com/news/2011-07-04/wal-mart-ikea-lead-retailers-push-in-china-land-buying-as-rentals-surge.html. Accessed 30 November 2011.
5. http://www.atkearney.com/index.php/News-media/downturn-has-increased-emerging-market-opportunities-for-global-retailers-says-at-kearney-study.html. Accessed 25 November 2011.
6. http://www.bloomberg.com/news/2011-07-04/wal-mart-ikea-lead-retailers-push-in-china-land-buying-as-rentals-surge.html. Accessed 22 November 2011.
7. http://www.propertywire.com/news/related-stories/shops-bring-in-investors-in-emerging-property-markets-20080419852.html. Accessed 25 November 2011.

Chapter 12

IT IS STILL easy for manufacturers to gloss over the impact on their businesses of online grocery sales as volumes are relatively small and successful retailer online business models few and far between. We estimate that online accounts for only 3% of US grocery sales and for every Tesco.com (grocery) and Tesco Direct (non-grocery) success (Tesco's total online sales increased by 15% in 2011[1]), there is a Webvan failure.

However, now that successful footholds have been gained in online grocery businesses, FMCG manufacturers and retailers need to plan for a world that will soon see a substantial proportion of their sales being generated and fulfilled online. In 2008, the Centre for Retail Research was predicting that, by 2015, approximately 13% of grocery sales would be online. We see this as still being realistic and predict 20% by 2020. The growth of online grocery is potentially the biggest seismic shift in the FMCG industry since the development of the supermarket.

Development of online sales

E-commerce became possible from 1991 when the Internet was opened to the public, but in reality 1994 saw the starting point, when Netscape launched the first commercial browser and Pizza Hut offered online

Definitions

E-commerce: all financial transactions online, i.e. all retail, payment, delivery, marketing, development, advice and services

E-retailing: (e-tailer, online shop) all selling of goods, anywhere a consumer buys goods or services direct, software, media, clothes, electronics, books, etc.

E-grocery: the selling of FMCG, food and non-food (detergents, cleaning materials, fresh food, drinks, etc.)

ordering from their Web page. Amazon commenced operations on 16 July 1995, followed shortly after by eBay.

Eighteen years after the first online order, JPMorgan have estimated worldwide 2012 e-commerce sales of $820 trillion. While that still only represents approximately 6% of total world retail sales, what is much more important is the continued acclimatisation of the shopper to buying online: according to Nielsen Global Online, 85% of the world's online population has made at least one purchase in 2011, a 40% increase over the previous two years. Amongst online users, online shopper penetration is exceptionally high, with South Korea at 99%; the United Kingdom, 97%; Germany, 97%; and Japan, 97%. There are currently (2012) an estimated 875 million online shoppers.

Location has always been a crucial component of retailing, so online is now a location no retailer can afford to be absent from for both its absolute size and its attractive growth rate. JPMorgan suggest that e-commerce is increasing at 19.4% a year compound and will reach sales of almost $1 trillion by 2013 (Table 12.1)

Across the world's leading 100 retailers, in 2010 online sales accounted for an average of 6.6% of their total sales.[2] Traditional retailers are seeing strong increases in their online sales, while their

Table 12.1 E-commerce is increasing around the world

Region	2010 ($ B)	Est 2013 ($ B)	Compound Annual Growth Rate (%)
USA	165.8	235.3	12.4
Europe	195.2	283.0	13.2
Asia	155.7	323.1	27.5
Rest of World	55.8	121.7	29.7
Global	572.5	963.0	19.4

Source: JP Morgan.

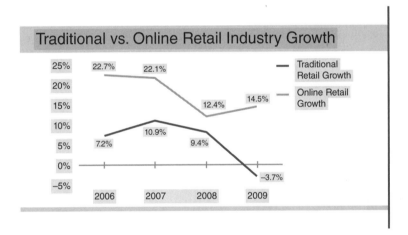

Figure 12.1 Traditional vs. online retail industry growth.
Source: EIU, Datamonitor, IMAP.

traditional store-based business has been hit hard by the combination of recession and the emergence of new online competitors (Figure 12.1).

Tesco attributed some of their underlying sales' decline of 2.3% in the last six weeks of 2011 to the speed by which clothing and electrical sales are shifting online. As grocery chains have moved into categories such as these only recently, it is less of a wrench for their shoppers to consider buying from someone else online, as the shopping habit is not yet entrenched.

Features and benefits of shopping online

In previous chapters, we have examined in detail the key elements that each retailer must balance to achieve success: service, value, convenience and price perception. So it is worthwhile comparing these to the factors online shoppers highlight as being the benefits of buying online. The most common reason for shopping online is because it saves time: 73% of shoppers choose this as a benefit, according to Marketingcharts.com (Figure 12.2). Second is the variety of choice (67%), followed by the ease of making price comparisons (59%), avoidance of crowds (58%), lower prices (55%) and then the money saved on petrol or transport (40%).[3] So convenience and value are the main drivers of consumer preference, which puts online shopping well within the realm of a bricks-and-mortar retailer's existing mindset.

Consumers like that they can easily search through large databases of products and services; they can see the actual price; they can build an order over several days; and, with the click of a mouse, they can

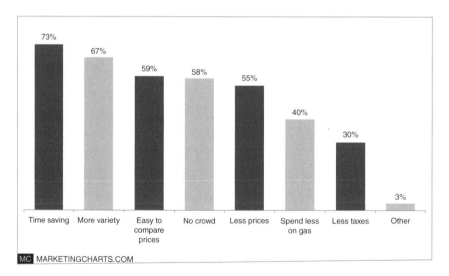

Figure 12.2 Reasons for online shopping preferences.
Source: Marketingcharts.com.

check the price and select the best-value option. Transparent pricing is a major advance for the shopper and something of a headache for the retailer, but it is fast becoming the norm. The Centre for Retail Research expect that by 2015 over 70% of all purchases will involve transparent pricing in some form, and this prediction was made before phone scanning of goods in store to compare price was possible.

But the scale of the timesaving benefit is substantial. Smartlife[4] estimate that the average American household spends 289 hours each year on grocery shopping, whereas the same shopping done online with home delivery would take only 13 hours. This scale of benefit makes the jostling between traditional retailers over who provides marginally faster checkouts pale into insignificance.

Grocery, because it has some significant challenges in developing online sales, has not been a leading factor in the emergence of e-retailing. Grocers see the attraction of being multi-channel retailers because it is a natural development as a growth strategy following hot on the heels of being multi-format retailers, where hypermarket, supermarket, convenience, forecourt and discount formats sit happily under the same banner. By 'multi-channel', they mean they will grow via online and mobile, with 'click and collect' or van delivery.

There are some significant barriers to growing online grocery sales. Not least is the desire of many shoppers to see for themselves the freshness of produce. In addition, given that many shopping occasions, both in-store and online, are currently on impulse, online purchases do not give the shopper the immediate gratification of having the product in their hands and restrict the ability of the retailer to increase basket size with impulse buys.

Intangible products such as airline tickets and hotel bookings, where there is no product to deliver, have consequently been at the forefront of the development of e-commerce and are involved in around a third of online purchases.

But, worryingly for the bigger grocers, categories that they see as being well within their domain are now well established online. Books are the leading online category, accounting for 44% of all purchases; clothing, including accessories and shoes, 36%; electronic items, 27%; cosmetics and nutrition, 22%; computer hardware, 19%; videos, DVDs and games, 18%.

Given the sensitivity of retailers' profits to small changes in top-line sales we discussed in Chapter 2, and that these categories have been significant drivers of growth in recent years for traditional retailers, they cannot sit back and see themselves losing sales by not being online. Add to that the fact that groceries are now the tenth-largest online category, at 18%, then the case for grocery retailers going online becomes mandatory, but the business model employed is absolutely critical. However, the online world increases the exposure of grocers to a rapidly developing breed of competitor, the specialist retailer. Diapers.com, Zappos and Pets.com have, to varying degrees, shown that the specialist can take sales and margin from the generalist. So it is not unreasonable to suppose that other high-value areas will come under attack: wine, spirits, perfumes, fresh, health foods, cheese, fish, personal care, coffee are all ultimately vulnerable areas for grocers to defend.

Learning from parallel categories and business models

Any aspiring online retailer would be foolish not to draw lessons from the undisputed market leader: Amazon. In its first week, Amazon grossed $12 500 and within five years had reached $2.8 billion, rising to a staggering £34.2 billion and a market capitalisation of $90 billion by the end of 2010. Amazon's growth continues to outstrip the average of the e-commerce market, having recorded a 39.5% increase in 2010 over 2009. In 2010, Amazon had 137 million customers who made 900 million purchase occasions from 320 billion monthly visits to their Web pages. So what were the big ideas that drove Amazon forward?

- **Inventory:** Digital enables limitless inventory (against the largest store in the world having over 100 000 SKUs).
- **Customer Service:** With digital, it's possible to customise service at the individual level.
- **Price:** The lowest price is always the most powerful retail proposition and is not incompatible in the online world with making a profit.

Traditional retailing, as we explored earlier, has location as a major feature and limitation of its competitive model. Innovation is difficult when so many stores have to be refitted. Range and inventory are also problematic in that a 30 000+ SKU store has a very long tail of a slow turnover of items: 55% of all products in a typical hypermarket achieve either one or zero unit sales in any given week. Also, while the combination of sales scanning and loyalty cards has been an information boon, such information is not always actionable in real time.

Conversely, Amazon have superbly exploited the major benefits of online retailing. Location is irrelevant, making the whole world a potential market together with the ability to test and experiment at minimal cost; negligible marginal costs enable limitless category possibilities and availability (especially when fulfilment of the long tail is outsourced), and real-time measurement coupled with perfect individual customer data enables customisation of the offer and optimisation of each individual sales visit. At Amazon, it's not just that the customer is king: they are the emperors! Amazon are able to reconfigure their virtual store based on daily or even hourly sales trends and individual customers' past buying behaviour. No customer need see the same offer as another or as the last time they visited. Amazon have always been motivated by a clear understanding of the key drivers for most buying decisions – low prices, large selection, good service and convenience – but have taken them to levels undreamt of by bricks-and-mortar retailers.

Amazon appreciated early on the need for world-class service levels. Two of their early appointments came from Wal-Mart: Richard Dalzell as CIO and Jimmy Wright as chief logistics officer. What Richard and

Jimmy brought was a deep and extensive knowledge required for a computerised supply chain and an integrated distribution and supply capacity. At the beginning in 1995, Amazon had 40 m² of garage space; by 1997, 30 000 m² in two centres; and by 2010, 2.6 million m² across 50 fulfilment centres. In 1997, there were three categories: books, music, and video, with one or two new categories added each year from 2000, until now, where Amazon represent almost a third of all US e-commerce sales, at prices cheaper than anyone else: on average 15% cheaper than Wal-Mart and 30–35% cheaper than specialist retailers.

Amazon essentially use the same formula for each market segment: the largest possible selection, the most convenient, customised and user-friendly search and low prices. Amazon are solution-neutral and will build, buy or partner as best fits with the opportunity. In May 2011, Amazon launched MYHABIT (offering free shipping for returns on selected items); bought Zappos.com, Quidsi, Diapers.com and Soap.com, and partnered with Toys "Я" Us. More customers and more channels equate to more bargaining power and then lower prices. Jeff Bezos once said that there are two kinds of company:

> those that work to try to charge more and those that work to charge less. We will be the second.[5]

Customer care is the big focus:

> Our competitors are never going to send us money . . . We start with the customer and work backwards, we build a great experience. We are looking for simple solutions.[6]

Amazon's customer service was ranked number 1 in 2009 and 2011 by *Business Week*, a key contributor to the fact that those customers spend an average of $220 each time they bought.[7] All the staff spend at least two days a year on the service desk, helping customers. Amazon were first with many of the now accepted best practices: customer reviews, looking inside the product, one-click ordering and free shipping (Figure 12.3).

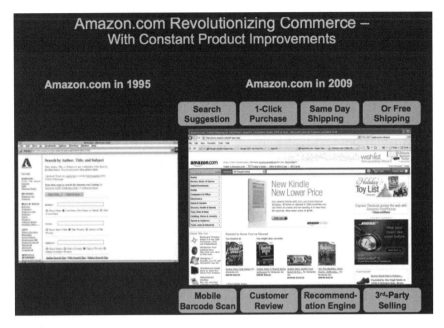

Figure 12.3 A comparison of Amazon.com in 1995 and 2009.
Source: Amazon.com.

Amazon's approach to going international has been both careful and sensible, not overreaching too early like many of the dot.com era's more famous crash-and-burn cases, such as Boo.com. Amazon have now launched in seven countries in addition to the United States: the United Kingdom, in 1998; Germany, 1998; France, 2000; Japan, 2000; Canada, 2002; China, 2004; and Italy, 2010. Unlike Wal-Mart, who had major problems in both Germany and South Korea, Amazon's international growth so far has been a success story.

Logistics is the critical unseen component behind their low prices. Their system chooses the cheapest source for each order in real time; fast-moving items are stored in all 50 fulfilment centres, hard-to-find are kept at one or two; and, where applicable, suppliers are asked to ship the product. This results in a very efficient system, on average a product only stays 33 days in an Amazon warehouse, against 70 days at Best Buy.[8] Savings such as these are passed on in lower prices, meaning that Amazon's operating margin is in line with traditional retailers, 4% in 2010 (versus 28% for Apple and 35% for Google).

Can't realise any profit

Amazon are a data-driven business. Starting in 2001, software was installed to measure the cost of each product shipped. As a result, Amazon were able to identify the losers, i.e. the rubbish.

In 2000, Bezos discovered it took 15 minutes to pack a best-selling folding chair, which wiped out the profit. He then re-negotiated with the manufacturer, who agreed to supply pre-packed. This is the advantage of instant data.

Amazon currently have a global audience comprising 20% of the world's Internet population and aim to be the only place where you discover and buy goods, which makes them a direct threat to any and all established retailers.

Other, more recent online successes have mostly drawn from Amazon's development and, in some cases, have been swallowed up by them, **Zappos.com** being a case in point. Launched in 1999, Zappos, an online shoe and clothing retailer, have grown to be the world's largest online shoe store. By 2001, Zappos had reached $8.6 million sales with minimal advertising costs as the company grew mostly by word of mouth. By 2003, Zappos had grown to $70 million and abandoned drop shipping, which accounted for 25% of their revenue base. This was a very important decision. 'Supplying superior customer service,' founder Hsieh said, 'I wanted us to have a whole company built around [customer service] and we couldn't control the customer experience when a quarter of the inventory was out of our control.' Zappos doubled their annual revenues each year, hitting $840 million in gross sales by 2007. They expanded their inventory to include handbags, eyewear, watches and kids' merchandise.

Zappos have 10 core values that define their culture, brand and business strategies. They are:

- Deliver WOW through Service
- Embrace and Drive Change
- Create Fun and a Little Weirdness
- Be Adventurous, Creative and Open-minded
- Pursue Growth and Learning
- Build Open and Honest Relationships with Communication
- Build a Positive Team and Family Spirit
- Do More with Less
- Be Passionate and Determined
- Be Humble.

However, following Zappos' reporting to their 24 million customers in mid-January 2012 that their computer system had been hacked,[9] they may soon develop an eleventh value . . . of protecting their customers' information. This, of course, is one of the main Achilles' heels in the relationship between an online supplier and its customers.

Rakuten are one of the top three e-commerce websites and one of the top 10 Internet companies in the world. They started in Japan in 1997 as an online retail marketplace, and in 2010 earned $4.2 billion by selling 85 million products from 36000 merchants. Rakuten are aggressively expanding via international acquisitions, including France's e-commerce site **PriceMinister** for $315 million, the United States' **Buy.com** for $250 million, Russia's online retailer **Ozon.ru** and Brazil's e-commerce firm **Ikeda**. The result of these acquisitions is that Rakuten now operate in every BRIC market.

Rakuten's biggest advantage over Amazon is that they are a B2B2C company, so they don't operate a warehouse. They also offer a wider range of goods, everything from four-ton trucks to local produce. They've been successful because of their ability to establish online storefronts for small businesses, as well as their aggressive pricing strategy, their focus on positive cash flow and their goal to be a global company. For example, they are the first Internet company based in Japan to make English their official language. Rakuten continued their global expansion, notably buying ebook company Kobo for $315 million in November 2011.

Elsewhere, while **eBay** may not be a direct competitor to the large grocery chains, they provide an alternative online sales channel analogous to the independent stores on the High Street in that the website provides a route to market for the small-scale online retailer of speciality products such as wine and jams.

Traditional retailers going online

There are an increasing number of bricks-and-mortar retailers making significant inroads online. Staples are the world's largest office products company providing products, services and expertise in the categories of office supplies, technology, furniture, copy and print (i.e. everything from paperclips to flip charts). Founded in 1986, they launched their Internet business in 1998. In 2010, Staples had annual sales of $25 billion, including $10.2 billion online, which ranked them second behind Amazon in the world in e-commerce sales. Their average online sale was $430, with an impressive 9.9% of all visitors buying. Staples are the leader amongst category-specific e-retailers, with 45 000 SKUs available, and a big commitment to making the process easy and helping the customer, both on and offline. In November 2010, they launched their twenty-first e-commerce site in Australia. Their main competitor, Office Depot, generated $4.1 billion of their total 2010 $11.6 billion sales online, with 19 million monthly visitors and a conversion rate of 9.6% spending $190. Sears, with 17 million SKUs available online, generated $3.1 billion sales in 2010 with 35 million monthly visitors, of whom 5% converted and spent an average of $150 a visit; this performance was in complete contrast to their failing and flailing traditional retail business.

However, when we look at the grocery sector specifically, one retailer stands out for their success in profitably building an online business, and that is Tesco.com, which is currently the clear leader globally in e-grocery. Starting in 1996 with investment in a few Dell servers, their internal analysis had shown that their existing retail infrastructure could cope with the anticipated volume. So there was no need for Tesco to go the route of building a dedicated warehousing and order-fulfilment infrastructure, which had been necessary for start-up online e-grocery businesses such as Webvan. In addition, Tesco made a strategic decision to charge £5 per delivery, as they believed the initial customers would be mainly working wives (from the Clubcard data they understood that these customers shopped in excess of 25 times a year with an average basket of £71), and hypothesised they would be prepared to pay the £5 for the convenience.

The service did more than sell groceries; books, electrical appliances, video and other products were also available. By 2000, the service was profitable in its own right and, by 2007, turnover was well through the first $1 billion. Today, their focus is absolutely on being a multi-channel business, as explained by Tesco's CEO, Phil Clarke, in their 2011 Company Report:

> Customers expect to be able to shop where and when they want – as shopping habits have changed over the years, we've changed too. As we've grown from a UK supermarket chain towards becoming an international multi-channel retailer we've continued to innovate every step of the way . . . We were viewed as pioneers when we first launched an online grocery business 11 years ago. It's now the largest, most profitable business of its kind in the world . . . Using their smartphones, our customers can now scan the barcode of grocery items, order online and have their shopping delivered to their home . . . As the combination of stores and online becomes compelling for customers, we aim to become a multi-channel retailer wherever we trade.

Tesco are currently the third-largest online retailer in Europe with an estimated $4.4 billion of online sales in 2010, behind only Amazon with $13.3 billion and Otto Group's $5.34 billion.

Less successful has been Walmart.com, which have struggled to develop an online business commensurate with their gargantuan size as a traditional retailer. In 2010, sales were $4.1 billion, with 97.5 million visitors a month – only a 2.41% conversion – spending an average of $140. In total, there are 1 million SKUs available, which may explain the average length of visit of 10 minutes 13 seconds. In August 2011, Wal-Mart carried out an extensive reorganisation of their management: e-commerce managers now report to executives in charge of the traditional stores in each country. Wal-Mart also announced they were ending their activities in the music area, having failed to make any significant inroads into the dominance of iTunes. However, in China, Wal-Mart have purchased Yihaodian.com, a significant online retailer, with currently 100 000 SKUs and a turnover of $464 million. It is anticipated that both these figures will grow significantly.

Industry observers had initially expected Wal-Mart to achieve the same kind of dominance in the virtual arena as they enjoy in traditional retailing, but the requirements for success online are very different. Not only are Wal-Mart dwarfed by Amazon – a situation they are completely unfamiliar with – but they are also lagging behind in growth rate.

Online-only grocers

Ocado is a UK-based pure online grocer. The UK grocery market, at $235.6 billion, is an attractive market in size but an intensely competitive one. The 3% of UK grocery sales currently online are fought over by not only the mighty Tesco but also Sainsbury's and Asda, who both rank in the top 20 of European e-retailers, all being bigger than Ocado, who are ranked nineteenth in Europe. Ocado have a somewhat limited range of 21500 SKUs, with an average order size of 55 items generating an order value of $198. In 2010, total sales were $859.6 million, a 29% increase on the previous year with 12% of orders coming via iPhone or iPad.

Ocado were set up in 2000 and went public in July 2010. They currently have 262000 active customers. They source a significant percentage of their products from Waitrose. They are developing their own private label range and match Tesco on 7200 products for price, buyers being advised of lower price options before checkout, which again highlights the importance of price in the online environment. Productivity is going to be key to their eventual success or failure. They are targeting 175 deliveries per week from each van (currently 133), with 94.95% of deliveries targeted to be on or before time and 99% correctly fulfilled. Simultaneously, there has been an ongoing drive towards providing greater consumer choice, particularly across a range of online food and non-foodstuffs (catering for issues around well-being, sustainability, provenance as well as greater differentiation across the value-premium spectrum).

Ocado reported their first profit in Q4 2010 and see a future world where, by 2025, 40% of sales are online. To achieve their fair share of that, they believe the following to be crucial:

- **Price:** broad price positioning attracts consumers.
- **Range:** range expansion increases consumer choice.
- **Availability:** real-time product availability increases consumer loyalty.
- **Freshness:** access to fresh product increases consumer confidence
- **Quality:** at least as good as in-store.
- **Ease of use:** convenience and intuitive ordering bring back customers.
- **Time:** freeing up consumers' most precious asset.
- **Reliability:** on time as ordered every time.
- **Information:** product information influences customer decision-making.

The Ocado model is different from most competitors', such as Tesco, who use their existing infrastructure and stores; Ocado have two principal customer-fulfilment centres that feed a number of spokes.

Launched in 1999, **Freshdirect.com** are an online grocery provider known for their convenient home delivery service of fresh food products that delivers to residences and offices in the New York City metropolitan area. Popular for their distribution of organic and kosher, chef-cooked food and locally grown items, their slogan is: 'Get fresher food and easy home delivery!' With an emphasis on higher-end customers with a large-than-average order size, FreshDirect custom-prepare groceries and meals for their customers. With a business model similar to computer maker Dell, FreshDirect deal directly with producers and make food to order, which undercuts their rivals. Orders are dispatched to the kitchen, bakery, deli as well as fresh storage rooms, produce-ripening rooms and production areas within the company's refrigerated facility. All order components are custom-cut, packaged, weighed and priced. In the case of dry goods or frozen foods, items are picked from storage before being placed inside bins that travel along conveyors to the sorting area. There, products in a customer's order are scanned and gathered in corrugated fibreboard boxes. The boxes are labelled, recorded and loaded into refrigerated delivery trucks.

Why are FreshDirect successful? Primarily through having avoided overly ambitious expansion plans, unlike other collapsed start-ups. FreshDirect, with 20% growth in 2010, were only planning an expansion beyond New York for 2011 and 2012. Like most online grocery start-ups, they initially faced problems with quality control and struggled to get orders correct, problems that have been solved by investments in better technology, such as SAP AG software to process thousands of orders placed on their website every night. Jason Ackerman, FreshDirect's founder and CEO, said:

> That's why we've been so slow to roll out across the country because we have been so focused on how to get this model right.

FreshDirect received a $50-million investment in 2011 from UK grocer WM Morrison, kick-starting the online food retailer's planned growth and expansion outside the tri-state area. FreshDirect will host a multi-disciplinary team of top Morrison managers, who will be embedded in FreshDirect at the company's headquarters. They will study FreshDirect's methods for storing, packaging and delivering groceries and take the system back to the United Kingdom for their own use to launch the e-commerce model.

Similar to Freshdirect.com, **Onlinegrocer.ca** became a success by focusing on one city, Ottawa. They were the first supermarket to offer an online grocery shopping and delivery service in Ottawa in 1999, and they have been supported by locals ever since. Online-grocer.ca has won countless awards, notably from the Canadian Federation of Independent Grocers Merit Awards and the National Silver Award, recognising them as the best store in Canada in their category.[10]

There is also a branch of online grocers that have been succeeding by exclusively providing ethnic foods, like **eFoodDepot.com**, which offer hard-to-find ethnic products to customers in the United States. Their success has been due to the investment in their inventory tracking system, which focuses on removing spoiled food from the supply chain. They also emphasise customer satisfaction by keeping certain foods, like halal and kosher foods, separate from other products – they even use a separate facility to store and ship them! Plus, they have a 'Savings Calculator' on their website, which encourages new visitors to shop online by calculating the cost it would take them (including time and petrol) to shop in the store.[11]

Other notable online grocers, like Schwans.com, have succeeded by focusing on niche private label products. Schwan's started in 1952 as a homemade ice cream delivery business in the United States, and now offer more than 350 different products, ranging from ice cream and dessert to meats and finger foods.[12] In 2011, they earned $3.7 billion, making them the largest branded frozen-food company in the United States. One of their founders, Alfred Schwan, was even inducted into the Frozen Food Hall of Fame in 2008 for his remarkable work in the frozen food industry.

The fact that such operations are becoming well established has prompted the likes of Safeway, Ahold and even Wal-Mart, currently testing their Wal-Mart To Go service, to get in on the act, undeterred by Publix and Supervalu having tried and then withdrawn.

It is worth mentioning that e-grocery in this format hardly exists at all in the emerging markets, such as India. This is because, essentially, the same service has long been offered by virtually all grocery stores in that the customer can phone them and the desired products will be delivered to their door by scooter or bicycle, usually within 30 minutes.

E-retailing failures

Webvan was launched in 1999 by Louis Borders, who thought he could revolutionise grocery shopping with automated warehouses. Offering to deliver grocery products to a consumer's home in 1 of 10 American cities within a 30-min window of their choosing, Webvan raised almost $500 million when they went public and then purchased their largest rival, HomeGrocer. But by July 2001, they were in liquidation, having burnt through $679 million of investor money. The business model was poorly conceived and executed, their main problems being:

- A massive investment in warehousing and developing a high-tech product-picking system (the problem is that in traditional shopping your customer does the selection for free).
- A high cost of customer acquisition at $210 per customer, who at best were spending an average of $81 gross and generating under $5 in net profit each per visit.
- Their size translated into a limited buying power, so they were not able to match the prices of major traditional retailers.

- Expensive new trucks, with drivers costing $30 an hour, stuck in traffic.
- No FMCG expertise in their management team.

All succinctly summed up by Bain Consulting president, Miles R. Coo, 'They've got an approach that's profit-proof.'

Webvan are a good illustration of the fact that retailing is in some ways a massive property business, where the requirements are for very significant investment into retail outlets, warehouses and logistics systems. The winners sell high volumes of goods at often very low margins. Tesco.com made a success of essentially the same process because they did not invest in expensive infrastructure; they used their existing supermarkets as warehouses and even existing night-shift shelf-fillers to pick the orders from the store shelves. They did not spend heavily on marketing but approached existing customers through their loyalty card communication channels. However, they did have the advantage of typical retail margins in the United Kingdom being 6 to 8% against 2 to 3% in the United States, but, since they have done more than any other grocer to create such margins, that is fair enough.

Homegrocer.com themselves were bought by Webvan when on the point of collapse. They had started in 1998, went public in 2000, opened eight distribution centres and had achieved sales of $1 million per day by June 2000 but, owing to high investment requirements, continued to bleed money. Their customers loved their 98% accurate delivery record, but to achieve that HomeGrocer staff often had to go to nearby traditional outlets and pay the full retail price for the last few items. Customer acquisition was costing an unsustainable $300 a time. They were always going to run out of money before they turned a profit, and were bought by Webvan on 26 June 2000.

Pets.com were launched in February 1999 and went bust 268 days later, in November 1999. This was another example of an online retail business model that had not been thought through, with $300 million invested mostly in infrastructure and high advertising costs ahead of significant revenues. Almost every sale lost money, not least because the pet category, being very high volume, operates at a 2–4% retail margin, the result being that sending heavy items like cat litters by post simply makes no financial sense. There are now a number of successful online pet businesses, but they all have more appropriate business models.

Current trends: What are consumers looking for?

Mobile is undoubtedly the major opportunity. Applications such as **ShopSavvy** are changing shopping behaviour by greatly simplifying the process of finding what you want to buy at the best possible price. Between 45% and 60% of smartphone users conducted 'due diligence' on store prices and inventory in 2010. Even more important is IE Market Research's prediction that more than $50 billion will be spent on merchandise using a smartphone by 2014.

However, the bricks-and-mortar retail world is fighting back. **Shopkick** bridge the worlds of mobile and physical retail in that you can be paid for walking into a store. In August 2010, shopkick launched the first mobile application that hands consumers rewards and exclusive deals at national retail partners simply for walking into one of thousands of stores and shopping centres. Shopkick created a new location technology that allows the app to verify the user is actually present inside a store (GPS being too inaccurate for that). In the same way advertisers pay Google for click traffic in the online world, they can pay shopkick for foot traffic in the real world. Partners include Best Buy, Target, Toys "Я" Us, Simon Malls (largest US mall operator), Procter & Gamble, Kraft Foods, Unilever, Coca-Cola, Intel, HP, Disney, General Mills, Colgate-Palmolive, Clorox, Revlon and Levi's. Shopkick is the only 100% performance-based marketing platform in the physical retail world, with measurable foot traffic and transactions at stores. The app grew to one million users in its first six months with the second million taking another four months to acquire.

Implications for manufacturers

So what are the implications for manufacturer brands in the move to online shopping? Mostly not good. At the macro level, online shopping is a terrific tool for retailers to enhance the strength of their brand in a way that manufacturers cannot. Even though Coca-Cola has had 5.1 million people 'like' its Facebook page, that is a transitory, relatively unthinking interaction compared to a positive shopping experience on Tesco.com. Some manufacturers do offer the opportunity to buy their products online but that has few benefits for busy shoppers, and is perhaps limited to the gifting arena.

Second, the online grocery store is a very different environment for the big brands. There is no real equivalent of shelfspace online other than the order in which products are shown. The visual power of multiple facings, which mostly exist so the shop doesn't run out of shelf stock during the day, is lost online. The online retailer can also use the online store to push their private label offerings even harder than they can in a real store. Manufacturers' claims as to the power of their brands, their advertising or their promotions to pull shoppers into stores are much less compelling in a virtual store, where the shopper never leaves the comfort of their home or office. For example, Ocado, at checkout, will automatically offer lower prices on all goods selected, which serves to confirm the commitment to helping the customer shop efficiently. One of the main beneficiaries of this service was private label offerings. For this and many other reasons, there can be little doubt that the move to online shopping will further accentuate the shifting of power from the manufacturer to the retailer.

Key learnings

- Worldwide e-commerce is **growing strongly**, nearly 20% annually, while traditional retailing is showing some decline and store closures.
- It is realistic to expect **30% of all worldwide retail sales to be online** in the near future.
- The growth of **mobile apps** will have a massive impact for both on- and off-line retail. Price-comparison apps will be a major driver in changing how we buy. The dominant players of the immediate future will be the online-only or online-traditional retailers who **best integrate their business** with the mobile opportunity.
- E-grocery was **a late-starter, but there are now profitable models** led by Tesco, and market penetration of what is the world's largest retail sector may reach 20% by 2025.
- The crucial success factors so far have been
  - size and quality of inventory
  - price
  - consumer care/consumer attention.
- Over 70% of all retail purchases will be influenced by information accessed online by 2015.
- The main cause of failure so far has been the lack of a clear business model and an understanding of where/when the income would arrive. These lessons have now been learnt.

The strength of the customer relationship being built by online companies should not be underestimated. Traditional brands may have fans on Facebook, but this is not driving significant business, nor is it a sign of undying loyalty. The **online retailer is becoming the brand**; nowhere is this clearer than with Amazon and Apple. And big brands make big profits. In January 2012, Apple declared Q4 profits of over $13 billion and had a market capitalisation only slightly behind Exxonmobil.

Notes

1. Tesco 2011 Annual Report.
2. Imap: retail industry global report 2010.
3. http://www.marketingcharts.com/direct/time-1-reason-for-shopping-online-18528/. Accessed 28 November 2011.
4. http://smartlifeblog.com/100-places-to-buy-your-groceries-online/. Accessed 27 March 2012.
5. Alef D (2010) *Jeff Bezos: Amazon and the eBook revolution*. Kindle.
6. Alef D (2010) *Jeff Bezos: Amazon and the eBook revolution*. Kindle.
7. Internet Retailer, 2010, http://www.top500guide.com/company/profile/?id=1, Accessed 2 February 2012.
8. http://blog.fabernovel.com/amazoncom-the-hidden-empire. Accessed 10 October 2011.
9. http://news.blogs.cnn.com/2012/01/16/zappos-com-hacked-24-million-customers-affected/. Accessed 23 November 2011.
10. http://www.onlinegrocer.ca. Accessed 18 August 2011.
11. http://www.efooddepot.com. Accessed 4 September 2011.
12. http://www.schwans.com. Accessed 29 November 2011.

Chapter 13

S INCE THE FIRST edition of this book appeared in 1995, the FMCG industry has been transformed.

- New markets have arisen: China is the second-largest grocery retail market in the world and Russia the fourth-largest in Europe.
- As FMCG retailers have eagerly adopted multi-format strategies, the retail industry has become much more concentrated: five retailers account for 88% of the market share in Sweden, Tesco take one in every seven pounds spent in UK shops and if Wal-Mart were a country, it would have the 25th-largest economy in the world.[1] Of the top 70 global retail companies, the top 10 account for 67% of the total net profit.
- In direct response, the brand manufacturers have begun a process of consolidation that must and will continue. Past giants of the branded era such as Nabisco, Gillette and Cadbury have been swallowed up by the new giants of the twenty-first century, such as P&G and Kraft. But the size gap has not closed: if P&G were a country, it would still only have an economy the size of Libya.
- The biggest brands in developed markets are now those of the retailers, who have focused their strategies on multi-channel availability purveying primarily multi-format private label brands. The retail chains have become brands in their own right. As Aldi and Tesco now have brand resonance, the days when the United Kingdom's

Morrisons would rebrand Safeway out of existence are coming to an end.

- The shopping experience has massively diversified. Highly successful hard discounters such as Aldi offer 2000 SKUs; the largest Wal-Marts, 100 000+; and Sears.com, 17 million. Both high-end and low-end formats are successful, even though neither depends on the cornerstone of twentieth-century FMCG retailing: traditional manufacturer brands. Michael Cullen's big-brand retailing model is past its 'best before' date.
- Retailers have a closer relationship with their shoppers than has been the case for 100 years. They use information technology to capture data on billions of individual shopping transactions, they analyse that data to identify thousands of customer segments and then they tailor their marketing to create exceptionally strong relationships with their best shoppers.

This seismic process of transformation has been massively accelerated by the emergence of e-commerce.

Most of these shifts have been uni-directional when it comes to the balance of power between manufacturers and retailers. FMCG retailers are now bigger, faster-growing, more complex, more sophisticated, better managed, better financed and more knowledgeable than their suppliers, to whom they previously played second-fiddle on all counts. Over the last two decades, whenever retailers have attempted to implement strategies that involve ousting or marginalising manufacturer brands, they have succeeded. This process has led retailers to compete, very successfully, with the traditional providers of brands.

But retailers are not more successful than manufacturers on one count: they are not more profitable. Despite all that has gone on and the palpable shift in power from manufacturer to retailer, the bulk of the profit from the sale of a branded product still ends up in the pocket of the manufacturer. There are two reasons for this:

- The intense horizontal price competition between retailers prevents any retailer from making too big a profit margin. They simply cannot afford to pocket too much of the transaction as it opens the door for a competitor to steal the sale and maybe even the shopper by selling for less. Thus, most of the funds retailers have squeezed from manufacturers actually get passed on to the shopper in the form of competitive prices. In this way, retailers act as a Robin Hood in the market, taking from rich manufacturers to distribute to poor shoppers.
- The very basis of branding is that the owner of the brand is entitled to make the bulk of the profit because they do most of the work in creating demand and take most of the risk, as theirs is the relationship of trust. So it is the rise of retailer brand strength that is the main strategic worry for brand manufacturers. It's not that they will keep on handing over more of their margin to retailers, which they will, but that more of the brands purchased will be those of the retailer.

The bottom line is that manufacturers are facing a competitive pressure from retailers for value-chain profits and brand mindspace the likes of which they have never felt before. This is not a blip, but a new reality. To avoid the power transference turning into a profit transference, manufacturers now have to learn how their brands can be best managed when retailers are competing very aggressively and successfully to provide brand reassurance. A key element of that learning process is to go back to the most basic rationale behind brands and see which can still be done better by the manufacturer.

The new focus of brand power

Brands are still needed by consumers because the function of brands hasn't changed: they solve many problems and without them shopping would be a nightmare. Brands simplify our life by providing, amongst other things:

- A useful **identification** as to what is inside the package. You only need to glance at a case of Coca-Cola to know what it is without having to read the small print.
- **Quality reassurance**. Before brands, shopping for butter, for example, was an open invitation for the retailer to sell rancid stock or lard at butter prices.
- Signals of our **identity**. This is one of the hardest brand benefits for retailer private labels to crack. It is unlikely, for example, no matter how strong the Aldi brand becomes that they will sell many t-shirts with one of their brand logos. Nike will sell plenty.

No shopper wants to make a hundred decisions every time they shop; the huge range of choice available in a modern supermarket makes the quick recognition and guarantees of consistent taste and quality that brands provide essential if the shopping trip is to be accomplished in a reasonable amount of time.

Of the main services that brands provide, retailers can satisfy the first: identification. The second, quality assurance, depends on the retailer being able to acquire high-quality products and then to reassure shoppers, credibly, that they have done so. In areas where the manufacturing technology is widely available, and the product assessment for the consumer is simple, retailers provide quality reassurance very well, for example, spaghetti. However, retailers have problems when the technology is complex, expensive and held by a few manufacturers who avoid supplying private label. Retailers also struggle when specific functionality is sought and its assessment prior to purchase is difficult in a store environment: a Wal-Mart motorcycle may not be an immediate hit.

The third branding service, identity, poses a special set of problems for retailers. Retailers have functional, good-value images, and when this fits with the branding requirements, they can provide satisfactory associations – there is no shame in buying a good retailer's bottle of wine, we trust that they will not allow vinegary plonk to be sold under their name. When the associations involve more aspirational imagery or a need for identification, retailers are limited by their broad, down-to-earth images. In these areas, the critical mass of the manufacturers allows them to create the desired images via brand-specific advertising and to invest in understanding their target markets to optimise their positioning and innovations.

The branding advantages held by manufacturers and retailers are shown in Table 13.1.

Table 13.1 Comparison of manufacturers and retailers in their competition to provide the consumer with branding in FMCGs

Area	Manufacturers	Retailers
Sources of power	**Critical mass and specialisation:** Technology Brand-specific advertising Consumer understanding	**Owning the stores:** Direct communication Control of marketing-mix variables Shopper data
Advantages	Image Variety/choice Novelty Ubiquity	Efficiency in branding for product areas where the advantages listed to the left are not dominant
Product fields where advantages dominate	Costly and rapidly evolving technology Specific function and hard to assess (e.g. toothpaste) Image important: brand name visible after purchase Variety, sense of choice important (e.g. hair care) Fun, novelty important	Real product differences small and easily assessed Spare capacity exists at manufacturer level Product is chosen and used without need for prestige/ communication value (e.g. spaghetti) Low-interest purchases, habitual
Distribution channels	Sold through variety of distribution channels (e.g. confectionery)	Products sold through all retail formats

Consumers will happily 'buy' branding from the organisation that can provide it most easily and cost-efficiently: we are willing to trade off some branding needs for a lower price or, to a lesser extent, convenience.

Each and every manufacturer brand needs to be reassessed in the new reality of eroded quality differences, blasé consumers, hyper-segmentation and resurgent multi-level private label offerings that have raised quality/value expectations. Those who have continued to operate under the traditional paradigm of manufacturer brand competing with manufacturer brand have to recognise this only now applies, if at all, for heavily differentiated, niche brands. Even their biggest brands face intense competition from private label me-toos, and the weaker secondary brands are doomed.

In addition to getting their own houses in order, can manufacturers constrain the ability of retailers to build their brands? They may be able to do so by exploiting the main weakness of all retailers: that they have very similar competitors and a business model very sensitive to changes in the top line. By aggressively seeking new distribution channels for their brands, manufacturers can and must always try to become less dependent on the big retailers. They may also be able to influence the way retailers position the big national brands. Perhaps the manufacturers' understanding of customer behaviour helps them influence shopping habits, especially now that new tools, like QR codes, have been developed to facilitate this. Manufacturers should certainly apply their experience and expertise developed in advanced retail markets to keep control of mindspace in emerging markets where retailers are not yet strong.

Meeting these challenges has huge implications for the way manufacturers operate.

Manufacturer responses

The shifts that have occurred since the mid-1990s place a huge burden on FMCG manufacturers to react if they are to survive and thrive.

The fundamentally different relationship between manufacturers and retailers demands that they implement new approaches to their individual strategy, brand portfolio, new product development, geographic structure, brand management and private label, which we will now consider in turn.

Strategy

Safeway, Loblaws, Tesco, Carrefour, Mercadona, Big Bazaar, Food World, Pick 'n Pay, Albert Hein, Wal-Mart and even hard discounters like Aldi now compete for the consumer's mindspace. Given that mindspace is a relatively fixed resource, then the more retailers build their brands and their multiple levels of private label, the less there is for manufacturers. In response, manufacturers must adopt one of three strategies:

- **Premium strategy:** In fields where technology, image or innovation is important, they can follow the value-adding tactics that have served them well for years. They can justify premium prices with higher brand satisfaction, both functional and emotional. Manufacturers should resist sharing their premium-brand technology with retailers at all costs.
- **Value strategy:** Manufacturers can compete directly with retailers on overall value if they leverage their scale advantage within their product field. With their global reach and cross-market sourcing opportunities, they can aim to provide the product to a global market, with its necessary branding, at a price that the retailer, constrained to operating in a handful of markets, cannot match.
- **Industrial strategy:** Manufacturers can accept that for certain products (even high-quality ones) the most efficient approach is through the retailer. The retailer will provide some or all of the branding services (name, reassurance, packaging, merchandising), and the manufacturer and retailer will share the profits.

There may well be no viable choice for second-tier brands. Manufacturers have to take a long, hard look at their brand portfolios and assess which ones cannot survive the squeeze between the premium, value and private label brands. Many manufacturers continue to treat minor brands as scaled-down versions of a major brand, with smaller budgets but the same objectives and marketing actions. The brand manager of a less successful brand is less senior than the brand manager of a power brand but has the same job and, if eloquent and persistent enough, can sometimes persuade the company to divert more resources their way. But to do so is almost always a mistake.

Each brand must be competitive in the value it delivers to retail customers. The value of premium brands is dependent on their consumer mindspace, and for these brands the most efficient way to motivate retailers is by winning the battle for mindspace. For second-tier brands, consumer pull falls below the threshold such that retailers believe they can safely ignore them, and they will.

For each and every brand, it is necessary to define an achievable and useful role with respect to the consumer and with respect to the trade. However, there is always a risk of falling between two stools: both consumer and trade objectives demand investment, and it is possible to spend in both areas without beating competitors in either.

Premium Brands

Premium brands have a strong enough consumer advantage to create an argument for the trade to value them (i.e. the perceived cost to the consumer of switching brands is such that non-stocking will reduce the appeal of the store). At the extreme, there are brands that have such strong loyalty that they become unavoidable for the FMCG retailer. Gillette is such a brand, which is why P&G bought it. In the world of manufacturer mergers and acquisitions, premium brands have become premium takeover targets. We predict that most of the world's premium brands will end up in the hands of the super-sized manufacturers who are not just amassing critical mass to match the retailers' size but also amassing premium brands to counter the retailers' brand power.

Premium brands have qualities retailers cannot match. For example, instant coffee is a weak area for retailers because the only people with the technical know-how are the big brand owners. As long as none of them agrees to share their best technology, the big brands are secure. But it only takes one manufacturer to waver for the dam to be breached.

The UK chocolate market was long assumed to be immune to private label as the technology and know-how to make excellent products was held by four main players: Cadbury, Rowntree, Mars and Terry's. Private label had less than a 2% share and was associated with poor-quality foreign chocolate. However, the purchase of Terry's in 1982 by United Biscuits (UB) changed the dynamic. UB were big private label suppliers and saw the volume opportunity for Terry's, who only had a 5% share of the branded market, to develop private label offerings. The strategy was a success for Terry's but, in providing high-quality offerings tuned to British tastes, their move allowed the leading retailers to gain a volume and then mindspace stake in the category. Private label share is now 10% of the total market and well over 20% in the main retailers.

Premium brands that depend on a heavily advertised image or personality are resistant to the retailer onslaught as retail image is neutral at best; hence Victoria Beckham has been more successful in the fragrance market than Costco. In other premium markets, such as toys and chilled desserts, variety and choice are best provided by manufacturer specialists, and there is a significant novelty sector that depends on innovation and brand-specific communication.

Traditional premium brands can still do well, but there is space for fewer of them. If a retailer procures a product comparable to the brand leader, and sells it at a lower price, it can set a new price-quality standard. If the ratio of quality to price improves, even brands that offer extra qualities have to reduce their price, or improve their quality, or both, to stay relevant. Over time, there is a trend for the value ratio to improve for the consumers, which is progress.

But even managers of the biggest brands can no longer afford to overestimate their brands' ability to justify a premium – the standard is being raised by retailers all the time. Aldi products are regularly rated by consumers in blind tests as being the best in their categories. The price margin between premium brands and their direct private label competition needs to be kept at a level that does not become too taxing to brand users.

For premium brands, manufacturers must work through the retail trade to hold onto control of the marketing-mix variables, which create usage, habit and mindspace. Cosmetic companies have been successful in managing which retailers sell their products and the ambiance in which their brands are sold. But this costs a lot of money. In general, given the increase in retail power, it is right that more marketing investment should be allocated to the retailer because they have increased their power to influence shopping behaviour. However, for premium brands, there is a risk that they will become weak by moving too much to the trade.

However, the rise of specialist e-retailers provides an excellent opportunity for premium brands to bypass the large FMCG retailer and retail their goods in a shopping environment uncluttered by tens of thousands of SKUs of dog food, carrots and shoe polish.

Birch Box are an e-retailer in the United States that connect high-end beauty products to customers, allowing them to bypass the traditional retailing experience. After discovering the biggest problem for shoppers was the huge selection of cosmetics and the inability to try them before purchasing, they created Birch Box, which mails women four to five deluxe beauty products every month for only $10. Shoppers benefit because they regularly test new products in the privacy of their home, and brands benefit from follow-up purchases when the samples run out and, more importantly, access to a channel that provides direct contact with their customers. Birch Box are expanding and planning to offer a similar subscription to target men.[2]

Nespresso, owned by Nestlé, also created a platform that skips traditional retailers and connects directly with their customers. Nespresso is a brand of espresso machines that brew single cups of coffee and other hot drinks from individual capsules. The capsules, sold exclusively by Nespresso on their website and in their boutique shops, are more expensive than ground coffee and represent one of the fastest-growing segments of the coffee market: they have sold more than 20 billion capsules since 2000 with sales growing at an average of 30% per year over that period.

Value Brands

Instead of trying to add value by targeting specific consumers with more tailored products, the value brand offers consumers the chance to compromise their preferences in favour of lower prices and superb value for money. Hard-discounting retailers follow this logic, and attract a significant and steadily increasing proportion of shoppers, so there is no reason why a manufacturer with all the cost benefits of global scale cannot do the same. It is essentially an EDLP strategy applied in the manufacturing field.

A value strategy can provide an effective platform for a manufacturer to compete against premium brands and the value proposition of retailers. Retailers are efficient in procuring products and providing branding, but manufacturers in any one category have greater critical mass. If, as a result of scale and commitment, manufacturers can obtain the most efficient cost structures, they may be able to beat retailers at their own game. For example, no one, manufacturer or retailer, has ever been able to match or beat the combination of quality and value of a Mars Bar (Milky Way in the United States) and still make money. In countries where retailers have no brands, only Basic private labels, a major manufacturer's occupying the value position may be the best way to inhibit private label growth.

In a value-oriented company, marketing drives have to be more sensitive to production when looking at the market. They must look for larger segments, find the common denominator and isolate the product functions that are essential to giving satisfaction (i.e. concentrate on features that create value to the consumer at an efficient cost). Consumer research can be devoted to finding new uses, new usage occasions, new countries or new target groups, rather than to finding niches for new products or brand extensions.

Another important role of value marketing is to iron out fluctuations in demand so that production capacity is always optimally used. Marketing for value brands has to plan pricing and promotional strategies that are efficient to implement, as promotions and quantity discounts cause fluctuations in demand, which create inefficiencies. As with EDLP for retailers, simplified pricing strategies are part of a manufacturer's cost structure and appropriate for a manufacturer obsessed with occupying the lowest cost position.

Value-oriented companies save on marketing and R & D because less of each is needed: it is easier to sell products offering exceptional value, so a technological consumer benefit is not needed. Value will move the product off the shelf. The company needs to be at the frontier in terms of production technology, but its products do not need to be the most sophisticated.

R & D is not directed to anticipating consumer wants but to serving existing wants more efficiently. Value-oriented companies eliminate non-essentials, design products that share components and transfer some of the costs (such as delivery, assembly) to the consumer. IKEA do as little as possible while the consumer does many of the tasks normally assigned to a retailer. Value-oriented companies streamline their product range, and are willing to drop last year's lines in favour of new, confident that they can make the best choice for the consumer.

In emerging markets, with less-affluent consumers, the value-oriented company will choose a quality and price at a lower level than in a high-income country, while retaining the same or better value ratio. Mobile phones are much cheaper in India than in America and have different features. Serving these lower-income consumers can lead to significant growth; low-income consumers spend more than $100 billion annually in Russia alone! Thus, companies like Hindustan Unilever have adjusted their portfolio and now sell over five billion pieces of penny candy each year in India, as well as cheaper soap and shampoo products. Danone also sell biscuits enhanced with calcium and iron in China at lower prices than they do in developed markets, which are popular as half of the Chinese population suffers from nutritional deficiencies.

This trend is common in other industries. In India, Renault and Tata introduced scaled-down versions of their cars for $3000 and $2500; Novatium introduced a personal computer for $100; and, in Africa, Vodacom introduced cheaper phones and 'pay as you go' rate plans.

Profit margins are not necessarily lower for value-oriented companies – the Walton and Mars families are among the richest in America. Low profits go to the companies that inhabit the netherworld between differentiated premium brands and cost-based value brands.

Second-tier Brands

The changing environment for FMCGs means that some brands are unable to compete as traditional premium brands or as value brands, and have no role beyond meeting the needs of a declining core audience. For these squeezed-out brands, an objective appraisal of their future is essential, or they will die.

Manufacturers with exhausted consumer brands have several options:

- **Recycle name with new product development (NPD):** If a name has consumer awareness and respect (i.e. a residual mindspace), it may be possible to exploit the name by transferring it to a new product with a more distinctive benefit. For example, Dove spent most of its life as a bar of soap. But the health and beauty market went through a technical revolution, leaving soap as a commodity. Unilever reused the names, colours and brand motifs with huge success across a wide range of bath and beauty products, including shampoo, body lotion and face cream.

- **Offer exclusivity to one retail chain:** Exclusivity is almost equivalent to selling the brand equity to a retail chain, except that the brand rights and production remain with the manufacturer. Target and Home Depot use this strategy quite extensively. Once a retailer has exclusive rights, it has the same interest in nourishing the brand's mindspace as it does with its own brands.
- **Target selected channel(s):** In some situations, where brands are distributed through a variety of different retail channels, there is scope for a brand that specialises in one of the channels. Smaller, specialised channels (e.g. hairdressers, beauty salons, boutiques and pharmacies) respond positively to a range that is exclusive to them and denied to the more price-oriented competition, a tactic long used by L'Oréal.
- **Fighter brand:** A small brand can sometimes justify its existence by being a strategic aid to a power brand, rather than being acceptably profitable in its own right. A fighter brand will often take a price positioning to protect a major brand. Normally, the financial objective of a fighter brand will be only to break even. In Holland, Van den Bergh markets a fighter margarine called Zeeuws Meisje, meaning 'Zeeland Girl.' Without its disruptive presence, competitors would be able to compete more effectively against Van den Bergh's premium brands.
- **Niching:** A small brand or competitor can choose a distinct part of a market that is either difficult or uneconomic for competitors to usurp. In such situations, small companies or brands can hold out in markets where economies of scale are otherwise important, an example of which would be Green & Black's organic chocolate. In those circumstances, the best solution for the mass producer is to buy the niche player, which was the case when Cadbury bought Green & Black's.

Managing second-tier brands demands a flexibility, imagination and entrepreneurial spirit that are a different skillset from the management of premium brands and value brands. They need to look for opportunities that fit with the resources of the brand: the cost of not being proactive and imaginative with these brands is their inevitable demise.

New Product Development

The most repeated conventional wisdom about new products is that the failure rate is huge. The second is that new products are vital for a company's long-term success. Thus, finding new products is risky but essential. A company that wishes to compete against the retailer has to do lots of it and exceptionally well, keeping in mind that this also means creating retailer value as well as consumer value.

Branding once allowed innovators to gain protection even if their innovation could be copied. Today, however, if a new product has no proprietary consumer benefit, the traditional branding approach will no longer provide protection. If the me-too is provided by a retailer, as it surely will be if the innovation is in any way successful, then the retailer will throw the weight of its shelfspace, shelf layout, pricing structure and merchandising behind its me-too to the detriment of the original. So innovation needs to be innovative.

It is sensible to steer clear of areas where retailers have the advantage, for example fresh salads and soups. Retailers are in a better position to react quickly to shopping information and are therefore the natural managers of fresh.

New products have to be presented to the retailer sometimes up to a year ahead of a planned launch to gain shelfspace. At the same time, retailers are always looking for innovative products to add to their own brand, so manufacturers worry that showing their hand too early will just result in a me-too appearing earlier. The retailer, on the other hand, does not see its request for an early sight of innovations as unfair, arguing that a genuine innovation is one they cannot copy anyway, so if they can easily copy it, it can't be very innovative.

When a manufacturer launches a new product, it should be as confident and knowledgeable about the likely trade reaction as it is about the consumer one. New products have to be successful not just in consumer appeal but also in trade appeal. Does the new product have a positive category effect? Is it easier to handle? Does it take up less space in-store than an existing product?

A double filter of consumer and retailer acceptance may seem to imply that testing will knock out a greater proportion of new brands: even fewer will get through the process. But this takes too narrow a view of the manufacturer's potential sources of business. A manufacturer with an idea for a new product should go to the retailer with a prepared answer to the question: 'Why shouldn't we source and launch that ourselves?' The answer might be:

- 'Because we are the only manufacturers who can make it, or market it (in the next, say, three years).'
- 'We are already working on your private label version, somewhat different, to be launched three months later.'
- 'You can have it as an exclusive private label on these terms.'

If the new product is one where retail reassurance is the most cost-effective way of branding, manufacturers should consider marketing the brand via a quality retailer, or selling the idea to a retailer for them to develop. Some large manufacturers already sell NPD projects that do not reach their own standards to retailers or private label manufacturers. The same logic applies to potential me-toos: the private label route may be the most economical. The manufacturer still has to ensure payment for its technical skills, but approaching the market in partnership with a powerful retailer may be a better route than the risks of a traditional launch.

Heinz have proved this strategy. Heinz, a world force in soup, never managed to prise the US soup consumer from Campbell's. After a valiant attempt to do so, Heinz decided to take the private label route to market in the United States. Given their technical quality, Heinz found market-oriented retailers ready to market their soups at prices reflecting both the quality of the product and the cheaper route to market.

Private label holds up a mirror to manufacturers. Who, for example, is the copycat? The top retailers are now innovating as well as, or better than, top manufacturers. To earn money, brand manufacturers have to develop and launch superior products more efficiently than their retail partners do. Manufacturers' emphasis on competitive bench-marking reduced their focus on innovative solutions and led to a mindset of 'me-tooing'. Retailers are the sure winners in an FMCG market where the only strategy is to copy. They can copy faster, cheaper, better and have a monopoly on being able to put their copies in front of their shoppers.

Geography

Company organisation has for a long time juggled with the dimensions of brand and country. Most large companies aim to globally harmonise brand management and international management, while giving enough autonomy to countries or regions to adapt to their consumers' desires. Unsurprisingly, these organisations have struggled to cope with the new dimension: the complex area of retail customers, who make life difficult by not being very global.

Thus, the need to market to distributors can be a countervailing force to globalisation or internationalisation. Consumers in different countries may be more similar to each other than retailers are to each other. Retailers in the United States are generally less concentrated than in Europe. In some countries, retailers have become very serious marketers and brand controllers; in others, retailers are in the 'selling phase'. In emerging markets, individual retailers are at different phases of development and changing very quickly. These differences have significant implications for manufacturers and their approach to the trade. Retailers are predominantly national, even regional in large countries, and so route-to-market strategies must be national or regional. Conversely, consumer marketing has become interested in synergy, opportunity and economies of scale across borders. The company has to consider ways of integrating these different geographical perspectives.

Brand Management

Focusing on the consumer is as critical as ever for manufacturers. Understanding consumer needs, owning consumer mindspace and developing innovative new products remain the core activities of management.

Brand management is evolving to become more flexible, with distinctions between premium brands, value brands, second-tier brand management and, if appropriate, private label. Each needs their specificity and culture. Top brands have to be handled differently from second-tier brands and industrial brands because their market is different. Companies should not just put junior people on smaller brands and give them smaller budgets. The separation of power brand and second-tier brand management recognises the different approaches and competencies required for the two tasks. The role of second-tier brand managers often involves expertise in wider business, financial and cost-control areas and a greater emphasis on tactical and trade marketing.

In particular, some process of review for defining the realistic management for each brand, by country, is essential. Depending on the power of the brand, and the country, sometimes brand management should have more say, and sometimes category considerations should dominate. The reviewing committee should not be afraid to drop squeezed-out brands in countries where the retailer is a mindspace competitor.

The role of premium brand managers is not only to build their brand but also to be involved with the international aspects, as these are the brands most likely to be relevant beyond national borders. Brand management also has to synergise with the company's overall category strategy in order to realise the full potential of the company's brands.

Private Label

Fitting private label management into a company's organisation raises difficult questions. There are good arguments for creating a separate function, with an independent director. This approach forces the private-label business to be fully profit accountable. It ensures appropriate costing and overhead allocations for private label and that the competition for production and R & D resources is more explicit. This structure is also suggested because private label business needs different core competencies than the brands' business. Management that is single-mindedly driven by low cost and efficient execution of retail demands may not be compatible with mindspace management and the rest of consumer marketing.

However, private label business has an impact on the company's consumer franchise, its route to market and its overall brand portfolio management. Therefore the views of these disciplines have to be represented in the development of a private label strategy.

Implications for retailers

It could be argued that, as the wind has been blowing strongly in favour of retailers, they need do nothing more than keep doing what they have been doing. That is largely correct when considered as a response to changes from the manufacturer side, in that there is very little that has been done by manufacturers that need cause retailers to implement radical changes to the way they do business.

But that has virtually always been the case, as most of the structural and strategic change in FMCG retail has come about because of innovation from other retailers or technological advances. The combination of geographic-based competition, ultra-sensitive bottom lines and few barriers to entry means that retailers must be permanently vigilant as to their competitive standing.

The biggest enemy for a retailer is not manufacturers but hubris. In the United Kingdom, Tesco showed in early 2012 that a two-decade run of unbroken success did not entitle them to sit back. They were resting on their laurels, as had Sainsbury's 20 years earlier. The result was that they let their competitors catch up, and in some cases overtake them. Ironically, Tesco's very success had come from seeing that the previous UK market leader, Sainsbury's, had grown complacent in the 1980s.

But while retailers will fight over every single scrap of market share, as they have always done, they cannot afford to ignore the combination of opportunity and threat posed by the emergence of e-retailing, which by 2020 we forecast will be taking up to a 30% share of purchases. Profitable e-retailing models are now essential for all mainstream FMCG retailers, no matter what cost or diversion of management focus is necessary for their implementation. They can no more afford to ignore the virtual shopping location than they could the out-of-town locations of the late twentieth century and the urban locations of the early twenty-first century.

Equally, the rise of the single-category e-retailing specialist poses a new, and enormous, threat. As FMCG grocery chains have expanded far beyond their traditional product ranges into areas like clothing, books and electronics, they have become more and more vulnerable to losing some of those recent gains to highly specialised online competitors.

Retailers, as ever, need to look after the basics in their vast collection of bricks-and-mortar stores. FMCG retailers are some of the largest property owners in the world, with billions tied up in their real estate. They cannot easily divest 30% of their vast holdings just because e-retailing has come along; they will still have to make a return on those assets for the foreseeable future.

Being competitive on price is a given, and will only increase the pressure put on manufacturers for more and deeper discounts. The old manufacturer arguments for their high profit margins – that they have huge investments in manufacturing facilities and mindspace – hold less and less water as manufacturing is increasingly outsourced and retailers are the big spenders on building mindspace.

As we have shown, virtually everything squeezed from the manufacturers will be funnelled straight through to the shopper by all players, so, for physical stores to thrive, they will have to increasingly concentrate on expanding and improving upon what they do best, such as fresh produce and high-quality pre-prepared meals. As Morrisons have shown, this is not easy to do well and entails massive commitments to an infrastructure to support such an approach.

Equally, retailers have to keep working at minimising the in-built negatives of bricks-and-mortar stores, such as a tedious and time-consuming shopping experience in massive stores far away from where most shoppers live and work. The era of the hypermarket is rapidly coming to a close: having 100 000 SKUs a 20-minute drive away is no longer a benefit when Sears.com have 17 000 000 you can purchase from your living room. Also, having large stores where half the SKUs sell one or zero units a week cannot be sustained indefinitely. Multi-format strategies of smaller stores more conveniently situated for busy shoppers are essential and victory will go to the retailers who get there first. More of the sales coming through smaller stores stocking fewer SKUs will add to the pressures on manufacturers' brand portfolios we examined earlier. Esselunga in Italy, seeing that the majority of their shoppers were time-starved working women, changed to reduce the number of SKUs they offered by 30% less than their competitors to decrease the shopping time.

In conclusion

A key purpose of this book has been to put into context and perspective the key events and changes that have taken place since the mid-1990s within the FMCG manufacturing and retailing industries. We began by reviewing the longer-term changes in the manufacturer–retailer dynamic and how changes have come about over time in their relationship, showing that there is no inevitability as to the outcome.

Just as every business needs to innovate to find an edge against its direct competitors; innovation and bold moves can also radically alter the vertical competitive picture between manufacturers and retailers. Innovations in products and store design are important because they create competitive advantage, but innovations such as P&G cutting out the distributors and Michael Cullen selling nothing but big brands at tiny margins changed the entire FMCG industry. Obviously, no one player has an obligation to take responsibility for the dynamics of an industry, but the rewards of doing so can be much more valuable and enduring. The pace of change has accelerated so much this century that the opportunities to create radical change have consequently multiplied

We stated in the Introduction that the friction between manufacturers and retailers is mostly brought about by the fact that they are very different organisations pursuing the same goals by very different means. In the developed markets, one of the biggest changes still happening is how the skillsets of these long-time opponents are increasingly overlapping. Up to the late 1990s, a marketing manager in a manufacturer could perform perfectly well by considering the retail trade as one relatively homogeneous body. Today, if managers do not intimately understand the individual strategies of their top 10 retail customers, they are doomed. Equally, while retail buyers could have only the haziest understanding of brand strategies in the past, today, they cannot perform at all without an equally intimate understanding of their employers' strategies across their many private label brands. But they still remain very different businesses pursuing the same goals.

Whether you are a manufacturer, retailer, student or academic, we hope this book has given you a much better understanding of both antagonists in this endlessly fascinating battle, particularly as hostilities spread to the vibrant emerging markets and the limitless battlefield of cyberspace. We shall sign off with our view as to some of the major changes we see ahead.

Looking to the future

- In developed markets, retailers now have an irreversible stake in **winning mindspace through their private label brands**; some retailers may continue to rise and some may fall, but the total mindspace held by retailers will continue to grow as they stake out their claims across more categories beyond traditional FMCGs. In emerging markets, manufacturers have a bigger mindspace advantage because of the huge head start they have had in terms of developing their businesses in those markets.
- It is clear that **retailers in emerging markets are evolving at a faster rate, and in different directions, from developed markets**. Retailing in the United States and Europe did not evolve down a pre-determined path to the logical optimised end-point; it evolved haphazardly, owing to a combination of changes such as radio/TV advertising and bar-coding, supplemented by inspirational ideas from retailers. Aldi and Costco were not inevitable: they were a product of their environments. Equally, given the different social and economic conditions of the emerging markets and the continued development of modern technologies, the only inevitability is that FMCG retailing and brand manufacturing in India and China in the year 2020 will not look like those of America and France in 2010. However, the large global retailers cannot ignore markets such as India and will buy locations and shoppers through the acquisition of local players as soon and as fast as they are able.
- **Retailer consolidation and multi-format strategies** are resulting in most key markets being dominated by a handful of major retailers, who will account for 60–70% of total sales. Manufacturers have to be completely transparent in their dealings with retailers and find ways of supporting each retailer's strategy with offerings of equal

value. To try to maintain relative critical mass, **manufacturers will consolidate** through mergers or acquisitions. We foresee 20–25 FMCG behemoths owning the vast majority of the premium FMCG brands, flanked by a multitude of medium to large-sized private label specialist supplies and a host of small innovators, filling gaps the giants cannot or will not. Within the giants, **overheads will continue to be cut dramatically** to deliver the price/quality mix that will be required not necessarily to succeed in future but merely to compete.

- **Private label** will continue to gain share. In 2011, the biggest brand in the United Kingdom was Tesco Finest. The second-largest was Tesco Value. As retailers' brand-building skills increase, so will their brand equities. Tesco now manage 23 distinct brand equities across their retail formats, product brands and private label pillar brands; brand management and the development of more powerful brands is a core part of their, and most other strong retailers', strategies. Manufacturers have to up their innovation and brand-building games or face extinction. Increasingly, the onus will be for manufacturers to demonstrate how their brands fit in with and complement retailers' brands.

- **Online** will continue to grow rapidly, both in terms of market share and in terms of research into buying decisions. If online is to become 30% of grocery, it will already have become 60% of books and 40–50% in many other categories. Manufacturers have to adapt to competing for sales in an environment that is both unfamiliar to them and one where they have far fewer means at their disposal to influence sales. One possibility is to structure their online operations vertically, becoming online specialists in those categories where consumers are committed or fanatical about product choice. For example, a Canadian company called BlackSquare built a platform that allows wine producers to sell directly to customers online. They make a higher profit margin on every bottle since they bypass traditional retailers, plus they give shoppers the ability to choose from larger collections. According to Jon Bonne, wine editor of the *San Francisco Chronicle*, 'What really counts is selection . . . access to a wide range of wonderful wines.' Not surprisingly, direct sales are becoming an important source of revenue for wineries: online sales are their fastest-growing profit source. However, wineries are not alone. Hundreds of retailers are also selling wine online, notably missionfinewines.com, northberkeleyimports.com and bounty-hunterwine.com, using their websites in addition to their stores to give customers a better experience by allowing them to compare thousands of wines, especially rare varietals, from global vineyards.

Another company that has structured its operations around being an online specialist is Indochino, the leader in custom online menswear. They make it easy and affordable for men to get tailored suits. They're unique because they control the entire supply chain, they sell their clothes exclusively online and pass the savings on to their customers. According to Indochino's CEO, Kyle Vucko, 'The Internet is enabling a new way for people to engage with brands and I am excited to see where our brand can push this. The combination of online retailing, the ability to connect globally, and leveraging a new supply chain will create a way of interacting with customers that is better on every level.'

Phone apps will push prices down, and history has shown that when prices go down, squeezing retailers' margins, there is only one place they can go to in order to restore their profitability: the manufacturer.

Notes

1. http://www.businessinsider.com/25-corporations-bigger-tan-countries-2011–6?op=1. Accessed 11 December 2011.
2. https://www.birchbox.com. Accessed 13 December 2011.

Appendix 1

Dean Foods are one of the largest private label producers: they have an estimated 8.5% of the private label market and operate two divisions, Fresh Dairy Direct and White Wave-Morningstar. They are the global leader in soy beverages, the largest processor and distributor of dairy products and the US leader in organic dairy. They also produce canned vegetables, relishes, processed pickles, salad dressings and frozen desserts. Dean Foods operate 100 plants with 25 000 employees and earned $12.1 billion in sales in 2010, selling more than 2.4 billion gallons of milk. They were named the 2011 US supplier of the year by McDonald's USA. Although they posted a $1.6 billion loss to reflect a lower value for their fresh dairy business in 2011, they are still positioned as one of the top global private label manufacturers.

Ralcorp Holdings Inc. are the largest private label producer of ready-to-eat cereal and one of the top global producers of dry pasta. They also make snack foods, chocolate, sauces and frozen bakery goods. Their focus is to create 'high-quality products that compare to national brands', so although they produce branded products, the majority of their portfolio is private label. Ralcorp Holdings Inc. operate 44 plants globally and have over 10 000 employees. In 2010, they generated $4.05 billion in sales, almost doubling their 2008 sales of $2.8 billion. Their main growth has been via acquisition: they've acquired 25 companies since 1997, including Post in 2008 and

American Italian Pasta Company in 2010. In late 2011, they were positioned to be acquired by ConAgra Foods, which valued Ralcorp at over $7 billion; however, no decision has yet been made.

Cott Corporation are one of the largest private label manufacturers based on market share (around 4.5%). They founded a business providing retailers with private label soft drinks, in particular a high-quality cola sourced from Royal Crown. Instead of operating as an industrial supplier, Cott provided retailers with a sophisticated private label packaging complete with name, design, merchandising and promotions. Many retailers jumped at this package, and Cott grew at an enormous rate, recruiting dozens of chains, including Sainsbury's and Wal-Mart. Cott's success indicates the potential that exists for developing private label in partnership with retailers. However, they have had difficulty securing long-term profits.

Treehouse Foods Inc. are the leading private label manufacturer in soups, dressings, pickles, powdered non-dairy creamers, powdered soft drink mixes and hot cereal, and second in spreads, salsa and dry mix pasta dinners. They produce over 9000 SKUs in 19 plants for 800 retail customers and they only operate acquired plants, which is unusual. Treehouse Foods Inc. is often referred to as the 'biggest company you've never heard of'. No other company has gone from $0 to nearly $2 billion in sales in five years and become the leader in its product categories (Figure A.1). They were founded in 2005 and have grown at a compound annual rate of 21%. Michelle Obama, wife to President Obama, sits on their board of directors.

Smithfield Foods are the world's largest producer and processor of pork and the leader in bacon, bone-in-ham products and meatballs. They make over 50 pork products and more than 200 gourmet foods, and will continue to focus their growth on packaged meats. Founded in 1936, Smithfield Foods have over 52 000 employees globally and sold $12.2 billion worth of products in 2010; this was an increase from sales of $11.2 billion in 2009, but less than their 2008 sales of $12.5 billion. Part of their sales' decline could be due to the scrutiny from the Humane Society for the alleged inhumane conditions in their

TREEHOUSE'S GROWTH

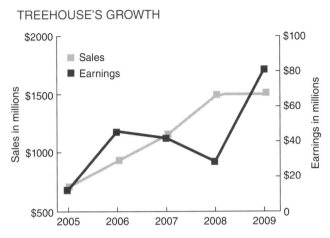

Figure A.1 Treehouse Food Inc.'s growth (2005–2009).
Source: http://www.treehousefoods.com.

pork processing plants. Smithfield Foods still use gestation crates, which companies like Safeway, Whole Foods, Wendy's, Burger King and Quizno's, among others, have discontinued. In 2007, Smithfield promised to phase them out, but in 2009 they reversed their statement following significant operating losses.

ConAgra Foods are one of North America's leading food manufacturers and a top global supplier to foodservice chains and distributors. They produce 40 brands, including PAM, Healthy Choice, Orville Redenbacher's and Chef Boyardee, as well as nine private label brands. ConAgra Foods specialise in frozen potatoes, sweet potatoes and other vegetables, and provide the broadest portfolio of whole grain ingredients in the world; 25% of their products are leaders or second in their category. Although private label only represents 35% of their business, ConAgra Foods are building their private label portfolio. In November 2011, they agreed to acquire National Pretzel Co, which make private label pretzel sticks, braids and twists. They sold $12.3 billion worth of products in May 2011 and were named Best Grain Products Supplier in *Food Processing* magazine's Reader's Choice Awards for the fourth year in a row.

Appendix 2

Brazil

Brazil has the most developed retail industry, with total sales of $150 billion in organised retail, and several global players already operate in the country. Food distribution in Brazil is very well organised by the retail trade compared to other BRIC nations and presents good opportunities for prospective importers.

Top Retailers

- **Wal-Mart:** Wal-Mart are the largest retailer there. They opened their first store in 1995, and by 2012 had 487 in 10 different formats. In 2008, they opened their first eco-efficient Supercentre in Rio de Janeiro, and since then have opened 13 more and one eco-efficient distribution centre.
- **Carrefour:** Brazil accounts for 10% of Carrefour's total global sales ($145 billion), and is projected to account for 20% by 2017, owing to an aggressive expansion and development programme.
- **Grupo Pão de Açúcar:** A local retailer formed from the merger of Companhia Brasileira de Distribuição and Sendas to compete against international players. They operate chains in different formats: Pão de Açúcar, Extra, Sendas, Assaí, CompreBem, Ponto Frio.

Trends

- Seventy per cent of the gross revenue of the top 500 retailers is from food products.
- Non-food retail sales are also expected to rise. For example, the cosmetics and personal care industry is expected to grow 13% by 2014 to reach $26.9 billion.
- Brazil's largest e-commerce company, B2W had sales of $3.1 billion in 2011.

Russia

Russian incomes have risen 14 times over the last decade and sales in virtually all consumer categories have followed suit. Russia is now the 11th largest consumer market in the world, according to Euromonitor International, and is already the second or third largest in Europe in most categories. Russia has become a middle-class country according to Citigroup, the chief strategist, rising wealth levels over the last decade mean that over 60% of the population can now be considered middle class. In 2011, Russia became the largest European market for milk ($14.6 billion) and children's goods. In 2012, it is expected to become Europe's largest dairy market, and in 2013 to take the top spot for advertising and apparel. A recent survey found that 71% of Russians would spend any spare cash, against 3% who would save it.

Russia is forecast to become number one in Europe in the following markets: cheese ($12.1 billion) by 2015; cigarettes ($20 billion) by 2015; cosmetics ($14.7 billion) by 2019; beer ($30.3 billion) by 2014. These figures highlight why manufacturers and retailers need to focus and grow in emerging markets (in reality-emerged markets). We expect the share of modern formats will exceed 50% of grocery retail trade by 2015.

Top Retailers

- **X5 Retail Group:** Have a 4% market share and use a multi-format strategy: soft discounters, supermarkets and hypermarkets. Their objective is to be the consolidator of the Russian retail food market and 'the absolute leader of Russian retail, able to compete with leading international chains as an equal'.

- **Magnit:** The largest food retailer in terms of the number of stores (4364 as of June 2011, with plans to open 1000 more in 2011) and geographical coverage (selling space varies from 6500 ft² to 41 000 ft²). Magnit have experienced a huge increase in sales: they rose 47% from 2010's level to $984.8 million in 2011 – and their total number of stores also grew 27% in the same period thanks to an aggressive store opening strategy. They operate a discounter chain and a hypermarket; their hypermarkets are located in the inner city, which makes them accessible to everyone, not just car owners.

- **O'Key:** Have 59 stores in two formats, hypermarkets (O'KEY) and supermarkets (O'KEY-Express); their hypermarkets have an average of 35 000 SKUs and their supermarkets 9000 SKUs. Most stores are in St Petersburg, where O'Key have the highest brand equity among their competitors. In 2011, they invested $366 million to increase their total selling space of 961 000 ft² by 30%.

- **Metro Group:** Entered Russia in 2001 and operate 88 outlets in three formats: Metro Cash & Carry (52), Real (15) and Media Market (21). In 2009, their sales fell by 10.4% to $5.4 billion, even though Real and Media Market recorded sales growth. Their focus is on logistics and improving relations with suppliers.

- **Azbuka Vkusa** is one of the most powerful and well-known Russian retailers. They offer a unique range of fresh produce, ready-to-eat meals and alcohol for consumers who want to choose from a variety of high-quality products. Azbuka Vkusa opened their first supermarket in 1997 and now operate 47 in the Moscow area; they have won several awards for their business, being the first Russian company in food retail to introduce a quality-management system based on ISO 9001:2000. Instead of cutting prices during the recession of 2008, they focused on sourcing hard-to-find items and charging a premium. According to their CEO, Vladimir Sadovin, 'The guarantee of success in the premium segment is the quality level of the food, production facilities, interior, staff and fresh air. People have to understand why they're paying more. It's not a secret that a number of the items we sell can be found cheaper somewhere else.'

Others

- **Utkonos.ru** is Russia's top online food retailer. Eighty per cent of online purchases are in cash – people prefer to place an order online, then go to the pick-up point and touch the goods to make sure everything is okay before they pay.
- In September 2011, **Wal-Mart** hired the former CEO of one of Russia's largest retailers, Lev Khasis, although they say that doesn't signal any immediate plans to enter the Russian market. (Wal-Mart closed their Moscow office in December 2010, creating speculation they had given up on Russia; the company isn't actively pursuing the Russian market but they say they are remaining open to the possibility. They have commissioned extensive research.)
- **Carrefour** entered Russia in 2009, but decided to leave after only four months, owing to weak sales and limited expansion potential; they were late to arrive (Metro Group entered in 2001 and Auchan in 2002). After not being able to sell their Russian business as one asset, they chose to sell their leasing rights to rivals in February 2010. Although official company reports claimed they abandoned the country in 2009, in September 2011 there were rumours that Carrefour were looking to re-enter Russia.

Trends

- Retail is one of the fastest-growing industries in Russia, and discounters are the fastest-growing retail format.
- Russia is also the fastest-growing market worldwide for luxury goods.

India

India is a difficult market to forecast as the government there still has not decided whether they welcome foreign retailers or not. However, we believe that, by 2020, India, already the fifth-largest retail market in the world, will see the fastest growth among all BRICs: the share of modern retail will increase from 6% to 20–25% of the country's total grocery sales and the revenues of major retailers will be $70–80 billion by 2015. For the last three years, India has topped A. T. Kearney's Global Retail Development Index.[1]

Top Retailers

NB: It is difficult to rank Indian retailers as it depends on which operations are included. The following are ones that have focus on food retail.

- **Pantaloon Retail (Big Bazaar):** Big Bazaar were launched in 2001 and were the first hypermarket in India, combining the look and feel of Indian bazaars with aspects of modern retail like choice, convenience and quality. They also own Food Bazaar and retailers in other industries, like Furniture Bazaar in home solutions and e-zone in consumer electronics.
- **Aditya Birla Retail (more.):** They acquired Trinethra Super Retail in 2007 and rebranded all of their stores 'more.' to reflect their new commitment to their customers. They operate the chain under two formats: supermarkets and hypermarkets; they have almost 600 outlets in India.
- **Tata Group (Star India Bazaar):** In 2004, they opened their first food retail chain, Star India Bazaar, a hypermarket with a large assortment of products at the lowest prices. In 2010, Star India Bazaar had $100 million in sales and 840 000 ft^2.
- **RPG Spencer (Foodworld):** They pioneered organised food and grocery retail in 1996 and currently operate over 60 stores in four formats.
- **K Raheja Group (Shoppers Stop):** Started as a menswear store in 1991, and became India's first department store in 2001. Launched India's largest hypermarket, Hypercity, which has 1.2 million ft^2 and $20 million in gross sales in its first year.

Trends

- Sixty-five per cent of growth is in the retail food segment. Biscuits, snacks, chocolates and confectionery are experiencing double-digit growth. Impulse, health and wellness, lifestyle and convenience have a more than 20% growth and are predicted to shape the direction of FMCGs.
- A shift from private label to branded products among lower-income population. Consumers from smaller urban areas are upgrading to branded products.
- Succeeding in rural environments is different from success in an urban environment: 90% of people in rural populations live in villages of 2000 or fewer people.

China

China has the best prospects among the BRICs: Wal-Mart, Tesco, Carrefour, Auchan and a dozen other global retailers operate here and consider China among their top priorities. This is unsurprising as the Chinese retail market is forecast to enjoy a double-digit compound growth over the next five years. The national retailers are also strong and have the vision and money to continue competing. The 10% share of modern retail is substantial considering that at the beginning of the century there were no hypermarkets. The share of modern retail will approach 35–40% by 2020, and the combined sales of domestic and foreign chain retailers will be $450–$500 million. Although e-commerce is doing well in China – the biggest player, Taobao.com, had sales of nearly $16 billion in 2011 – none of the international retailers has a strong online business here.

Top Retailers

- **Wal-Mart:** Entered the market with their first Supercenter and Sam's Club in 1996, and opened their Global Procurement Office in 2002.

They purchased a 35% interest in Trust-Mart in 2007 and recently beat Carrefour to take full ownership, catapulting them to first place with a 3.6% market share.

- **Wumart:** Beijing based Wumart started in the 1990s and is one of the top local retailers. In 2011, they had 469 stores and generated $2 billion in sales. Wumart are noticeably cheaper than Wal-Mart; in fact, Wal-Mart are considered fancy to many Chinese shoppers!
- **Carrefour:** Were ahead of Wal-Mart because of their strategy to give almost total independence to local managers to meet local preferences, but they fell to second place with a 2.3% market share after Wal-Mart took full ownership of Trust-Mart.
- **Tesco:** Have a 1% market share and are in the early phase of development. They are opening their first multi-level shopping centre in Forshun in 2011, with a further 17 in various stages of development.
- **Auchan:** Entered the market in 1999 and are growing fast. They are opening an average of two stores a month and have a 0.7% market share. Most outlets are a joint venture with a Taiwanese company and operate under the brand RT Mart.
- **Shanghai Bailian:** One of the biggest retail chains in China, they have more than 6000 outlets in a variety of industries and own 11% of the total retail market.
- **Li & Fung Group:** Founded in 1906, they operate some of the largest local retailers, including Convenience Retail Asia Limited (540 convenience style outlets), Trinity Limited (40 high-end retail outlets) and Toys Holding Limited (operate Toys "Я" Us chains in nine Asian markets), which together sold $1 billion in 2010. (Their entire company had sales of $18.5 billion in 2010, mostly through other ventures.)

Trends

- More than 25 of the world's largest retailers are in China.
- China now has the third-largest economy in the world. The FMCG industry is strong, with market leaders developing quickly, overseas

brands doing well, plenty of mergers and acquisitions and more competition.

- Consolidation is low, owing to the large distances between cities. The top five players only represent 13.4% of the market.
- Different cities and regions are at very different stages of development (both economically and regarding market saturation).
- Growth is in smaller cities. Lower-tier cities are home to 87% of the country's population but represent only 64% of retail sales. Growth in smaller cities will double by 2017.
- Chinese consumers are:
  - Habitual, 56% of people go to the same store.
  - Much more sensitive to price than Westerners are, placing price as a higher priority than store ambiance, service and facilities. Best Buy failed in China as they did not allow price haggling, whereas their local competitors did. A third of shoppers actively search out promotions in their regular store and a quarter switch brands because of promotions.
  - Not very brand loyal. Chinese consumers do not consistently buy the same products and are not willing to pay much in premium prices for the leading brands.
  - Spoiled for choice. Owing to the low brand loyalty, shoppers are swamped with competing offerings. A typical Chinese hypermarket will have up to 40 brands of shampoo and conditioner (vs. 15 in the West) and more than 20 different toothpastes.
  - Brand lovers: private label remains small. Sixty per cent of shoppers think private label is only for people with a serious budget problem.

Note

1. http://www.ideasmakemarket.com/2011/05/supply-chain-challenges-in-indian.html. Accessed 11 November 2011.

INDEX

STOREWARS IS THE WORLD'S LEADING BUSINESS MANAGEMENT SIMULATION PROGRAMME

Management in the Retail and FMCG marketplace face a daily barrage of new demands; the aim of StoreWars is to develop a more diverse set of skills to help managers adapt and survive in the race to the top.

Seventy per cent of the world's leading FMCG companies and 60% of the world's top consultancies and retailers have used Store-Wars. **Over 20 000 directors and executives in 43 countries have taken part in StoreWars**; many of them consider it the best training and coaching they have ever received. StoreWars is available in eight languages.

In a StoreWars programme, 25–34 participants run a virtual business worth $500 million. They develop the company's strategy, negotiate and make decisions that determine the success of their business.

On the first day of the programme, participants are divided into five teams, two of which operate the retail business while the other three operate as a manufacturing business. All teams compete and interact with each other to win the greater market share and to make more EVA. A detailed analysis by the coaching teams helps participants make strategic and tactical solutions in the market, and consolidate the key lessons and conclusions.

Why is StoreWars Unique?

As a Business Model	**As an Educational Tool**

- ▶ Compound vertical market model showing trade relations along the **complete supply chain**
- ▶ Comprehensive retailing and manufacturing business model
- ▶ **Live negotiations** and their effect on business outcomes
- ▶ **No golden strategy** implied: results are dependent on each team's actions
- ▶ **Dynamic extensions switching**: shop leasing and acquisition, supply chain automation, private label subcontracting, POS activities, inventory holding costs, refinancing etc.

- ▶ **Top and middle** management
- ▶ Practical extension of basic management skills
- ▶ Overall testing and development of **managerial competence** and skills in four major areas:
  - Managing Own Job
  - Relating to Others
  - Building the Team
  - Thinking Clearly
- ▶ Professionals of sales, marketing and trade marketing, purchase and logistics, production, finance and HR

Kimberly Clark, Henkel, L'Oréal, Pepsi, Coca-Cola, Danone, BAT, Ikea, Nokia, HP, Wal-Mart, Wrigley, GSK, Reckitt Benckiser, Unilever, Tesco, Beiersdorf, Bacardi, JTI, Philip Morris, Metro C&C, Kraft Foods and SAB Miller have used StoreWars for staff training and development.

Visit www.storewars.net to learn more about StoreWars, or contact:

Sarah Thain	sarah.thain@storewars.co.uk	Marketing and business schools
Anastasia Lavrenyuk	alavrenyuk@storewars.net	Asia and Far East
Ekaterina Voitenkova	evoitenkova@storewars.ru	Russia and CIS
Veronika Klamar	veronika.klamar@storewars.co.uk	Europe and UK
Ludmila Belokonova	ludmila.belokonova@storewars.co.uk	Middle East and ROW
Dariusz Kepczynski	dariusz.inc@sfr.fr	Programme's technical support